PENGUIN  CLASSICS

PRAISI
LETTER TO MA

DESIDERIUS ERASMUS, born   da,
Utrecht and Deventer. He be   the
Northern Renaissance and led the humanist reform in theology, education, rhetoric and classical studies. He was a brilliant satirist whose
evangelical humanism led him into conflict both with the scholastics and
with Luther. Erasmus travelled widely. He studied and taught in Paris,
and at the invitation of one of his pupils, Lord Mountjoy, came to
England, where he spent the happiest years of his life and became a close
friend of Thomas More, with whom he translated Lucian, and to whom
he dedicated the *Praise of Folly*. Italy, where Pope Julius II was
conducting his military campaigns, disappointed him, and he ended his
life, saddened by the sharpening of the religious conflict, in Basle, where
he died in 1536. He published the first Greek text of the *New Testament*,
the *Adages*, the often ironic *Colloquies*, the satirical *Ciceronianus* and
numerous editions of classical and patristic authors. His vast correspondence shows that he was in touch with all Europe's leading princes and
scholars and his prolific writings make him a figure not only of
scholarly interest but also of outstanding literary importance.

BETTY RADICE read classics at Oxford then married and, in the
intervals of bringing up a family, tutored in classics, philosophy and
English. She became joint editor of the Penguin Classics in 1964. As
well as editing the translation of Livy's *The War with Hannibal* she
translated Livy's *Rome and Italy*, the Latin comedies of Terence,
Pliny's *Letters* and *The Letters of Abelard and Heloise*, and also wrote
the introduction to *The Odes and Epodes* by Horace, all for the
Penguin Classics. She also translated from Italian, Renaissance Latin and
Greek for the Officina Bodoni of Verona. She is the author of the
Penguin reference book *Who's Who in the Ancient World*. She was an
honorary fellow of St Hilda's College, Oxford. Betty Radice died in
1983.

A. H. T. LEVI was born in 1929. He studied philosophy in Germany
and modern languages at Oxford before taking a degree in theology. He

taught at the universities of Oxford and Warwick before becoming Buchanan Professor of French Language and Literature at the university of St Andrews. He has published extensively on the Renaissance and the seventeenth century in France as well as more generally on literary and theological topics. He hopes shortly to complete a *Guide to French Writers* and then to return to projected books on sixteenth- and seventeenth-century French literature.

PRAISE OF FOLLY

AND

LETTER TO MAARTEN VAN DORP

1515

ERASMUS OF ROTTERDAM

TRANSLATED BY
BETTY RADICE
WITH AN INTRODUCTION AND NOTES BY
A. H. T. LEVI

PENGUIN BOOKS

PENGUIN BOOKS

Published by the Penguin Group
Penguin Books Ltd, 27 Wrights Lane, London w8 5tz, England
Penguin Books USA Inc., 375 Hudson Street, New York, New York 10014, USA
Penguin Books Australia Ltd, Ringwood, Victoria, Australia
Penguin Books Canada Ltd, 10 Alcorn Avenue, Toronto, Ontario, Canada m4v 3b2
Penguin Books (NZ) Ltd, 182–190 Wairau Road, Auckland 10, New Zealand

Penguin Books Ltd, Registered Offices: Harmondsworth, Middlesex, England

This translation first published 1971
Reprinted with a revised Introduction and updated notes 1993
3 5 7 9 10 8 6 4

Typeset by Datix International Limited, Bungay, Suffolk
Printed in England by Clays Ltd, St Ives plc

CONTENTS

PREFACE TO THE 1993 EDITION

The cooperation between translator and editor that led to this edition of the *Praise of Folly* was conceived in 1969, the quincentenary year of Erasmus's birth, and grew out of the interest in Erasmus stimulated by the centenary. Editor and translator each carefully revised and accepted joint responsibility for the work of the other. The flurry of scholarly activity, symposia, colloquies, collective and individual volumes carried on for a number of years after the centenary, creating among its lasting monuments the great Amsterdam critical edition of the works and the Toronto *Collected Works of Erasmus* in English. Further translations of the *Praise of Folly* also appeared. However, the Toronto editors selected Mrs Radice's translation, which also appeared in the 'Folio' collection, and the editor was invited by the Toronto University Press to undertake the general editing of the two volumes of *The Collected Works* in which this translation of the *Praise of Folly*, together with five other Erasmus texts, appeared in 1986.

Since the Toronto edition of the *Praise of Folly* was prepared, three things have happened, each of which on its own would have been sufficient to demand a revision of the original Penguin Classic. First the magisterial critical edition of the Latin text by Professor Clarence Miller, published in Amsterdam, demonstrated that in 1514, after the death of Pope Julius II in 1513, Erasmus had strengthened his text considerably in two important ways: by sharpening the attack on the scholastic theologians, and by increasing his perfectly serious insistence that Christian sanctity is folly to the world. Other modifications were made to the text later, one of which reflects the growing inevitability of the schism, but for practical purposes it is now necessary to distinguish three states of the text. These are the first authorized state as printed a year after the original 1511 editions by Josse Bade in 1512, the augmented text printed by Matthias Schürer in 1514 and the virtually final text printed by Johann Froben in 1521.

The last text corrected by Erasmus before his death was that of Froben and Bischoff (Episcopius) of Basle 1532.

Second, since the 1987 publication by Francis Clark of his two-volume work the *Pseudo-Gregorian Dialogues* it has been impossible to uphold the very great authority with which much popular medieval teaching on purgatory and demonology used to be invested. It had previously been believed mistakenly that the *Dialogues* to which coarsened late-medieval Christian piety looked for support were the work of the last of the great Latin Fathers, Pope St Gregory the Great. In other words, the superstitions witheringly satirized by Erasmus turn out not to have had the backing of the very considerable authority of Gregory after all.

Third and most important, historians familiar with late-medieval spiritual traditions have shown that Erasmus's piety needs to be evaluated in a way that has become fully apparent only in the late 1980s. The whole thrust of Erasmus's single most forthright statement of his own spirituality as expounded in what he referred to as the *Folly*, strengthened by the 1514 and subsequent additions to the text, was directed towards the mockingly humanistic restatement of the unlettered pious ideals in which Erasmus had been brought up. This was the spirituality of the *Imitation of Christ*, a collection of four treatises written by Thomas à Kempis in the third decade of the fifteenth century.

It needs additionally to be noted that in her 1993 *Erasmus, Man of Letters*, Lisa Jardine has proposed a new image of Erasmus's activity, emphasizing that this 'itinerant producer of textbooks and translations' 'self-consciously created his own reputation as the central figure of the European intellectual world'. That Erasmus carefully promoted, adjusted, and cultivated his own image, creating a literary identification between himself and St Jerome, whose life he wrote, seems indisputable. It is possible that what seemed like the real debates in which he took part were often orchestrated performances, the product of a back-scratching conspiracy building on a humanist ideal itself known by the humanists who paid lip-service to it to be a chimera.

Humanism in much of northern Europe included little admiration of antique culture, but was limited to the study of the languages in which the scriptures were originally written, so providing the protagonists of evangelical religion with the weapon needed to overthrow the authority of the Vulgate Latin text as exploited by the Paris theology faculty. But Erasmus himself certainly went further, genuinely exploring a new vision of human personal and social potential, to bear visible fruit in a cultural movement which lasted for at least three centuries. He was, however, always conscious of his reputation, and he calculated the effects he strove for.

Erasmus's own first manual of piety, the *Enchiridion militis christiani* (*The Handbook of a Christian Soldier*), written in 1501 although not published until two years later, derives from the spirituality of the *Imitation of Christ*, although in form it is apparently based on the rules for the spiritual combat drawn up by Giovanni Pico della Mirandola (1463–94), whose piety may well also be reflected in its content. Pico's devotional rules for the spiritual combat together with his life by his nephew Gian-francesco Pico della Mirandola (1469–1533), and three letters, of which two were to his nephew, were to be translated by Thomas More (1478–1535) into English. More translated this material at about the time that he decided to remain a layman. He had received spiritual direction from John Colet (1467–1519), and he had also taken Pico as his spiritual ideal. Likewise, Colet and Pico had a profound influence on Erasmus, who was to write the *Folly* for More.

À Kempis, like Erasmus, was an Augustinian canon, although the way in which Erasmus developed an interest in classical literature in reaction to the official spirituality of the monastery at Steyn, where Erasmus lived as postulant, novice and monk from 1485–6 until 1493, suggests that the affinity of Erasmus's spirituality with that of à Kempis was based not so much on their common membership of the same Order of canons regular as on their joint roots in the *devotio moderna*, 'modern devotion'. The *devotio moderna* was practised by the Brethren of the Common Life in the Low Countries, the Rhineland and the eastern part of what is now Germany. This was the spirituality in which Erasmus had been brought up at Deventer (1478–9 to 1483–4) and 's Hertogenbosch before entering the monastery. In spite of his classical enthusiasm, for which the *Folly* shows signs of serious doubt if not actual repentance, Erasmus was to remain faithful to the *devotio moderna* until the end of his life.

Folly's final panegyric of unlettered Christian piety is the entirely serious if now mature derivative of his boyhood piety. It was only superficially neoplatonist, although permeated with a devotion to the authentic text of Scripture that by 1514 made a virtually public announcement of the forthcoming edition of the New Testament in Greek which Erasmus was to publish in 1516. The Pauline folly seriously praised by Folly at the end of her mock sermon, essentially derived from the spiritual combat as envisaged by à Kempis and Pico, can now be seen to have become the point of Erasmus's text and the focus of scholastic hostility towards it.

The introduction and notes have been brought up to date in the light of all three of these developments. The translation was revised by Mrs Radice to accord with the last text revised by Erasmus himself, the 1532 Basle edition by Froben and Bischoff. The very early editions, from July 1511, are all faulty. The text here presented, although based on that of 1532, indicates all that was added after that of 26 July 1512 by Josse Bade. That was the first authorized edition, careful and almost certainly corrected by Erasmus himself. Additions made in 1514 are shown by inclusion between pointed brackets, ⟨and⟩, while all additions made in later editions are shown by bold pointed brackets ⟨and⟩. Because some of the insertions are long, the newer material that runs over more than one line is indented and a rule runs down the margin showing the extent of the insertion. A fine rule denotes 1512 additions, and a heavy rule indicates later material. Words, phrases and quotations in Greek in the original, often single words coined by Erasmus himself, are printed in single inverted commas, while all Latin quotations, whether from Scripture or elsewhere, appear between ordinary double inverted commas. The style of the Toronto edition has been followed for the titles of works written by or atttributed to classical authors. The eighteenth-century chapter divisions have been abandoned, and the text has been divided into paragraphs to conform with the usage introduced by Clarence Miller in his critical edition (Amsterdam 1979).

INTRODUCTION

I. THE IMPORTANCE OF THE *PRAISE OF FOLLY*

The *Praise of Folly* has long been famous as the best-known work of the greatest of the Renaissance humanists, Erasmus of Rotterdam. It is a fantasy which starts off as a learned frivolity but turns into a full-scale ironic encomium after the manner of the Greek satirist Lucian, the first and in its way the finest example of a new form of Renaissance satire. It ends with a straightforward and touching statement of the Christian ideals which Erasmus shared notably with his English friends John Colet and Thomas More.

It was written in 1509 to amuse Thomas More, on whose name its Greek title *Moriae Encomium* is a pun, as a private allusion to their cooperation in translating Lucian some years earlier. It was a retreat into the intimacy of their friendship at a moment when Erasmus, just back from Italy, was ill, disillusioned at the state of the Church under Julius II and perhaps uncertain whether he had been right to turn down the curial post of apostolic penitentiary and promise of further preferment offered him if he stayed in Rome. He tells us that he wrote the *Praise of Folly* in a week, while staying with More and waiting for his books to turn up. It was certainly revised before publication in 1511, and the internal evidence leads one to suppose that it was considerably augmented and rewritten. Almost one sixth of the text here translated was added after the first edition, almost all before 1522. The text as we have it now moves from light-hearted banter to a serious indictment of theologians and churchmen, before finally expounding the virtues of the Christian way of life, which St Paul says looks folly to the world and calls the folly of the Cross (I Corinthians i, 18 ff.). It is situated at the nodal point where Renaissance Christianity, having broken with medieval religion, already manifests those characteristics which will later make inevitable the split between the majority of the evangelical humanists who inaugurated the early sixteenth-century return to scripture and the leaders of the Reformation.

The bantering tone, the attack on the theologians and the satire on widely practised religious observances provoked a re-action of shocked hostility during Erasmus's lifetime. Erasmus regarded the *Praise of Folly* as a minor work and, in his letter to Dorp (p. 138), said that he almost regretted having published it. But Leo X was amused by it, and both More and Erasmus defended the work in long formal letters to the representative of the Louvain theologians, Maarten van Dorp. Erasmus himself was surprised at the satire's success and at the strength of the reaction it provoked. As he pointed out, it contained, cast in an ironic mould, much the same views as he had already published in the *Enchiridion Militis Christiani*. But the *Praise of Folly* with its bantering and incongruous irony was a much more potent vehicle for conveying the same message.

It was certainly a success. By Erasmus's death in 1536 it had been translated into French (Galliot du Pré, 1520), Czecho-slovakian and German (Schoeffer, 1520), and thirty-six Latin editions had been printed. From 1515 onwards it was accom-panied in all the editions printed by Froben by the learned commentary of Gerard Lijster, to which Erasmus substantially contributed. It was subsequently translated into English, notably by Thomas Chaloner (1549), John Wilson (1668), White Kennet (1683) and J. Copner (1878). More recently interest has increased and, when this translation was first published, three other English translations had appeared in the USA since 1940, Hoyt Hudson (1941), Leonard F. Dean (1946) and John P. Dolan (1964). The present translation first appeared in 1971 and was updated for the Toronto *Collected Works of Erasmus* (1986), and it has been followed by the translations of Clarence H. Miller (1979) and Robert M. Adams (1989). Between 1950 and 1962, fifty-two new translations or printings of the *Praise of Folly* in various languages have been listed.

Several reasons for the recent increase of interest suggest themselves. Erasmus, for all his tortuous subtlety and waspish irony, produced an extremely intelligent and articulate response to what was perhaps the fundamental value-shift in modern

European history. In a world slowly rejecting its medieval moorings, a new and intoxicating vision of man's potentialities had opened up. Predictably, the results ranged from a theological backlash of unprecedented severity to the wild millenniarist expectations of such figures as Charles de Bouelles and Guillaume Postel. They included the Reformation and the rise of national consciousness in northern Europe, and were not diminished either by the exploitation of the newly discovered printing press or the wave of economic prosperity and inflation which spread eastwards form Spain, as western European economies reacted to the influx of precious metals from the new world.

In an era such as our own, in the grip of a value-shift no less bewildering and of changes in systems of transport and communication no less disturbing, the northern European Renaissance must necessarily represent a historical paradigm of interest and importance. Looking back over the course of Renaissance history, we may feel that Europe had to pay dearly for the failure of its spiritual and temporal leaders to heed Erasmus's advice. If, instead of returning to England to write the *Praise of Folly*, Erasmus had stayed in Rome, where Leo X was shortly to be elected to the papal throne, it is difficult to suppose that Rome's reaction to Luther would not have been different.

The technical difficulties of penetrating behind Erasmus's writings to the imaginative and intellectual constraints which explain his mind are formidable. He was an accomplished classical scholar, but was also learned in the history of the Church and the writings of its early Fathers. He was devoted to the study of the scriptures, but was also familiar with the scholastics. He was an educational reformer in touch with all the major European humanists, a satirist and a political thinker. He was an original and important moralist and no mean theologian. He was interested in the arts and held strong views on most of the issues which concerned his contemporaries. Well over three thousand of his letters have been preserved, but the letters occupy only one large volume in the ten-volume edition of his writings. Totally to understand the contours of his thought in so many different fields demands a rare and complex competence unlikely to be found in any individual modern scholar.

Partly for this reason, and because he founded no school or sect, and partly because the serious study of the Latin authors of the Renaissance is only now beginning to find room on university syllabuses, Erasmus's work was for a long time more neglected than it should have been in view of his known historical importance. The *Colloquies*, the *Praise of Folly* and perhaps the *Enchiridion* were all that were known, and Erasmus was erroneously judged on evidence small in volume, humanist in content and haphazard in survival. Recently, however, and largely owing to the decisive step forward marked by the publication of P. S. Allen's remarkable twelve-volume edition of the letters, a much fuller and more balanced view of Erasmus's mind has emerged. There are still too few reliable monographs, and Erasmus's technical and moral achievements as a Renaissance humanist have been emphasized to the detriment of any balanced assessment of a figure whose piety, at least, never moved far from its medieval moorings. But some recent historical monographs have been excellent, and they have totally changed the old view of Erasmus as an intellectual dilettante uncommitted to the great struggles of his time and fastidiously ironic about its religious, social, imaginative and political life.

The *Praise of Folly*, considered inside the huge corpus of Erasmus's writings, is a slight work. It would be wrong to expect from it either an understanding of the mature Erasmus, struggling despondently on as the religious schism between Rome and the Protestant churches became more irreparable, or a systematic exposition of his views even in 1511, when he was forty-two. The body of the satire catches Erasmus in a moment of melancholy, but even as satire it is less caustic and sure of touch than some of the *Colloquies* or the 1528 *Ciceronianus*. The collection of commentaries on antique proverbs known as the *Adages*, first published in 1500, had grown from 838 in 1505 to 3,260 in the Aldine edition of 1508, but was still without the long essays and the biting criticism of contemporary society to be introduced after 1515. The 1508 edition had still represented a compromise between religious and classical interests rather than a bridge from one to the other, and in this the *Praise of Folly* scarcely marks any advance. The learned references and newly coined Greek terms accord ill with the unlearned piety praised in the final pages, and although these pages are aimed more against the fourteenth-century theologian Duns Scotus and his followers than against the humanists, there is in them a melancholy tinge of self-denunciation.

Although affirmed by Erasmus from the beginning, the link between the religious attitude or *philosophia Christi* and classical learning becomes much closer in the *Colloquies*, while only the later works show clearly the integration of the whole spectrum of Erasmus's religious, educational, political and social attitudes. The grand programme for reform in all these spheres unfolded more slowly than is often realized. It was unified by the application to different situations of a series of constant values that became articulate only in reaction to concrete situations or occurrences. It was scarcely discernible even in outline before 1516.

The *Praise of Folly*, however, despite its imperfect unity of tone, does contain comment on a very wide range of Erasmus's interests, and, if the unifying principle of his attitudes is not yet completely apparent, the satire does at least allow a clear glimpse into the constraints which bore on their elaboration. For this reason, it is still the best introduction to Erasmus's thought. No other single work reveals quite so clearly the alternatives between which he was moving or gives such insight into the reasons for his final position. The *Praise of Folly* has a historical importance which transcends its considerable literary merit. It is not a flawless masterpiece, but it is an exciting feat of literary virtuosity. Folly, considered blinded by the self-love that impels her to sing her own praises, turns out to be wise with Pauline as well as with Shakespearean folly. The technique is self-consciously stretched to explore the limits of its potentialities, and it provokes in the reader a reaction of intellectual appreciation before it moves him. But what warrants its accustomed place in the front rank of Renaissance satire is the brilliance of its technique, the sharpness of its aim, the daring of its implications and, not least, the insight it gives into the mind of its author.

It starts off in relaxed mood when Folly, dressed in the 'unaccustomed garb' of a jester, steps forward to claim that she is mankind's greatest benefactor, an assertion that is substantiated with great energy and ingenuity in an amusing parody of a classical declamation. Born in the earthly paradise of Plutus, the young and intoxicated god 'hot-blooded with youth', and of Youth herself, 'the loveliest of all the nymphs and the gayest too', Folly was nursed by Drunkenness and Ignorance. She represents freedom from care, youth, vitality and happiness. Her followers include Self-love, Pleasure, Flattery and Sound Sleep, and she presides over the generation of life.

Even Jupiter has to join her retinue when he wants to beget a child. Not even the stoics can achieve fatherhood without her. Happiness, which Folly bestows, is the prerogative of the young, the foolish and all those subversive of dignity, hierarchy and authority. The enemies from whom Folly offers release are propriety, 'which clouds the judgement', and fear, which draws back from danger. Woman, 'admittedly a stupid and foolish sort of creature', is Folly's particular pride. The 'incessant outcry' of the severe stoics leads only to what is 'dreary, unpleasant, graceless, stupid and tedious' in life, and Folly maliciously asserts that even the stoics, like the rest of mankind, are secretly intent on pursuing the pleasure over which she presides. Folly, helped by Flattery, alone binds human society together, and she cites Socrates as an example of 'just how useless these philosophers are for any practice in life'. Who would ask a wise man to dinner? Stripped of every emotion 'by that double-dyed Stoic Seneca', the wise man is no better than 'a marble statue'.

The first forty-six pages follow this vein of inspiration and may well have been all that Erasmus wrote immediately on his return from Italy, Lucianic more in content than in form. The humour is straightforward and gay. More, for whom it was written, will have understood the allusive jocularity. Erasmus is of course conscious that he is parodying himself. He admired Seneca, whom he was about to edit. He takes an advanced position about the role of women in society and he knows that he passes in the world for a wise man, that flattery was a social evil in all the courts of Europe. He admires Socrates and was elsewhere to remark on the spiritual stimulus to be gained from reading Seneca and Plato. But in these early sections the sense of self-parody does not obtrude or weigh down the text. It is a clever and frivolous mixture of wit and fantasy, swift in pace and gay in tone.

The first striking metamorphosis in Folly's role comes when she has boasted of her role in politics and the arts, and the parade of people on whom she confers her benefits moves on from the young and the hot-blooded to the pitiful and the grotesque, whose folly is to preserve their illusions. They include old men with wigs and dyed hair and old women running after young men 'exposing their sagging, withered breasts'. Folly has come down to earth 'as Homer does', and discoursed on her role in human affairs, relationships and wars.

Folly's note is lower and her voice graver as she praises ignorance and lunacy. She forgets for a moment that Flattery is one of her attendants in a passage celebrating court fools, and it is clear that the declamation's ingenious virtuosity takes precedence over depth and consistency. Folly has to cover herself by suddenly distinguishing between good and bad sorts of flattery as she had already made the all-important distinction between the two sorts of madness, modelled on the two sorts of love distinguished by Pausanias in Plato's *Symposium*. The original gaiety is replaced by a consciousness of paradox as Folly deals with the benefits of insanity, although the mood continues to switch back without warning to the most light-hearted banter, as in the passages on hunters, builders, seekers after the fifth essence and gamblers. Already by page 65, under the guise of continuing frivolity and without any change of tone or style, Erasmus has thrown in a list of pious superstitions, quite long enough to make any theologian's hair stand on end. And, as Folly continues, the banter turns to acid. By the end of this chapter Erasmus is calmly arguing in something very like his own voice with nothing but an occasional reference to folly to remind us of the framework into which it is all supposed to fit. Then he switches back again to the grotesque parade as Folly resumes her second voice, to claim for her own those obsessed with their ancestry or their funeral arrangements, and those made happy by their delusions.

This section ends when Folly, having enumerated her powers to confer happiness through the gifts she bestows from love to insanity, begins in the paragraph starting 'We won't go into every kind of life . . .' (p. 75) to list her followers. She uses her most solemn voice, and the tone is harsh as she indicts the follies of the human race as seen by the gods and passes in review those who on earth seem to be wise. This section, with its attack on pretentiousness of all sorts, forms the heart of the satire. There is no parody, and the subdued humour yields to the catalogue of fatuities that plague the affairs of men. The section culminates in the treatment of the theologians and monks, a full-scale attack from which banter almost disappears after the original reference to the theologians as 'a remarkably supercilious and touchy lot'. Folly is decidedly in her third role, that nearest to the role of Erasmus himself. The issues at stake are discussed in the next section of the Introduction.

The long insertions into the post-1514 text start with the paragraph about the 'jack-of-all-trades' put in after the schoolmasters, and not until 1516. The reference is to Thomas Linacre, and the pretended attack is friendly in tone, as when Folly makes remarks about Erasmus's own pedantry. The long insertions of 1514 concern the abstract scholastic arguments and abstruse concepts which had come to have no apparent bearing on the moral values that, for Erasmus, were the essence of the Christian message. It was clearly neither very difficult nor very daring to make fun of the scholastic attempts to give a coherent rational substructure to Christian belief in the name of religious devotion. The scholastics had applied Aristotelian notions of causality to the theology of the sacraments, defining the psychology of cognition in such a way as to preserve the human spiritual principle's independence of corruptible flesh. The scholastics had laid down norms for moral behaviour that they had conceived outside the situations in which actual moral decisions were generated, according to abstract principles whose applications could be shown to be grotesque.

What is noteworthy is that it is in the name of the simple piety of the *devotio moderna* that Folly here attacks the scholastics in earnest. Folly, like Erasmus before he entered the monastery, is not interested in supporting religious attitudes with rational scaffolding of any philosophical provenance at all, but only in following the example of Christ, the warrior against temptation of the *Imitation of Christ* who was the exemplar of charitable simplicity. When, in the final section of the declamation, Erasmus – in 1514 and subsequently – strengthens Folly's defence of the Pauline folly of the cross, he keeps adding further short allusions, references and scriptural tags, as if anxious at every rereading to buttress the argument even further, as he had earlier constantly added classical examples to increase the erudite humour of the list of antique mock encomia.

After the attack on theologians, the parade of apparently wise followers of Folly continues with princes and courtiers. But we are soon back to prelates in a development that ends with a savage attack on Supreme Pontiffs, in particular when they have recourse to war. Erasmus is careful not to name Julius II, to whom, however, he is clearly alluding. It is only after the section on Folly's followers, in the paragraph beginning 'To start with ...' (p. 114), that Folly makes the two-paragraph transition to the declamation's final section in which she will speak with yet another voice, her fourth, the most complex and paradoxical of all. As Folly proclaims the virtues of the religious ideal in which Erasmus was brought up, in terms which exclude the possibility of defending it in the way Erasmus has dedicated his life to defending it, Erasmus indulges in a whimsical and melancholy ironic comment on his own behaviour. Did he more than half-regret the security of a boyish piety for which learning had seemed the path to pride? Or did he simply ironize his present position whimsically, by pointing to what could prove to be its internal contradiction? What is certain is that in 1511 Erasmus published Folly's earnest and touching praise of the Christian folly of St Paul, quite conscious that Folly expressed it in terms which excluded from it his own intellectual endeavours. In case we miss the point, it is explicitly made when Erasmus is identified by Folly with the Greek pedants.

It is never safe to identify Folly, not even when she is using her third voice, with Erasmus, who might always have been more prudent were he not projecting his view through Folly's mouth. Nor can we use the satire as a guide to Erasmus's world, which Folly caricatures. Careful literary analysis reveals only ambiguity in the continuously varying relationship between Folly and Erasmus. Indeed, since we know how often and carefully Erasmus corrected his text, it is clear that Folly's inconsistencies are deliberately exploited in the interests of achieving the extraordinary control of satirical nuance and ambiguity that Erasmus required. Neither in 1509, nor in 1511, nor in 1512, nor even in 1514, did Erasmus quite know what he thought should be done to reform the Church. He could not identify the dangers to be avoided, nor how to solicit such reform without setting fire to a revolution. The ambiguities are necessary, deliberate and effective, but they detract from the literary unity of the satire. The refusal to establish a clear tonic key in which a totally consistent Folly speaks with an identifiable and steady relationship to the voice of Erasmus makes the satire as tentative as it is sharp and subtle. What happened between 1514 and the condemnation of Luther in 1520 was to leave Erasmus sadly aware of what in 1514 was still to go wrong.

2. ERASMUS, SCHOLASTICS, HUMANISTS AND REFORMERS

The customary presentation of Erasmus as the single principal figure in the evangelical renewal of Christianity, the leader of the northern Renaissance and its outstanding humanist in the technical sense, implying textual and linguistic competence, rhetorical skills and educational preoccupations, has led to the overemphasis of the importance for Erasmus of Renaissance Italy and to the contemptuous dismissal of the Parisian scholasticism against which the *devotio moderna* affirmed and defined itself.

Erasmus had not much enjoyed or profited from his eagerly anticipated journey to Italy, where he spent the period from 1506 to 1509, although he was impressed by the manuscripts, the scholars and the friends he made among the community of ecclesiastical diplomats in Rome. Such spiritual stimulus as he derived from Renaissance Italy had already been absorbed through the mediation of Colet and More, and he was more interested in the Greek scholars of northern Italy, especially Venice, where Aldus had set up his famous press, than in the

Florentine neoplatonism that had so impressed Colet. Within a few years of the turn of the century Colet in England, like Jacques Lefèvre d'Étaples in France, was to transform essentially neoplatonist spiritualities into a close preoccupation with the Pauline epistles, increasingly the focus of all that was new and exciting in devotional practice on the eve of the Reformation.

In order to understand Erasmus and the huge religious upheaval presaged by the *Praise of Folly*, it is, however, also indispensable to understand the scholastic intellectual substructure supporting late-medieval piety. The scholastics were not the mere quibblers on whom Folly pours scorn, and their concerns were of fundamental religious importance. In the end, in spite of Folly's derision, virtually all their disputes concerned the elaboration of a rational system of thought that would make intellectually comprehensible individual survival after death and the doctrines of creation, fall and redemption. Paris had been the intellectual centre of the Christian world since the thirteenth century, during which every single scholastic theologian of note either taught or studied at its new university. Even well before the thirteenth century the debate about universal ideas had essentially been a dispute about the immortality of the soul.

The realists stipulated that during the process of cognition the mind 'abstracted' some universal essence or quiddity that really existed in the objects of perception, but this analysis seemed to leave the mind's spiritual powers dependent on bodily sense organs that decomposed at death. The realist view allowed more easily for the transmission of the guilt of original sin, since each human being was an individual modification of the universal humanity, which after the fall was sinful, but it also seemed necessarily to imply the incarnation of all three divine Persons, since they shared a single essence. The nominalist position that only individual things existed, allowed for an explanation of knowledge that left human spiritual powers independent of the body that was subject to corruption on death, but it easily led to three separate godheads, and seemed to make God responsible for the creation of guilt when he created each individual soul. What was at stake was simply the attempt to make the Christian revelation rationally intelligible, a problem the Christian theologians inherited from Islam whose theologians, like those in thirteenth-century Paris, regarded the philosophers, in Paris the masters of arts, with distaste and disdain.

In the thirteenth century the full-scale exploitation of Islam's Aristotelianism in the interests of elaborating a rational system capable of supporting the Christian revelation was finally undertaken by Thomas Aquinas (c. 1225–74). Aquinas was impelled by the old problems in the psychology of cognition raised by the controversy between realists and nominalists, and he provided the basis for a more optimistic understanding of the world and human experience than that inherited from Augustine, whose later writings had emphasized the effects of original sin on man's natural powers. In particular, Aquinas believed in a rationally ordered universe that reflected the rationality of the divine mind in its laws and structure. Since the human intellect was a created derivative of the eternal mind of God, it was itself capable of judging what was and what was not in accordance with 'right reason', or the rational norms imprinted on the cosmos by its creator. In other words the human intellect was capable of making moral judgements that necessarily accorded with divine law because both were based on the same rational norms. For Aquinas the norm of morality was the conformity of some particular object with the rationally perceived end of man, and this norm was necessarily in accordance with the divine law and the natural law, which was its reflection.

Aquinas's use of the related concepts of reason and law therefore made it possible for him to regard man's perfection as something towards which his own rational nature necessarily tended, rather than as something to be achieved in accordance with norms discoverable *only* by recourse to revelation or authority and anyway extrinsic to the internal exigencies of human moral aspiration and rational experience. There were limits to the lengths to which Aquinas took this conclusion. He would not, for instance, concede that, while it was certainly wrong to act against an erroneous judgement of conscience, it was therefore necessarily right to follow it. He argued against the necessity of invincible error in a world in which he thought everyone came into contact with the gospel message. But the implication that man's perfection was by and large to be achieved in accordance with the moral aspirations with which his rational nature endowed him was a clear and important step forward from Augustine towards a more humane moral and theological system.

The Thomist synthesis was too daring and its theological implications too dangerous for Christianity for it to win widespread acceptance in the schools until the sixteenth century, by the end of which Aquinas's *Summa Theologica* had universally replaced the *Sentences* of Peter the Lombard as the basis for commentary in the theology schools. A series of condemnations at Paris in 1277 seemed possibly to have pointed to heterodox implications in Thomist psychology, and Duns Scotus (*c.* 1265–1308) reacted strongly against Aquinas by restoring in psychology primacy to the will over the intellect. He thereby emphasized both the freedom of the human will at the expense of the rationality of the act of choice and, what was worse, the arbitrary nature of a divine law no longer linked, as in the Thomist psychological system, to the moral aspirations of rational human nature. The link between divine law, natural law and the judgement of conscience was severed, and human perfection was no longer necessarily linked to moral aspiration or fulfilment.

Scotus's emphasis on the freedom of the will might itself have led to heterodox consequences. The heresy of Pelagius, who had come from Britain to Rome in the late fourth century and had been strongly attacked by Augustine, centred on his aristocratic view that the human will could attain to religious perfection, define its own values and reform society. Pelagius held that man could merit his salvation unaided by grace. The 'semi-Pelagian' heresy consisted in holding that man, by his unaided efforts, could at least merit the first gratuitous gift of God which, if accepted, could lead towards the subsequent state of justification in the eyes of God. By extension, it was also semi-Pelagian to hold that man by his own unaided efforts had the power even to accept grace that was offered to him, but this was the conclusion to which Scotus's emphasis on the will's freedom seemed naturally destined to lead.

Scotus, however, guarded against any such implication of his psychology by affirming God's 'absolute' predestination of the elect, that is without reference to any foreseen merit. God first decides to save Peter and then *quasi posterius* (as if afterwards) decrees the grace which in fact determines Peter's salvation. Such a system had its difficulties, for while it was orthodox to assume the absolute predestination of the elect, it was a lot less orthodox to assume the absolute reprobation of the damned without reference to their demerits. And it is very difficult to explain how absolute predestination of the elect could be reconciled with reprobation of the damned only after taking account of their sins.

Scotus's theological bulwark against Pelagianism was eroded by the 'nominalist' logician and theologian William of Ockham (c. 1285–1341). The nominalists had needed to do away with any distinction between essence and attributes in God. But this understandable desire left no room for the quasi-chronological sequence of divine acts on which Scotus's doctrine of absolute predestination depended. The nominalist tradition was therefore left with a Scotist theory of will, but without the Scotist safeguard against Pelagianism. At least one nominalist, Gregory of Rimini (?–1358) solved the difficulty by accepting the absolute predestination of the elect at the price of accepting also the absolute reprobation of the damned. God, even if he did not directly cause human sin, created souls whom He predestined to an eternity of torture. Other extremely complex safeguards against Pelagianism were invoked by the nominalists, but it seems certain that, from Ockham onwards, and with exceptions like that of Gregory of Rimini whose solution was unacceptable on other grounds, the Pelagian implications of the nominalist theory of the will were in fact not avoided. Behind the great emphasis in late-medieval theology on divine transcendence, the arbitrary nature of the law and the inability of man to fathom the purposes of the divinity except by recourse to the extrinsic norms of revelation, the Pelagian principle of the late fifteenth-century schoolmen looms. Grace was *necessarily* bestowed on those 'who did all that lay within them'. The Pelagian implications of this position were not in fact finally to be overcome until, in 1588, Molina went back on the whole nominalist tradition and reintroduced the quasi-chronological distinction of acts in God, clearly a philosophical absurdity.

The current theology of the late fifteenth century was therefore Pelagian in that it allowed man to earn his salvation by his own efforts, providing they were sufficiently intense. 'To those who do what lies within them', ran the great principle of nominalist theology, 'God will not deny grace.' On the level of popular religion, in spite of the mystics and the more spiritually inclined religious movements, the result was great moral tension. Since, in the scholastically inspired spirituality of the late fifteenth century, religious perfection was no longer considered to be intrinsic to moral achievement, it was clearly impossible to know whether one had satisfied the requirement of doing all that lay within one. There were no criteria in the realm of experience on which one could rely to know whether or not one was justified. The inevitable consequence was the growth of the religion of 'works'. The typical devotional forms created in the late fifteenth century like the rosary, the Stations of the Cross, the Angelus, all have to do with making possible the performance of repeated acts. The rise at the same period of charity bequests and of indulgences applicable to the dead increased the sense that salvation depended not on moral achievement but on something extrinsic to it, even works or acts performed by another.

The frankly superstitious religious practices attacked by Folly were those of the kind that looked to the *Pseudo-Gregorian Dialogues* for support. The four books are chiefly devoted to miracle stories, to other extraordinary supernatural phenomena and to heroic feats of religious edification. They were intended to reinforce in the faithful the salutary fear of hell. They originated in the very late seventh century and purported to be an account of Gregory's relaxed narration of the stories to the deacon Peter. They were not a mistaken ascription, but a deliberate forgery, with snatches of authentically Gregorian material.

Gregory had died in AD 604. The dialogues are alleged to have been composed in AD 593–4, but there is no reliable evidence for their existence until well after AD 680, when their dissemination was sudden and widespread. They were translated into virtually all known vernaculars and became the best-known single source for the piety, iconography, art, literature and popular culture of the middle ages. They clearly implied that hell was eternal

(IV, 44), that the soul, although spiritual, suffered physically from burning (IV, 29), and that absolution could be granted after death through the mediation of alms-giving by the living (II, 23). Commonsense objections are parried, and the relationships carefully explained between purgatory, hell, heaven, the individual judgement of the soul at death, and the general judgement at the end of the world.

Being buried in consecrated ground does not help if you are in hell. The doctrine of purgatory is discussed without reference to what has come to be called the 'temporal debt' remaining after the remission of sin which, in later theology, removes the need for supposing that the prayers or alms of the living can affect the moral status of the dead. The resurrection of the body is understood quite literally (IV, 25), as are the grossly realistic depictions of the state of the dead. The efficacy of the prayers, Masses and alms-giving offered by the living for the everlasting fate of those already dead is not so much taken for granted as triumphantly proclaimed. Dante drew extensively on the *Dialogues* and its influence on popular piety was greater than that of any other single work of piety in the history of western Christendom. It obviously distorted popular piety into superstition by its assumption that religious perfection was something extrinsic to moral fulfilment. Pico himself is said by his nephew to have appeared to Savonarola after death, tortured by the flames of purgatory. More's translation of Gianfrancesco's life of his uncle reads, 'Now sith it is so, that he is adjudged to that fire from which he shall undoubtedly depart into glory, and no man is sure how long it shall be first: and may be the shorter time for our intercessions.'

It was precisely against this assumption that the *devotio moderna* rebelled. Considered as a moral, cultural and educational phenomenon, essentially a value shift that the intellectual apparatus of scholastic theology could not accommodate, the Renaissance in northern Europe was quite different from that in the south. Although they were contemporaneous, the Renaissance in the north was not originally either classically or, in the technical sense, humanistically based to anything like the same extent. The form of the Renaissance south of the Apennines was moulded by the relationship between the papal Curia and Byzantium, and the proximity of Venice and Greece had a similar impact on the Renaissance in Venice and the Po valley. There were also reasons of economic geography for the Alps proving much less of a cultural barrier than the Apennines. Culturally Munich was nearer to Venice and Lyons to Rome than Bologna was to Florence. Partly for political reasons intellectual traffic between Oxford and the Italian peninsula probably flowed more freely than that between Paris and Rome. Nevertheless, by the late fifteenth century the unlettered repudiation of the superstitious popular piety of the late-medieval ages by the *devotio moderna* had been reinforced by the neoplatonist forms of humanism to be found both in Florence and, in a more eclectic form, north of the Alps. The two streams came together in the Pauline contention that grace, which was earned uniquely by Christ, affected behaviour and experience.

The return to scripture was not uniquely inspired by the humanists, as is testified by the success of the various spiritual movements and of such works as Ludolph the Carthusian's vast folio of meditations on the life of Christ, the *Vita Christi*, written around 1500. But the evangelical humanist movement, as represented by such figures as John Colet in England, Jacques Lefèvre d'Étaples in France and Johannes Reuchlin in Germany, which Erasmus was to lead, is of particular importance in the present context. It bore a special relationship to the Platonist humanism of such fifteenth-century figures as Nicholas of Cusa (1401–64) and Marsilio Ficino (1433–99).

Ficino was an ardent Christian apologist, convinced that the neoplatonist authors had provided the most suitable philosophic substructure to mediate an understanding of the Christian revelation. His system is in fact generally based on that of the neoplatonist Greek philosopher Plotinus, and his most famous work, the commentary on Plato's *Symposium* written in 1469, incorporates the Plotinian theory of the soul's alienation in space and time. The soul, in its quest for reunification, is stimulated by one or more of the four Platonist 'furies' (the poetic fury, extended to include the effects of music, the religious, prophetic and erotic furies) and ascends through the four degrees of the universe (matter, nature, soul and mind) to achieve final reunification in the beatifying union with God.

The commentary on the *Symposium* was an immensely influential work. It gave birth to a whole spate of treatises on love, and its doctrine was exploited by countless sixteenth-century authors. It was the first formal theory of love to allow the compatibility of the love that is spiritually perfective with that which is expressed in physical relationships, and it was Ficino who coined the term 'Platonic love' to describe the spiritually perfective affection. But in Ficino's Plotinian account of the soul's ascent to beatitude there is no formal separation of natural and supernatural and, in this system, religious perfection therefore becomes clearly intrinsic to moral fulfilment. This explicit link goes a long way to explain how and why the commentary on the *Symposium* was so frequently exploited by the humanists of the sixteenth century.

In particular, however, Ficino's doctrine was taken up into the eclectic syncretism of Pico. Pico's direct relevance for Erasmus comes partly from Erasmus's reliance for the *Enchiridion* on the famous letter from Pico to his nephew (May 1492) and partly from Erasmus's reliance on Pico, and especially the *Apologia*, for the defence of the third-century Greek Father Origen, who was later condemned on account of his largely neoplatonist heresy. But there is much indirect influence as well, and it is important to note that Pico, slightly modifying the Ficinian tradition, puts forward in his celebrated parable *Oration on the Dignity of Man* (written in 1486) the view that man is capable of autonomous self-determination to both good and evil. The *Oration* was written to introduce the 900 theses which Pico offered to defend at Rome in January 1487. In it he gives an account of the creation according to the testimony of 'Moses and Timaeus' and puts into the mouth of God these words to man:

Confined within no bounds, you shall fix the limits of your own nature according to the free choice in whose power I have placed you. We have made you neither mortal nor immortal, so that with freedom and honour you should be your own sculptor and maker, to fashion your form as you choose. You can fall away into the lower natures which are the animals. You can be reborn by the decision of your soul into the higher natures which are divine.

In the evangelical humanism that Erasmus inherited through Colet from Pico, not only was man's perfection intrinsic to his moral achievement but, outside a formal theological context and the difficulties about Pelagianism it imposed, moral self-determination was clearly put into man's autonomous power. Erasmus never ceased to hold this view, and it explains his final rejection of Luther.

John Colet probably came to Oxford in 1483. His great friend, the theologian and Greek scholar William Grocyn, had been to Italy, as also had Thomas Linacre, the future physician of Henry VIII. It was probably on their advice that Colet undertook the journey in 1493. He corresponded with Ficino but did not meet him. On his return to Oxford in 1496 he lectured for three years on the text of scripture, probably substituting a series of 'free public' lectures, like those of Grocyn on Greek, for the traditional disputations he would otherwise have been obliged to take part in. He was to become Dean of St Paul's in 1504 and, in 1510, to found St Paul's School. Some of his Oxford lecture notes have been preserved. He examined the historical and grammatical meaning of the text as a whole, related it to the circumstances of its composition and used strongly Platonist language to illustrate St Paul's points, sometimes almost paraphrasing Ficino and Pico, on whom he drew especially for his commentary on Genesis. Later on, before becoming Dean of St Paul's, Colet substituted in his commentaries examples from St Paul for those from Plato and Plotinus that he had taken from Ficino. His interest in evangelical Christianity had taken him towards Ficinian Platonism before, in the end, he rejected it in favour of a more severe emphasis on the Pauline theology of the redemption.

It was Colet, at the time of his Platonist enthusiasm, who welcomed to Oxford the 'young poet' Erasmus, whom he subsequently persuaded to devoted his life to the study of scripture. Erasmus was at first hesitant. He knew better than Colet how much fruitful study of scripture depended on a knowledge of Greek and Hebrew. In 1499 he wrote to Colet of his intention to devote himself to scripture as soon as he had acquired the necessary technical knowledge. In 1504 he could write that his whole attention was turned to scriptural studies.

The *Enchiridion*, published before Easter that year, had not only drawn heavily on Pico. It had also verbally quoted from the Ficino translation of Plato. Its whole background was neoplatonist, from the Socratic exhortation to self-knowledge to the psychology of spiritual progress. But however remarkable the combination of Pauline theology and Platonist spirituality may seem today, it must be remembered that at this date the neoplatonist corpus of 'Denis the Areopagite' was commonly considered to have been a primitive elaboration of the theology of St Paul made by Denis, his first convert at Athens (Acts xvii, 33). Erasmus was later to challenge the identification of Denis as the author of this material.

Erasmus's early dependence on the Platonist tradition is important because that tradition contains both the belief in intrinsic human perfectibility, which was the pole of Erasmus's opposition to the scholastics, and the belief in an autonomous power of self-determination, which was to be the pole of Erasmus's opposition to the reformers. It also explains much about Erasmus's preference for Origen, condemned for refusing to admit the eternity of hell, and the more Plotinian works of the early Augustine. The achievement of the evangelical humanists generally, and of Erasmus in particular, was to be the anchoring of the values which were transmitted by the Platonist tradition and might otherwise have seemed heterodox in their implications firmly in the text of the Church's own revelation.

The scholastics regarded themselves as the defenders of a traditional orthodoxy and judged the new attitudes according to rigidly conservative criteria. To their minds, the relevance of the traditional norms of belief and behaviour to moral experience was unimportant. Their training was professional, not pastoral, and they could honestly feel themselves justified in obtaining recantations from heretics by the employment of gross physical torture, because they believed that faith, which they identified with the acceptance of their own orthodoxy, opened the way to eternal salvation. The way to salvation was through the acceptance of norms of belief and behaviour extrinsic to the mind's need to understand its experience and to the moral aspirations of the individual. Against this view, Erasmus cautiously urged a confidence in nature and its highest impulses which he expressed both in the prefatory material to his edition of the Greek text of the New Testament in 1516 and, even more strikingly, in the second *Hyperaspistes* letter against Luther from which Rabelais later borrowed the famous '*Fay ce que voudras*' passage on Thélème for *Gargantua* (chapter 57).

The touchstone in the dispute was the view to be taken about pagan virtue. The scholastics were well aware that the ancient pagans had been capable of the highest moral achievement, but by definition, they did not have 'faith' in the sense of Christian belief. Since grace was always dependent on faith, they could not therefore have had grace, been justified or been saved. The identification of the theological virtue of faith with assent to the Creed therefore precluded them from allowing that justification and grace could be intrinsically connected with a moral stature obviously attainable without them. The evangelical humanists, as if to confirm that it was precisely the issue of intrinsic perfectibility which split them from the scholastics, groped towards an exploration of the possibility that the ancient pagans on account of their moral achievements were justified and saved. They were aided by the recent discovery of whole peoples in the new world who had had no opportunity to receive the gospel through no fault of their own, although for centuries more the heroism of Christian missionaries was to be based on the supposition that acceptance of the Christian revelation was an ineluctable precondition of salvation.

In 1512 the French evangelical humanist Jacques Lefèvre d'Étaples wrote in his commentary on the Pauline epistles that those who, in ignorance of the gospel, keep the divine and natural law and, with the significant exception of the rites and ceremonies they prescribed, served their neighbours and repented of their faults, would surely be saved. This doctrine represents only a relatively slight advance on that of Aquinas, but was revolutionary in a late fifteenth-century context. Erasmus himself notoriously allowed the term 'Saint Socrates' to appear in the 1522 colloquy *Convivium religiosum*, tentatively borrowing from an important letter of Ficino on the sanctity of Socrates. In the same colloquy 'Eusebius' says that he is helped by reading Cicero and Plutarch but that he rises from the reading of Scotus 'and others of his sort' 'somehow less enthusiastic about true virtue but more contentious'. Between them, the speakers in the colloquy emphasize the conformity of Virgil, Horace, Cicero and Cato to the Christian spirit. In the 1523 preface to his edition of Cicero's *Tusculan Disputations* Erasmus, now writing clearly in his own name, takes the argument further, asserting that the reading of Cicero has stimulated him to moral progress and improved his ideals. There was in Cicero 'something divine', and it is permissible to hope that he is now in heaven. Morally speaking, Erasmus argues, many of the patriarchs were less blameless than Cicero.

The whole controversy about the salvation of the pagans, which merges into an even wider one about the exceedingly vulnerable channels of transmission invented to explain the conformity of their doctrines with the Old and New Testaments, still awaits its definitive historian. But Erasmus's position is clear, and it accounts for his hostility to the Scotists, the pre-eminently moral content of the *philosophia Christi*, the lack of enthusiasm for mysticism and institutional loyalties and the perpetual primacy of the moral, spiritual and interior whether in theology, education or scholarship. The ultimate source of Erasmus's attitudes in all domains lay in his own discernment of what was and what was not conducive to moral enrichment, undertaken with great imaginative daring and tempered only by a critical scholarship which prevented him going against the evidence, however awkward, but which did allow him to base his conclusions on the technical exegesis of scripture as well as on moral and satirical arguments.

There can no longer be any real doubt that the central feature of Jesuit spirituality, the celebrated 'rules for the discernment of spirits' at the heart of Ignatius of Loyola's *Spiritual Exercises*, derives from Erasmus. Ignatius's personal religious ideal was the related *discreta caritas*, which implies choice made under the inspiration of grace, and he made an aptitude for the discernment of divinely inspired spiritual movements a presupposition running through the official Jesuit documents, including the *Constitutions*, felt in the sixteenth century to be dangerously based on direct religious experience. Ignatius's *Spiritual Exercises* existed as a document of some form by 1527, and they are ultimately the result of a mystical experience undergone by Ignatius in the autumn of 1522 by the Cardoner river. On 14 January 1522 Erasmus in Basle had hurriedly written a prefatory letter to fill a blank page in the commentary on Matthew's Gospel for Froben. That letter contains all the major features of Ignatius's spirituality embryonically, including the principle of the *discretio spirituum* ('the discernment of spirits') and, among much else taken by Ignatius, the idea of imaginatively reconstructing the episodes of Jesus' life for meditative prayer that was to form the body of the *Spiritual Exercises*. The probability is that Ignatius read Erasmus's text at Alcala early in 1526. He certainly drew on it for the literary expression of his own spirituality.

Erasmus had written in his preface of the difficulty of the discernment of spirits, and of the challenge of distinguishing between the promptings of Christ and those of the world or the devil. The problem had already preoccupied him in the *Enchiridion* (Rules 9 and 20) and, although there is no reference to the discernment of spirits in Pico's *Rules*, the subject was mentioned by More in his celebrated letter to Batmanson of 1519–20. Erasmus was also to use the term again when, in a very important letter to Zwingli of 31 August 1523, he concluded, 'How rare is the gift of the discernment of spirits.' Rabelais refers to the same spiritual principle at the end of chapter 14 of the *Tiers Livre* in 1546. His source, too, can only have been Erasmus. It seems probable that historians have attached altogether too much weight to dogmatic disputes as the cause of the Reformation, when the real explanation lies in a clash of spiritual movements between the various reformers and the different schools of scholastics and evangelical humanists.

Erasmus's dependence on the discernment of spirits and the circumstances in which he advocated his view that man's perfection was intrinsic to his moral achievement explain why he so often preferred to make his points satirically and with an apparent lack of directness. To have spoken out would have compromised an orthodoxy he was reluctant to relinquish. The circumstances explain, too, why Erasmus was touchy about criticisms of his orthodoxy, at any rate when they were too important for him to disdain. His view naturally brought him into conflict with the scholastics, and it is a tribute to his patience, ingenuity and forbearance that he escaped serious condemnation. The *Colloquies* were banned and accusations of heresy, normally from a lunatic fringe, were frequent. But Josse Clichtove of the Sorbonne, Edward Lee the archbishop of York, the Spanish theologian J. L. Zuniga, Pierre Cousturier who had left the Sorbonne to become a Carthusian, to say nothing of the Carmelite Nicholas Baechem and Noël Beda, leaders respectively of the conservative reactions in Louvain and Paris, were serious opponents. Erasmus was compromised by the unfaithful French translations of various of his works by Berquin who was executed in 1529. After his death, various of his works were banned in Spain and burned in Milan. They were all put on the Roman index of prohibited books in 1559. The *Praise of Folly* in particular was banned in Franche-Comté, in Spain, in Rome and by the Council of Trent. But the early Jesuits, at least, came very near to venerating his memory, and the Jesuit St Peter Canisius spoke very highly of him. Most of his educational theory was taken up into their own carefully elaborated educational programme expressed in the *Ratio Studiorum* which was to be the immensely influential charter for their schools after its elaboration in the late sixteenth century.

What has here been called the spirituality of intrinsic perfectibility not only alienated Erasmus from the scholastics. It also alienated him from Luther. The Wittenberg theses of 1517 were mostly concerned with indulgences and ritual practices and were by no means clearly heretical. Rome took a long time about issuing the condemnatory bull *Exsurge Domine* (1520) and the Paris faculty hedged until Rome had spoken. Erasmus had agreed with much of what Luther said, but carefully kept his distance from Luther's total position in an important series of letters. His support was solicited by both sides, and pressure was put on him to prove an orthodoxy on which criticism of ecclesiastical practices in the *Colloquies* had seemed to cast doubt by speaking against Luther. When he did finally and reluctantly take up his pen against Luther, Luther had already attacked five of the traditional seven sacraments and listed many other ways in which the Church had fallen away from its revealed function. Erasmus, however, pinpointed in what was now a mass of material Luther's one departure from orthodoxy which was to provide a doctrinal criterion throughout the century for deciding to which side of the schism any individual by right belonged. At the suggestion of Henry VIII and with startling accuracy he picked on the essence of Luther's spiritual position, the denial of any autonomous power of self-determination in man.

Luther's rebellion against fifteenth-century religion had been less humanistically motivated but more sudden and more radical than that of Erasmus. Above all, he had attacked the Pelagianism of the scholastics and the religious tension which it had bred. For Luther, justification consisted in the non-imputation of guilt. The need for straining to do all that lay within one was thereby removed. Justification had become a clearly gratuitous act of God, and Luther's concept of faith as trust and confidence in God further removed the need for moral tension. It made it possible for the truly devout to be virtually assured of their salvation. In the treatises of 1520, Luther had clearly gone beyond the bounds of orthodoxy in his outright condemnation of works and merit as well as of the sacraments and practices whose importance Erasmus had been careful merely to downgrade. In particular, however, Luther had held in the Heidelberg Disputation of 1518 that man by his own free will, so far from earning his salvation, necessarily committed mortal sin. This anti-Pelagian denial of the autonomous power of self-determination to good was confirmed in the *Freedom of the Christian Man* (1520). No doubt Erasmus misunderstood Luther. But the point of attack he chose was also that which split More from Tyndale, Budé from Melanchthon and Sadoleto from Calvin in their respective controversies. Much more than Eucharistic theology, it was the divisive force behind the schism.

The difficulty was clear. Both humanists and reformers wished to reject the Pelagianism of the scholastics and the deleterious

religious extrinsicism which it promoted. But while the humanists as such were dedicated to defending man's intrinsic perfectibility in accordance with his self-determining moral choices,
the reformers could find no logical answer to Pelagianism, short
of denying to free will any power in the order of grace.

It is not difficult to see how this situation arose. If man's
'nature' is capable even of accepting, to say nothing of meriting,
grace, the result is at least semi-Pelagian theology and a religion
of tension. If, however, it is not, man is necessarily deprived of
any power of self-determination to a good which, on any
theory, is supernatural, and he is incapable of influencing his
own eternal fate. The dilemma is rigid. Erasmus's treatise against
Luther, the *de libero arbitrio* (On Free Will, 1524), accuses Luther
of denying free will. Luther's reply, the *de servo arbitrio* (On
Unfree Will, 1525), accuses Erasmus unjustly of scepticism, but
also of Pelagianism. Although Erasmus had never made a formally Pelagian utterance, it was true that there was no known
way of reconciling the autonomous power of self-determination
to good in which Erasmus believed with a non-Pelagian theory
of grace. The ultimate solution depended on assuming that
justified man was a compound not of pure nature and grace, but
of a nature which itself bears in its supernatural aspirations the
mark of its redemption and the grace which confers on it formal
justification. Once it is accepted that nature itself is affected by
the redemption, it becomes possible to allow all men's power of
accepting grace, in virtue of a power bestowed on his nature by
the redemption, without thereby incurring Pelagian implications.
But this avenue of solution was blocked in the early sixteenth
century, however near the evangelical humanists edged towards
it, because it would have implied allowing grace to the pagans
and therefore apparently abandoning faith as a prerequisite for
grace. When, at the very end of the sixteenth century, the Jesuit
Lessius put forward a theory in which the power of accepting
'efficacious' or justifying grace was attributed to human nature as
it in fact exists in man, it was suppressed even inside his own
order. It was also strongly contested by the faculties of Louvain
and Douai, as later by the Jansenist theologians in France.

The rigidity of the dilemma in the early sixteenth century is absolute and immensely important, but it need not further detain us. It is sufficient to see that Luther chose one of its horns and Erasmus the other. Erasmus's religious position is well defined by his stand against the scholastics on one hand and against Luther on the other. But the implications of his position would certainly have been dangerous for him had they been spelled out in a formal theological account of how grace acts in the will. He retained the position of Pico but, with the example of Pico before him, understandably preferred to make his points more in terms of conformity to the scriptures or in terms of ironic comment than in formal scholastic debate. There were other issues, notably his concern for the primacy of rhetoric over dialectic, on which Erasmus took the opposite line from Pico, and in terms of direct influence on his thought, others were more important. But the religious position of the evangelical humanists, elaborated on the basis of scriptural arguments, none the less owes a great deal to the personal and social values which the Florentine neoplatonist tradition not only brought into prominence, but was in a large measure erected to support.

3. THE *PRAISE OF FOLLY*, DORP AND THE SPIRITUALITY OF ERASMUS

Desiderius Erasmus, as he came to be known, was born either in 1466 or, perhaps a shade more probably, in 1469, the illegitimate son of a future priest and a physician's daughter. He was brought up at first by his mother and went to school at Gouda for one year. It was probably immediately after Gouda that he spent a year as a chorister at Utrecht. From at least 1478 to 1483 he was at the famous school founded by Gerard Groote at Deventer where he learned Latin and developed a taste for Latin literature. When Erasmus was thirteen his mother died of the plague. A year later he left Deventer when twenty of his school companions died of the same disease, and he was admitted to the school of the Brethren of the Common Life at 's Hertogenbosch. Erasmus's father also died of the plague and his elder brother Pieter joined the Augustinian Canons in their monastery at Sion when Erasmus himself went to Steyn.

Deventer was already an intellectual centre and under Alexander Hegius, who arrived in the year in which Erasmus left, it was to become a cradle of Dutch humanism. Its alumni already included Nicholas of Cusa, the cardinal who taught the 'learned ignorance' of passive neoplatonist mysticism, and Thomas à Kempis. Its founder, Gerard Groote, had emphasized the religious experience of the individual, cultivated an ethical and Biblical piety, and remained largely indifferent to sacraments and monastic vows. Closely associated with the spirit of the modern devotion in which Erasmus was brought up were the Brethren of the Common Life, also founded by Groote as a lay congregation devoted to the schooling of the young. Their piety, however, like that of the *Imitation of Christ*, was anti-intellectual and, if they helped to create the situation which was to require and to produce the learned Christian humanism of Erasmus and his friends, they themselves had little influence on the development of humanism. Groote himself had admired Seneca and Cicero, and it is arguable that Rudolf Agricola, brought up at Groningen in the atmosphere of the modern devotion, remained true to Groote's spirit by going to Italy and returning imbued with the ideals of humanist rhetoric to be employed in the service of religion. Hegius was his friend and younger contemporary. Erasmus in his early days admired both, and took the term *philosophia Christi* from Agricola. In later years he reacted somewhat against them but it is possible, especially in the *Praise of Folly*, to see the devotional ideal of the Brethren rather uneasily clad in the richly embroidered humanist trappings of the early part of the satire. Throughout his life, Erasmus was to regard his knowledge of ancient languages and lore of ancient literature as something to be put at the service of a religious ideal which does not differ substantially from that of Groote, although he no doubt went further than any of his predecessors in attributing valid religious and moral ideals to classical authors.

In the monastery Erasmus pursued his studies, and wrote two treatises. One was on the contempt of the world, a subject which attracted several Parisian humanists who entered contemplative monasteries at about the same time, and which was not without humanist overtones, since the peace required for contemplation was also that which favoured study. The other treatise was the *Anti-Barbari* ('Against the Barbarians'). Both were humanist works in their original texts, although they were not to be published until 1521 and 1520 in texts which had later been rewritten. About 1492 Erasmus entered the service of Henry of Bergen, Bishop of Cambrai, by whom he was ordained priest in that year and whom he hoped to accompany to Italy.

Erasmus's monastic career is controversial. He benefited from many exceptions from the more ascetic parts of the rule. He contracted an intimate and emotional friendship with a fellow monk, Servatius, and he looked for support to a wealthy widow active in good works, Berthe de Heyen. He was the source of a humanist enthusiasm in the priory, and the *Anti-Barbari* in its original form was the result of his superiors' desire to restrain his humanist enthusiasm. It seems certain that he had no real monastic vocation, but only a boyish and rather timid devotion that made monastic disciplines less than totally uncongenial and at any rate tolerable for the sake of his studies and his religious life. For some years after his profession in 1487 Erasmus seems to have made a largely successful attempt to find a *modus vivendi* with the monastic life. He was to remain a canon even when dispensed from wearing the habit or residing in a monastery. He was pious as well as prudent throughout his life and if later he was occasionally bitter or stinging, he none the less showed a control of the aggressive reactions by which many of his contemporaries were overcome. Without his monastic years Erasmus might never have found the patient and comparatively tranquil intellectual firmness that kept him faithful to his own true vocation.

Henry of Bergen was not made a cardinal and his journey to Italy was cancelled. Erasmus's years with him were frustrating, although he became an accomplished poet and discovered a manuscript of Augustine that gave him great joy. In 1495 he was released by the bishop to go to Paris, where he became a poor scholar at the College de Montaigu, recently reformed by Standonck and linked in spirit with the Brethren of the Common Life. The discipline was harsh, the food bad, the conditions dirty and the asceticism obligatory and rigorous. Furthermore, the orthodoxy was Scotist. Erasmus broke down and was cured, he declared, not by the help of the doctor but by the intercession of St Geneviève. He returned to the bishop and then to Steyn, where he was encouraged to return to Paris. This time he took private lodgings.

Largely by flattery, Erasmus now entered into relations with the humanist rhetorician and general of the Maturins, Robert Gaguin, through him meeting the quarrelsome Fausto Andrelini, with whom he quickly became the closest of friends, and other humanist visitors to Paris. When the subventions of Henry of Bergen ran out, Erasmus took pupils and began writing for them the *Colloquies*, first published without his consent in 1519 and then reworked by him into his most popular book. There are over six hundred known editions. At this time, too, Erasmus started other pedagogical works, in particular the *Adages*, of which a small collection was published in 1500. Erasmus seems to have entered into an emotional relationship with one of his pupils. Another, William Blount Lord Mountjoy, the future tutor to Henry VIII, was to be his lifelong patron, and first invited Erasmus to England, which he visited in 1499.

That autumn found him living at the Oxford house of his order. He met Colet, already a theologian of note and firmly devoted to scripture. Colet certainly exercised a strong influence over Erasmus, but Erasmus was probably telling the truth when he later wrote to Colet that he had never had the intention of devoting himself solely to profane letters. Colet encouraged an inclination which was already there, helped to give it a definite purpose and imbued Erasmus with a lasting devotion to peace.

When staying with Mountjoy, Erasmus had even taken up riding and hunting. He clearly enjoyed his stay in England. He met William Grocyn, Thomas Linacre, William Latimer, future tutor of Cardinal Reginald Pole, who was the king's cousin, and above all Thomas More, at this date still undecided about the possibility of a monastic vocation. Through More, Erasmus met the family of Henry VII, including the nine-year-old prince who was to become Henry VIII. It was at Oxford that Erasmus first came into serious contact with Florentine neoplatonism. More himself, who had learned Greek from Grocyn, had translated the letter from Pico to his nephew on which Erasmus was to draw for the *Enchiridion*.

In January 1500 Erasmus returned to Paris to see the first edition of the *Adages* through the press. The work, dedicated to Mountjoy, was printed in Roman type and contained 818 adages with Greek versions of 154 of them. As he left England Erasmus had had his savings confiscated at Dover, restrictions on the export of currency being no modern hazard, and there began a period of assiduous courting of patrons. He went to Orléans, possibly to avoid the plague, and then went for the same reason to Holland where he stayed for a month at Steyn before travelling widely. He spent his time immersed in Greek and working on Jerome and Cicero.

This period in Holland from 1501 to 1504 is notable for Erasmus's discovery of the manuscript of Lorenzo Valla's critical notes on the New Testament, which Erasmus published in Paris in 1505. He was already enthusiastic about Valla's *Elegantiae* and the discovery of the philological notes on the New Testament excited him greatly. The prefatory dedication to Christopher Fisher, an English papal diplomat, formally enunciates the principle of correcting the Latin Vulgate from the Greek text and the Septuagint version of the Old Testament from the Hebrew. In Valla's timid critical notes, Erasmus found the encouragement he would need to embark on his own critical Greek text of the New Testament.

While in Holland Erasmus also wrote the *Enchiridion*, first published in the *Lucubratiunculae* of 1503 (or perhaps early 1504) and republished, notably in 1518, with a new programmatic preface. The *Enchiridion* shows a deepening interest in the third-century Greek Father, Origen, which may well derive from a new friend, the humanist Franciscan prior John Vitrier. Even when in later life Erasmus admitted that Origen's neoplatonism had led him into theological error, he followed Origen's great admirer, Pico, in defending him. The most interesting features of the *Enchiridion* are the emphasis on interior, evangelical piety and its use of a Pauline but also frankly neoplatonist psychology to support its description of the spiritual combat. It is essentially a guide to Christian living, in spite of the fact that Erasmus goes so far as to recommend to his ordinary Christian the study of Origen, Ambrose, Jerome and Augustine rather than the scholastics.

Embryonically, however, the *Enchiridion* contains the whole Erasmian programme, advocating a religion of interior conversion in place of ritual observances, a return to scripture and the Fathers and a demand for social harmony and peace between nations. The neoplatonist psychology allows Erasmus to spiritualize the significance of observances and dogmas to so great an extent that his opponents were understandably uneasy about the lessened weight he put on them as fitting aids for those who had not yet reached spiritual adulthood. Erasmus allegorizes his interpretation of the Old Testament and deliberately exploits the Pauline distinction between interior piety or the spirit and the ritualism of the early Christian Judaizing party or the letter. Learned humanism is not absent from the *Enchiridion*, but the place taken in it by the imitation of Christ links its spirit to that of the modern devotion. Christ appears above all as the exemplar of patience, humility and the passive virtues.

The *Enchiridion*'s criticism of rites and observances is audacious, as is its final affirmation that life under religious vows does not necessarily sanctify. But Erasmus is careful not to discredit praying to the saints or the devotional cult of relics completely. It is simply more important to live the interior Christian virtues than merely to observe the outward forms of devotion. The only really new note to be heard in the *Praise of Folly*, which is perhaps less openly reliant on Plato, is the satire's final and paradoxical attack on intellectual endeavour.

Late in 1504 Erasmus returned to Paris, and by late 1505 he was back in England, where he stayed until 1506. He met William Warham, the Archbishop of Canterbury, and became an intimate friend of Thomas More, with whom he made a series of translations of Lucian. These were published in a joint volume of 1506, although Erasmus himself went on translating Lucian until 1512.

Erasmus was to borrow much from Lucian apart from exploiting the potentialities of Lucianic satire in order to create a defence of ambiguity. The very notion of praising Folly, the mock encomium, is itself Lucianic. The 1517 *Complaint of Peace*, which is put into the mouth of Peace, shows however that giving the mock encomium to Folly herself is not the chief source of irony in the *Praise of Folly*, since the *Complaint of Peace* is not an ironic work. No doubt encouraged by Folly's success, other Renaissance authors were to write mock encomia. Notable later examples include Ulrich von Hutten's *Letters of Obscure Men* (1515) purporting to congratulate the scholastics responsible for the attack on Johannes Reuchlin, the German Hebraist and lawyer admired by the Erasmian humanists, the *Encomium of the Ass* at the end of Cornelius Agrippa of Nettesheim's *On the Vanity of the Sciences* (1526) and, best known of all, Panurge's harangue in praise of debt at the beginning of the *Tiers Livre* of Rabelais (1546).

In addition to the form, Erasmus takes from Lucian the technique of making serious points in bantering tone and mixing the frivolous with the serious. In the preface to Lucian's *The Cock* in the 1506 volume Erasmus explains what attracts him in Lucian. He likes the vividness of Lucianic satire, but above all he delights in the mixture of serious satire with banter, of vinegar with sweetness, of the trivial with the important, and the light-hearted treatment of sacred and solemn subjects. The absurdity of the prayers reaching Mary in the 1526 colloquy *A Pilgrimage for Religion's Sake* recalls the contradictory prayers reaching Zeus in Lucian's *Icaromenippus*, just as, in the *Praise of Folly*, Folly adopts Menippus' vantage point to comment on men as seen by the gods.

More, who had led Erasmus to Lucian, knew precisely how to understand the *Praise of Folly*. His reply was to be the similarly Lucianic *Utopia*, which puts a serious exploration of advanced personal and social values into the mouth of Ralph Hythlodaeus or Ralph the fool. Like the *Praise of Folly*, *Utopia* is a fantasy, not a programme. Both have serious imaginative purposes, both explore seriously the compatibility and implications of the enlightened social and personal ideals that were the heritage of Colet. Needless to say, Erasmus and More are in total agreement. More defended Erasmus to Dorp, and everything in *Utopia* can be matched from Erasmus's works.

Not very much comes from the non-ironic *Ship of Fools* (1494) by Sebastian Brandt, whose passenger list includes most members of the human race. Brandt's accusations of folly in human affairs are accurate enough, but they are conveyed in the ordinary late-medieval style, with none of Erasmus's ironic cutting edge.

From 1506 until 1509, Erasmus was in Italy. For a year he supervised the studies of the two sons of Henry VII's physician. He received in Turin the doctorate of theology for which he had worked in Paris. The party then settled in Bologna but, soon after their arrival, were obliged by the advance of the papal armies to retreat hastily to Florence. Bologna capitulated and Erasmus arrived back in time to see the pope's triumphal entry on 11 November. On 17 November Erasmus, already beginning to show signs of disillusion with the Italy he had longed to visit, wrote that studies there had given way to war and that the pope was fighting, conquering, triumphing and imitating Caesar, a description of Julius II he was often to use subsequently. He later commented on the extortionate taxation of the poor in the newly reconquered papal territory.

In late 1507 Erasmus arrived in Venice to stay with Aldus Manutius. He stayed to see a newly enlarged edition of the *Adages* through the famous Aldine press in 1508. After Venice came Padua and Rome, where Erasmus made some important friends, including the future Leo X, but where the corruption and sycophancy of the papal court, the neglect of the faithful and the greed of the clergy depressed him. Then in 1509 came news from Mountjoy that Henry VIII, who had twice written to Erasmus in Italy, had become king and had explicitly declared his desire to build up a scholarly entourage. William Warham promised a benefice and enclosed travelling expenses. Cardinal Grimani suggested that he should stay in Rome where he ranked a number of cardinals among his friends. A curial appointment could be arranged. Erasmus hesitated, drawn no doubt by the prospect of the Roman libraries and eventual preferment. On the other hand, he could look forward to friends, a benefice and leisure to work in England. It seems likely that his disappointment with the state of the Church in Julius II's Italy tipped the balance in favour of England. On his arrival he stayed with More and wrote the *Praise of Folly*, as he recounts in the letter to Dorp.

It is important to remember the frame of mind in which

Erasmus wrote the *Encomium Moriae* (at once the 'praise of Folly' and the 'praise of More'). He had just returned from Italy, the country which had first experienced the Renaissance, which had seen the rebirth of letters and the rebirth of classical rhetoric, the country of Ficino, Valla and Pico. For many years Erasmus had dreamed of undertaking the Italian journey from which so many of his fellow humanists, Colet, Grocyn, Agricola, Lefèvre d'Étaples and the others, had drawn inspiration. Erasmus had not enjoyed his stay. He was stimulated by the libraries, the manuscripts and the scholars, but he had been unhappy with Aldus at Venice and deeply shocked by the irreligion of Julius II. The pagan atmosphere of Rome, where the pope was intent only on territorial aggrandizement and revaluing the coinage, must have seemed to him as distasteful as the superstition into which a Scotist orthodoxy and a clergy without pastoral interests had allowed the faithful to lapse in France.

The result in the *Praise of Folly* was indulgence in a whimsical lack of confidence. On arriving in England Erasmus retreated into what was at first intended merely to be a clever Lucianic frivolity which he knew his friend would understand and which became for him an imaginative catharsis. The banter is occasionally weighed down by bitterness, if not invective, and the final praise of Pauline folly, however moving, also sounds a harsh note of self-parody. The religious ideal remains that of the modern devotion, even of its anti-intellectual wing, but the end of the *Praise of Folly* is disingenuous in its advocacy of an ideal which Erasmus knew could only prevail with the help of the learned humanism he shared with Colet and More. When searching the *Praise of Folly* for the spectrum of Erasmian attitudes it contains, it is important to remember that it is tinged with a melancholy that does not draw back from self-parody and in which intellectual confidence is betrayed by emotional uncertainty.

Erasmus stayed in England, mostly with Mountjoy and More, from 1509 to 1511, when he went to Paris to see the now corrected *Praise of Folly* through the press. More had recently remarried on the death of his first wife. His second wife, Dame Alice, spoke no Latin and did not get on well with her husband's friends, however good she might have been to his children. On his return from Paris Erasmus went to Cambridge where he began to worry about regularizing his situation and obtaining dispensations from wearing his habit and residing in his monastery, and from the incapacity to accept a benefice as a result of his illegitimacy. All were to be forthcoming from the future Leo X. After some delay, William Warham paid him a substantial pension. But ironically enough it was Julius II who finally drove Erasmus back to Holland. He had by now made peace with Venice and wished to form an alliance with England against the French, still entrenched in north-west Italy. It was the ensuing preparations of Henry VIII for war which so changed the climate in England that Erasmus preferred to leave, although he did not actually depart until his friend Leo X, whom he later acclaimed as having restored peace, had been pope for over a year.

Leo X was elected pope in March 1513. Julius II had crushed the Borgia domination in northern Italy and, although Venice had as usual successfully defended itself, the lost papal territory had been reconquered by 1510. He then aimed to unite Italy behind him and to oust Louis XII of France from Italian territory. By Easter 1512, Henry VIII's troops were ready to sail against France. Colet was momentarily in disfavour for preaching a pacifist sermon to the court on Good Friday. A Christian prince, he had said, would do better to imitate Christ than Caesar. Erasmus waited long enough to see if Leo X would succeed in restoring instant peace. In 1514 he wrote of his disappointment to Henry of Bergen and made arrangements to leave for Holland where he hoped for the patronage of the future Charles V. What finally decided him to publish the *Praise of Folly* in 1511 may well have been his wish to support the growing opposition to Julius II in Gallican France.

From 1514 to 1521 Erasmus made Holland his base. He visited England in 1515, 1516 and 1517, on the last occasion receiving the dispensations he sought. He also made six journeys to Basle in order to see his works through Froben's press. Financially he was in difficulties. Friends helped, and he was made a councillor of Charles V, but the stipend was in arrears. In 1516 he was offered a bishopric in Sicily but commented that he was unwilling to give up his studies for any bishopric, however splendid. At Easter of that year he had been made a canon of Courtrai, but in the winter he wrote to More of the danger that, although he was well clad, he might still die of hunger. It should however perhaps be said that his poverty was relative to the task he knew he had to perform. He normally travelled with an amanuensis.

During these years in England and Holland Erasmus had been engaged on the Greek version of the New Testament and on editions of Seneca and Jerome. The edition of Seneca's *Lucubrationes* was published by Froben in 1515 and need not detain us, except perhaps to note that Erasmus draws attention in his preface to Jerome's very high opinion of Seneca, so justifying the continued utility of classical authors to Christian readers. The Greek New Testament on the other hand is relevant in two ways to the *Praise of Folly*.

First, it makes clear that Erasmus viewed his own contribution to the restoration of evangelical religion in terms of technical and critical expertise. He saw perfectly well that unlettered piety on the medieval model, unless it was interior and evangelical, led easily to superstition. But the prefatory material made it clear that, however bold Erasmian criticism of the text of scripture might have appeared, its intention was to mediate a popular and vernacular diffusion of evangelical religion, as the Brethren of the Common Life had tried to do.

Second, the publication of a critical Greek text of the New Testament provoked opposition from the same sources and for the same reasons as the *Praise of Folly*. Just as the *Praise of Folly* more sharply than the *Enchiridion* had manifested Erasmus's serious desire to shift the theological centre of gravity towards scriptural exegesis and so threatened theological tenets and religious observances that were part of the current orthodoxy, so, too, the appearance of the Greek New Testament threatened the ascendancy of the Latin Vulgate which had been the Church's official text of scripture since Jerome in the fourth century. The *Novum Instrumentum*, as Erasmus called his Greek text, was intended and understood to have a religious relevance. It was to provide a scriptural rather than authoritarian base for theology and religion.

If the Vulgate Latin was faulty or inaccurate, then the Church and its theologians were compromised by having for centuries backed with their authority an unauthentic or at least seriously imperfect version of scripture. What Erasmus was doing was less radical than what Luther was to do and perhaps not much more audacious than what was being done by other evangelical humanists elsewhere. But it is important to realize how real a threat to the establishment was the programme which emerged from the *Enchiridion* through the *Praise of Folly* to the *Novum Instrumentum*.

Critical work on the Bible was being undertaken notably at Alcala and in Paris. The publication of Lorenzo Valla's notes had given notice that Erasmus did not regard even the text of scripture as exempt from the application of rational critical norms. In France Jacques Lefèvre d'Étaples, while he continued to publish Aristotle, the medieval mystics and the neoplatonist theologians, was to devote himself to the textual criticism and then increasingly to the vernacular diffusion of scripture. His mind, however, was very different from that of Erasmus. His spirituality was less moral than mystical, passive and nourished on paradox. He was devoid of irony and even of humour. His *Psalter* of 1509 contained five Latin texts of the psalms, but both in this work and in the 1512 edition of the Pauline epistles, the boldness is mystical rather than critical. Lefèvre thought that the Vulgate text, because clearly faulty, could not on that account be the work of Jerome, and that St Paul could not really have quarrelled with St Peter. The edition of Paul's epistles includes the 'correspondence' with Seneca known already to be spurious. Lefèvre not only accepts with Colet the authenticity of the Pseudo-Denis, rejected by Valla, Grocyn and Erasmus, but he identifies St Paul's first convert with Denis the first martyr of France, so providing apostolic authority for the French Church and a continuity between Athens and Paris which was to be a weapon of sixteenth-century French humanists against the Italian boast of continuity between ancient and modern Rome. There was to be an acrimonious dispute between Lefèvre and Erasmus on a point of textual criticism in which Lefèvre tardily and tacitly conceded defeat. In the end however, Lefèvre was both bolder and more effective in the vernacular dissemination of evangelical religion than Erasmus himself.

At Alcala the Erasmian critical techniques of A. Lebrixa were suppressed by the Inquisition, and the Polyglot Bible of Cardinal Ximenes de Cisneros did not permit the correction of the Latin text against Greek or Hebrew manuscripts. But the Polyglot Bible did print a Greek text and the type was finer, the printing better and the manuscripts older than for Erasmus's edition. Only Erasmian critical techniques were lacking. But although the Polyglot New Testament was ready in 1514, pontifical authority for the Polyglot Complutensian Bible did not come until 1520 and it was not on sale until 1522, by which time Erasmus had published three editions of his Greek text with his new Latin translation, itself dating back to 1506.

Erasmus's own work was far from perfect, as he himself knew, due to lack of manuscripts. Many of the criticisms it provoked were valid, although Erasmus, nettled at criticisms on purely theological or ecclesiological grounds, tended to reply either with unconcealed disdain or at testy length. He was quite rightly criticized for translating some missing verses of the Apocalypse into Greek out of the Vulgate Latin, although the Complutensian Bible opened itself to the same sort of reproach. But the *Novum Instrumentum* appeared in 1516 with a prefatory dedication to Leo X along with three introductory works, later expanded, to give the gist of the whole Erasmian programme for religious renewal.

Meanwhile Erasmus had also edited the letters of St Jerome in the first four volumes of the nine-volume edition of Jerome's works published by Froben in 1516. Jerome was the patron of the Brethren of the Common Life and Erasmus's interest in him stems from his earliest days. He had begun work on the text of the letters by 1500 and in 1511 he was lecturing on the letters at Cambridge. The preface to the whole edition is a letter from Erasmus to William Warham in which Erasmus recapitulates his total aim. In an age, he says, in which princes behave like barbarians and bishops are wordly, the task of instruction has been left to the ignorant. From the neglect of ancient authors whom Erasmus lists – the list includes Origen and omits

Augustine – Erasmus wants to rescue Jerome, the patron of learned and eloquent piety, by using the same critical techniques as he has applied to the *Novum Instrumentum*. Erasmus is not unaware of the similarity of the role he has chosen for himself with that of Jerome. Both admired Origen, although Jerome's early enthusiasm turned to opposition in AD 394. Both were learned in the ancient languages and devoted themselves to scripture. Both learned from the pagan authors of antiquity. Both were apt to be tart and waspish in their reactions and neither enjoyed criticism. And in the third preface to the second volume of the Jerome edition Erasmus justifies his own critical approach to the Vulgate by pointing to Jerome's attitude to the Septuagint in spite of the conservative reaction of Augustine.

The edition of Jerome's letters in the same year as the Greek New Testament is no doubt fortuitous, but Erasmus certainly thought his own critical activity justified by Jerome, and the edition of the Jerome letters was intended to further exactly the same cause as the *Novum Instrumentum*.

Erasmus had written to Leo X, from whom he hoped for a restoration of peace and for protection for his own task, to ask him to accept the edition of Jerome. Leo X acceded and warmly wrote on Erasmus's behalf to Henry VIII. The new era looked as if it might have dawned. Erasmus was on good terms with Henry VIII of England, Pope Leo X and Charles V of Spain. He was soon to include François I of France and Ferdinand of Austria among his patrons. All of them were either humanists or at any rate wished to protect humanists of Erasmus's calibre. He had many other friends in high places. It is true that he could not prevent himself from provoking a theological reaction which he was too sensitive to endure with equanimity, and that his chosen enterprise would have fared better if he had not been obliged to loyalty to any prince. But none the less the controversy with Maarten van Dorp was a cloud in a sky that must otherwise have seemed bright. Other opponents rattled him, but Dorp was the representative of powerful Louvain, and having lost Paris he was concerned to win him over.

Maarten van Dorp (1485–1525) was a humanist theologian at Louvain who acted as spokesman for his colleagues. He wrote little, but was rector of the university in 1523. Erasmus remained friendly with him. In the important 1521 edition of Erasmus's letters by Froben the references to the 'stolid' Dorp are omitted, attenuated or made anonymous in deference to their reconciliation. At Dorp's death, Erasmus composed an epitaph.

Dorp's first letter, probably sent in September 1514, is much more concerned to prevent the edition of the New Testament in Greek than to prevent a re-edition of the *Praise of Folly*. Dorp represented the sort of conservative humanism typical of the more daring members of the Paris faculty. His letter draws attention to the theological obloquy Erasmus has drawn on himself. He dislikes the bantering treatment of serious matters but is prepared to be enthusiastic at the prospect of a good edition of St Jerome. On the New Testament he refers to Lefèvre and Valla. The argument rests on the implication in publishing any new Greek text that the Vulgate was wrong. The reactionary Cousturier ('Sutor'), who had been prior of the Sorbonne before becoming a Carthusian, claimed that any error found in the Vulgate could ruin the authority of scripture and the Church.

The reply to Dorp is the letter of May 1515 translated here after the *Praise of Folly*. Erasmus begins by saying that he is in a hurry, that he 'almost' regrets publishing the *Praise of Folly* which only puts into ironic form what was in the *Enchiridion*, that he was only following the advice of Augustine's *de doctrina christiana* in making the evangelical message attractive, that he had arrived ill from Italy and while staying with More had written the *Praise of Folly* in seven days, that it was published by friends without his permission in a bad copy; but that there had been seven editions in some months (pp. 138–43). It is difficult to guess how many of these statements are true, since some certainly are not. Erasmus did publish a carefully revised text of his satire himself, but he was ill when he returned from Italy. The debt to Augustine is disputed but seems doubtful. It is difficult to believe that More's house contained no books with which Erasmus could have worked on something else, but he is correct about the work's success. There are at least six known editions in thirteen months.

Erasmus did not send the whole letter, which was written for publication, but it is impossible to say exactly what portion of it was sent, and the whole letter is so important in the context of the *Praise of Folly* and in the total undertaking of which it is a part that it has become usual to print it as an appendix to the satire. Dorp replied in August, pressing the conservative objections, pointing out that the Jews did not know Greek nor the Greeks Latin, so that one could not argue that true religion required a knowledge of all three. He asserts that the 'new' theology is old enough, that scholastics like Thomas Aquinas and St Bonaventure were not enemies of the Church. He alleges with care the doctrine of St Augustine, but is careful not to point out that the *de doctrina christiana* recommends the study of Greek and Hebrew, and declares the source of the dispute to be the inerrancy of the Vulgate. Dorp's quotations are not totally honest. He runs together phrases from different chapters of Jerome and does not mention Augustine's reserves. He is unfair in saying to Erasmus that he cannot pretend to be the only theologian to have understood the Bible.

To this reply the answer came from More dated 21 October 1515. It carefully says that Dorp's technical arguments are not worth refuting and that no one of importance agrees with them, but takes him to task for attacking Erasmus in person. The letter is a delicious pin-prick. Who, after all, is Dorp? What right has he to speak for the theologians? And above all to patronize Erasmus? How can anyone speak for the scholastics who are at daggers drawn with one another over the question of universal ideas? More devotes some time to attacking the basis for instruction in dialectic, the *summulae logicales* that Peter of Spain, later Pope John XXI, composed about 1250, and which consists in a hideously complex set of logical rules to be learned by heart, rather as if the whole of today's symbolic logic should be written out without the symbols. This, says More, is not grammar. His letter is a masterpiece of intelligent controversy. No trick is missed, no weakness goes undiscovered.

Dorp's opposition moderated. A congratulatory letter from Erasmus, perhaps of 1516, is extant, and there is a letter from Dorp of possibly the same year. The reconciliation seems to have come about early in 1517, and thereafter relations were cordial. In the end, we should be grateful to Dorp for eliciting Erasmus's letter, without which we should have inadequate means for elucidating Erasmus's changing relationships with his Folly.

A. H. T. Levi

SELECT BIBLIOGRAPHY

This translation of the *Praise of Folly* was made for Penguin Classics from the text of J.-B. Kan (1898), but then revised for the University of Toronto Press edition of *The Collected Works of Erasmus* to accord with the critical text by Clarence Miller published in the *Opera Omnia* by the North-Holland Publishing Company (Amsterdam 1979). The Latin text of the letter from Erasmus to Maarten van Dorp is taken from P. S. Allen's edition of the *Opus Epistolarum* (vol. 2, Oxford 1910, pp. 90–114). The text of Gerard Lijster's commentary, where referred to, is that printed in the Froben 1515 edition of the *Praise of Folly*.

The notes in this edition have drawn on those of Clarence Miller for his critical edition, as well as those supplied by J.-B. Kan, H. Hudson, and by Maurice Rat for the French translation by Pierre de Nolhac.

Among the other works used for the introduction and notes are the following:

P. S. Allen (ed.), *Erasmus: Opus Epistolarum*, 12 vols., Oxford 1906–58

Roland H. Bainton, *Erasmus of Christendom*, New York 1969

M. Bataillon, *Erasme et l'Espagne*, Paris 1937

L. Capéran, *Le Problème du salut des infidèles. Essai historique*, Paris 1912

Francis Clark, *The Pseudo-Gregorian Dialogues*, 2 vols., Leiden 1987
Contemporaries of Erasmus, ed. Peter G. Bietenholz, 3 vols., Toronto 1987

Richard L. deMolen, *The Spirituality of Erasmus of Rotterdam*, Nieuwkoop 1987

Lucien Febvre, *Au cœur religieux du XVIe siècle*, Paris 1957

Richard Förster, 'Lucian in der Renaissance' in *Archiv für Literaturgeschichte*, Leipzig 1886

H. Humbertclaude, *Erasme et Luther. Leur polémique sur le libre arbitre*, Paris 1908

Lisa Jardine, *Erasmus, Man of Letters: the Construction of Charisma in Print*, Princeton 1993

Sears Jayne, *John Colet and Marsilio Ficino*, Oxford 1963

Walter Kaiser, *Praisers of Folly*, London 1964

A. H. T. Levi, 'Erasmus, the Early Jesuits and the Classics' in *Classical Influences on European Culture, AD 1500–1700*, pp. 223–38, Cambridge 1976

— 'The Breakdown of Scholasticism and the Significance of Evangelical Humanism' in *The Philosophical Assessment of Theology*, pp. 103–28, Tunbridge Wells/Washington D C 1987

Raymond Marcel, '*L'Opera e il pensiero di Giovanni Pico della Mirandola nella storia dell'umanesimo*' in the *Acta* of the Convegno Pico, Florence 1965

Clarence H. Miller, 'Current English Translations of the *Praise of Folly*. Some Corrections', in *Philological Quarterly*, pp. 718-33, Iowa 1966.

Thomas More, *The Works*, London 1557

H. A. Oberman, *The Harvest of Medieval Theology: Gabriel Biel and Late Medieval Nominalism*, Cambridge, Mass. 1963

Rudolf Pfeiffer, *Ausgewählte Schriften*, Munich 1960

Margaret M. Philips, *The Adages of Erasmus*, Cambridge 1964

R. R. Post, *The Modern Devotion: Confrontation with Reformation and Humanism*, Leiden 1968

I. Pusino, 'Der Einfluß Picos auf Erasmus' in *Zeitschrift für Kirchengeschichte*, pp. 75-96, Gotha 1927

A. Renaudet, *Etudes Erasmiennes*, Paris 1939

— *Erasme et l'Italie*, Geneva 1954

— *Humanisme et Renaissance*, Geneva 1958

M. A. Screech, *Ecstasy and the 'Praise of Folly'*, London 1980

Craig R. Thompson, *The Colloquies of Erasmus*, Chicago/London 1965

James D. Tracy, *Erasmus. The Growth of a Mind*, Geneva 1972

D. P. Walker, '*Origène en France au début du XVIe siècle*' in *Courants religieux et humanisme à la fin du XVe et au début du XVIe siècle*, Paris 1959

PRAISE OF FOLLY

During my recent journey back from Italy to England, not
wishing to waste all the time I was obliged to be on horseback
on 'idle gossip' and small talk, I preferred to spend some of it
thinking over some topic connected with our common interests
or else enjoying the recollection of the friends, as learned as they
are delightful, whom I had left here.[1] You were amongst the
first of these to spring to mind, my dear More. I have always
enjoyed my memories of you when we have been parted from
each other as much as your company when we were together,
and I swear that nothing has brought me more pleasure in life
than companionship like yours. And so since I felt that there
must be something I could do about this and the time was hardly
suitable for serious meditation, I decided to amuse myself with
praise of folly.[2] What sort of a goddess Athene put that notion

1. On the circumstances of the composition of the *Praise of Folly*, see the
Introduction. The references to idleness and writing on horseback, like the
date-line 'from the country', should not be taken literally. They are conventional scholarly disclaimers, like that of Petrarch who claimed to have
written his own discourse on his ignorance on a boat, or that of More who
had claimed to have composed his *Utopia* at odd moments. These are
conventional warnings that we should not regard the ensuing work as
totally serious. Erasmus's reference here to 'idle gossip' is the first of many
Greek words in the original Latin text (indicated by single quotation marks
in the translation). These Greek words, many of which Erasmus himself
coined, emphasize that the introductory epistle, like the work it prefaces,
was a formal literary exercise, however serious or however light-hearted.

2. The word Erasmus uses for praise, 'encomium', is simply the Latinized
form of the Greek word for a laudatory composition in prose or verse,
originally denoting a song for athletic victors. As a literary form the
encomium soon became a sophisticated *genre* used to praise legendary
heroes or for purposes of satire or fantasy. Lijster ponderously distinguishes
it from the hymn in his commentary, pointing out that hymns are only used
for praising gods. *Moriae* in the Latin title *Encomium Moriae* is simply a Latin

into your head, you may well ask. In the first place, it was your own family name of More, which is as near to the Greek word for folly, *moria*, as you are far from it in fact, and everyone agrees that you couldn't be farther removed. Then I had an idea that no one would think so well of this *jeu d'esprit* of mine as you, because you always take such delight in jokes of this kind, that is, if I don't flatter myself, jokes which aren't lacking in learning and wit. In fact you like to play the part of a Democritus in the mortal life we all share. Your intelligence is too penetrating and original for you not to hold opinions very different from those of the ordinary man, but your manners are so friendly and pleasant that you have the rare gift of getting on well with all men at any time, and enjoying it.[3] I am sure then that you will gladly accept this little declamation of mine as a 'memento' of your friend and will also undertake to defend it. It is dedicated to you, so henceforth it is yours, not mine.[4]

There may well be plenty of critical folk rushing in to slander it, some saying that my bit of nonsense is too frivolous for a theologian and others that it has a sarcastic bite which ill becomes Christian decorum. They will clamour that I'm reviving Old Comedy or Lucian, carping and complaining about everything. Well, those who are offended by frivolity ⟨and fun⟩ in a thesis

---

transcription of the genitive of the Greek word for folly. The pun on More's name was of course deliberate.

3. The reference to the goddess Athene is a quotation from the *Odyssey* (21, 1). Democritus, the Greek philosopher of the fifth century BC, is said by Juvenal (10. 28–30) and Seneca (*de Ira*, 2, 10, 5) constantly to have been amused by the spectacle of humanity. The Latin for 'getting on well with all men at any time' (Suetonius, *Tib 42* and Erasmus, *Adages* 286) was translated by Richard Whittinton in 1520 and applied to More as 'a man for all seasons'.

4. Erasmus uses a diminutive for his 'little declamation', but the word still denotes a formal rhetorical exercise. The word for 'memento' is in Greek in the Latin text, as it is in the text of Catullus (12, 13) to which Erasmus alludes. More did take the *Praise of Folly* to himself, and defended it in a letter to Maarten van Dorp written in October 1515, just as Erasmus took to himself More's *Utopia* by procuring its publication at Louvain in 1516. Erasmus was right about his detractors but, as he well knew, it was not merely his frivolous tone they would attack.

may kindly consider that mine is not the first example of this; the same thing has often been done by famous authors in the past. ⟨Homer amused himself ages ago with his *Battle of Frogs and Mice*, Virgil with his *Gnat* and *Garlic Salad*, Ovid with his *Nut*,⟩ Polycrates wrote a mock eulogy of the tyrant Busiris ⟨and so did his critic Isocrates⟩, Glauco spoke in favour of injustice and Favorinus of ⟨Thersites and⟩ the quartan fever; Synesius praised baldness and Lucian the Fly ⟨and the parasite. Seneca was joking in his *Apotheosis* of the Emperor Claudius, as Plutarch was in his dialogue between Gryllus and Ulysses. Lucian and Apuleius both wrote in fun about an ass, and someone whose name escapes me about the last will and testament of the piglet Grunnius Corocotta: this is mentioned by St Jerome.[5]⟩

5. This erudite list of precedents is not merely pedantic, although its humour is learned. It was a fairly well-known catalogue, repeated with various additions and subtractions by a number of Renaissance satirists, but in Erasmus it also constitutes a semi-serious bid to protect himself against the inevitable charge of irreverence, and it fits in well with the technique of exploiting great learning in the interests of amusement, a technique in which Erasmus was to be followed and superseded by Rabelais. The number of relatively short additions shows the meticulous care which Erasmus actually bestowed on his joke.

'Old' Comedy, represented typically by Aristophanes, centred on personal invective, or on the fantastic and the burlesque. Lucian of Samosata was the author of a series of satirical dialogues, some of which were translated by Erasmus and More, which were extremely influential in the Renaissance. From such works as Lucian's *Encomium of the Fly* and *On the Parasite* derives the Renaissance mock encomium as a literary *genre*.

The Battle of Frogs and Mice is in fact a parody of Homer from the fourth century BC. The *Gnat* and the *Garlic Salad* are both from the apocryphal *Appendix Virgiliana*. The gnat awakened a peasant in danger from a snake, was crushed by him and appeared to him in a dream to demand proper funeral rites. The *Garlic Salad* describes the first part of a day in the life of a peasant.

The *Nut*, ascribed by Erasmus to Ovid, is a probably apocryphal complaint by a nut tree, wounded by the stones thrown at it to knock off the nuts.

Polycrates, a rhetorician of the fourth century BC, composed several encomia, some of them strongly criticized by Isocrates who wrote a rejoinder to his *Busiris*, the name of a legendary Egyptian king who slaughtered all foreigners entering Egypt until he was himself slain by Hercules.

Glaucon is a character in Plato's *Republic*, where he is said to have written

⟨If they want⟩ they can imagine I've been amusing myself all this time with a game of draughts, or riding my stick if they like that better.⁶ How unjust it is to allow every other walk of life its relaxations but none at all to learning, especially when trifling may lead to something more serious! Jokes can be handled in such a way that any reader who is not altogether lacking in discernment can scent something far more rewarding in them than in the crabbed and specious arguments of some people we know – when, for example, one of them endlessly sings the praises of rhetoric or philosophy in a botched-up oration, another eulogizes some prince, and a third sets out to stir up war against the Turks. Another man foretells the future, and yet another invents a new set of silly points for discussion about goat's wool.⁷ Nothing is so trivial as treating serious subjects in a trivial

---

a dialogue on injustice. Favorinus was a favourite of Hadrian whose works have not survived. Thersites, a character in the *Iliad*, said to have been the subject of Favorinus' encomium, was ugly, deformed, low-born and foul-tongued. Synesius was a bishop of the early fifth century AD who wrote a mock encomium on baldness, sometimes printed with the *Folly*. Seneca's *Apocolocyntosis* is a skit in prose and verse on the deification of the emperor Claudius, under whom Seneca had been banished.

Plutarch, whose influence on the Renaissance was probably greater than that of any other single author, wrote a dialogue in which Gryllus, turned into a pig by Circe, tries to persuade Ulysses that an animal's lot is happier than a man's. Apuleius is the author of *The Golden Ass*, the only surviving whole Latin novel. Grunnius Corocotta is a hybrid animal whose testament, composed in the third century AD, was used for the amusement of schoolboys. It is mentioned by St Jerome, whose letters Erasmus was to edit in 1516.

6. Lijster gives references from Martial and Ovid to the game of 'thieves' played with pieces on a board like chess or draughts. The reference to riding a stick comes from Horace (*Satires*, 2, 3, 248).

7. The term 'scent' is an implied reference to Horace (*Epodes*, 12, 3). The Latin term for 'botched up' comes from Aulus Gellius (13, 25, 19 and 2, 23, 21). Lijster comments that lots of speeches have been composed to urge the princes to war against the Turks for the financial advantage to be gained, when it would have been more appropriate to urge Christians to war against vice. The point about goat's wool in the next sentence is a reminiscence of Horace (*Epistles*, 1, 18, 15). Erasmus, like Pico della Mirandola from whom he derives much, disapproved of the superstitious and determinist overtones of astrology and not infrequently attacked its professional practitioners.

manner; and similarly, nothing is more entertaining than treating trivialities in such a way as to make it clear you are doing anything but trifle with them. The world will pass its own judgement on me, but unless my 'self-love' entirely deceives me, my praise of folly has not been altogether foolish.[8]

Now for the charge of biting sarcasm. My answer is that the intelligent have always enjoyed freedom to exercise their wit on the common life of man, and with impunity, provided that they kept their liberty within reasonable limits. This makes me marvel all the more at the sensitivity of present-day ears which can bear to hear practically nothing but honorific titles. Moreover, you can find a good many people whose religious sense is so distorted that they find the most serious blasphemies against Christ more bearable than the slightest joke on pope or prince, especially if it touches their daily bread.[9] And to criticize men's lives without mentioning any names — I ask you, does this look like sarcasm, or rather warning and advice? Again, on how many charges am I not my own self-critic? Furthermore, if every type of man is included, it is clear that all the vices are censured, not any individual. And so anyone who protests that he is injured betrays his own guilty conscience, or at any rate his apprehensions. St Jerome amused himself in this way with far more freedom and sarcasm, sometimes even mentioning names. I have not only refrained from naming anyone but have also moderated my style so that the sensible reader will easily understand that my intention was to give pleasure, not pain. Nowhere have I stirred up the hidden cesspool of crime as Juvenal did; the ridiculous rather than the squalid was what I set out to survey. Finally, if anyone is still unappeased by all I have said, he should at least remember that there is merit in being attacked by Folly, for when I made

8. Erasmus takes the word for 'self-love', *philautia*, from Plutarch and Horace, both of whom emphasize the blindness it causes. Rabelais, who also entertains by treating trivialities with a strengthening undercurrent of seriousness as his novel proceeds, was to take over the term *philautie* which, in the *Tiers Livre* becomes the reason for Panurge's blindness and his inability either to answer his question or to resolve his uncertainties by action.

9. Lijster maintains that the honorific titles referred to are the customary forms of address such as 'most victorious and serene' for kings, 'most reverend' for cardinals and 'venerable' for abbesses.

her the narrator I had to maintain her character in appropriate style.[10] But why do I say all this to you, an advocate without peer for giving your best service to causes even when they are not the best? Farewell, learned More; be a stout champion to your namesake Folly.

From the country, 9 June 1508[11]

10. Erasmus is here offering a somewhat elaborately disingenuous excuse for his satire on the grounds that, since it is put into the mouth of Folly herself, consistency demanded an attack on what was wise. Those who feel themselves attacked in the *Praise of Folly* should therefore take it as a compliment to their wisdom. Juvenal, to whom he refers, was the Latin satirist known for his ruthless diatribes on the corruption of Roman society.

11. The date of the letter preface has been the subject of much controversy. The notation 'from the country' does not need to be taken as establishing more than the *genre* and is not necessarily a statement of fact. The date 1508 given by the 1522 Basle edition of Froben is impossible, and no earlier edition gives any year. The *Praise of Folly* was written at More's house in Chelsea during July and August 1509. At the beginning of July that year, Erasmus was still in Rome, so that the month-date excludes any year before 1510. The most probable view is that Erasmus wrote the letter-preface with the *Praise of Folly* itself in the late summer of 1509, but that he added 9 June (without a year) when he corrected the text for publication in 1511, when Erasmus went to Paris from More's residence at Bucklersbury to see the *Praise of Folly* through the press. It is likely that the first, and very faulty, edition appeared in the early part of July. The erroneous year-date of 1508 added by Froben in 1522 may possibly derive from an apparent reference in More's letter to Dorp of 1515 to the fact that the *Praise of Folly* had appeared seven years previously. But the number seven may be a manuscript misreading.

MORIAE ENCOMIUM

THAT IS

THE PRAISE OF FOLLY

A DECLAMATION BY ERASMUS OF ROTTERDAM[1]

Folly speaks:

Whatever is generally said of me by mortal men, and I'm quite well aware that Folly is in poor repute even amongst the greatest fools, still, I am the one – and indeed, the only one – whose divine powers can gladden the hearts of gods and men. Proof enough of this is in the fact that as soon as I stepped forward to address this crowded assembly, every face immediately brightened up with a new, unwonted gaiety and all your frowns were smoothed away. You laughed and applauded with such delightfully happy smiles that as I look at you all gathered round me I could well believe you are tipsy with nectar like the Homeric gods, with a dash of nepenthe too, though a moment ago you were sitting looking as gloomy and harassed as if you had just come up from Trophonius' cave.[2] Now, when the sun first shows his handsome golden visage upon earth or after a hard winter the newborn spring breathes out its mild west breezes,[3] it always happens that a new face comes over everything, new colour and a kind of youthfulness return; and so it only takes the mere sight of me to give you all a different look. For great orators must as a rule spend time preparing long speeches and

1. Lijster points out that a 'declamation' announces wit, frivolity and enjoyment.

2. The phrase about the smoothing away of frowns is taken from Terence (*Adelphi*, 839). 'Nepenthe' is the herb mentioned in Homer (*Odyssey*, 4, 220) whose juice, mixed with wine, drove away all care. Trophonius, murderer of his brother Agomedes, was buried in a cave which became the seat of an oracle famous for filling with gloom all those who came to consult it. He is mentioned by Homer and Pausanias, and is referred to by Erasmus in the *Adages*.

3. The reference to mild west breezes is a reminiscence of Horace (*Odes*, 1, 4, 1; 3, 7, 3; 4, 5, 6).

even then find it difficult to succeed in banishing care and trouble from your minds, but I've done this at once – and simply by my looks.

Why have I appeared today in this unaccustomed garb? Well, you shall hear the reason if you have no objection to lending me your ears – no, not the ones you use for preachers of sermons, but the ears you usually prick up for mountebanks, clowns, and fools, the sort of ears that once upon a time our friend Midas listened with to Pan.[4] I've a fancy to play the sophist before you, and I don't mean by that one of the tribe today who cram tiresome trivialities into the heads of schoolboys and teach them more than feminine obstinacy in disputation – no, I shall follow the ancients who chose the name sophist in preference to the damaging title of wise men.[5] Their concern was to provide

4. Erasmus, having noted at the beginning that Folly herself is speaking and having drawn attention in the preceding section to the instantaneous effect of her appearance, now emphasizes once again that the declamation is put into the mouth of Folly by drawing attention to the dress in which she appears. Holbein portrayed her in the margins of one copy in a cap and bells, but in a pulpit. Folly later says she is not in theologian's garb, but she forgets from time to time who she is, and may well be made by her puppeteer to forget where she is, or what she is wearing. Since it is Folly who is praising herself, and since therefore she might be taken to be blinded by self-love, Erasmus can pretend, as he did in the letter-preface, that he does not intend anything she says to be taken seriously. The word for 'fools' is another pun on More's name. Folly refers to the story of Midas, whose ears were changed by Apollo into those of an ass for preferring Pan's flute to Apollo's lyre (Ovid, *Metamorphoses*, 11, 153 ff. and Herodotus, 7, 33). Midas was at some pains to hide his ears, but his barber betrayed him. There is another reference to Midas in the *Adages*.

5. The ancient sophists were itinerant teachers, often of oratory, sometimes even of virtue. But the premium put by most of such teachers on the ability to defend any point of view, irrespective of its truth or moral value, explains the pejorative overtones which the term 'sophist' developed. Folly here touches on a theme frequent in the writings of Erasmus, whose blistering comments on the scholastic educational system focus on the accusation of 'sophistical cavilling'. In the middle ages the term 'sophist' could refer to a student as well as to a professor. There is a sense in which the humanist reform of education was always Erasmus's central concern. When, a little later on, Folly refers to speech as the least deceptive mirror of the mind, the reference is to a central tenet in the humanist philosophy of education, as

eulogies in praise of gods and heroes, so it's a eulogy you are going to hear now, though not one of Hercules or Solon. It's in praise of myself, namely, Folly.

Now, I don't think much of those wiseacres who maintain it's the height of folly and conceit if anyone speaks in his own praise; or rather, it can be as foolish as they like, as long as they admit it's in character. What could be more fitting than for Folly to trumpet her own merits abroad and 'sing her own praises'.[6] Who could portray me better than I can myself? Unless, of course, someone knows me better than I know myself. Yet in general I think I show a good deal more discretion than the general run of gentry and scholars, whose distorted sense of modesty leads them to make a practice of bribing some syco-phantic speaker or babbling poet hired for a fee so that they can listen to him praising their merits, purely fictitious though these are. The bashful listener spreads his tail-feathers like a peacock and carries his head high, while the brazen flatterer rates this worthless individual with the gods and sets him up as the perfect model of all the virtues – though the man himself knows he is nowhere near that; 'infinity doubled'[7] would not be too far away. Thus the wretched crow is decked out in borrowed plumage, the 'Ethiopian washed white', an 'elephant created out of a gnat'. Finally, I follow that well-worn popular proverb which says that a man does right to praise himself if he can't find anyone else to praise him.

---

well as to one of Erasmus's own *Apothegmata*. Eloquence, or style, not only mirrors intellectual qualities, but can become the means of inculcating and developing them. From this central tenet, clearly implied by Erasmus in an important series of letters to Colet, derives the importance of the Renaissance debate about the relationship between eloquence and philosophy (or between dialectic and rhetoric).

6. Folly here quotes a Greek proverb in Greek, as she does three times more in the following lines. Most of the proverbs are commented on in the *Adages*.

Solon, the law-giver who reformed the Athenian constitution, is famous for the introduction of humane and liberal legal, social and political systems.

7. The Greek phrase for 'infinity doubled', actually 'through two octaves' indicates, says Lijster, the greatest interval in musical harmony, known popularly, he says, as 'the double octave'.

Here, by the way, I can't help wondering at the ingratitude (if I may say so) or the dilatoriness of mankind. Everyone is only too anxious to cultivate me and freely acknowledges the benefits I bring, yet throughout all the ages nobody has ever come forward to deliver a speech of thanks in praise of Folly. Yet there has been no lack of persons ready to spend lamp-oil and lose their sleep working out elaborate speeches in honour of tyrants like Busiris ⟨and Phalaris⟩, quartan fever, flies, baldness, and plagues of that sort.[8] From me you're going to hear a speech which is extempore and quite unprepared, but all the more genuine for that. Still, I wouldn't have you think I composed this to show off my talent, as the common run of orators do. As you know, they can spend thirty whole years elaborating a speech which even then may not be theirs at all, and then swear they wrote it for a joke in a mere three days or even dictated it extempore. For my part, I've always liked best to say 'whatever comes ⟨ill-timed⟩ to the tip of the tongue'.[9]

None of you need expect me to follow the usual practice of ordinary rhetoricians and explain myself by definition, still less by division. It wouldn't bode well for the future either to limit and confine one whose divinity extends so far, or to cut her up when the whole world is united in worshipping her. And what purpose would it serve for a definition to produce a sketch which would be a mere shadow of myself when I am here before you, for you to look at with your own eyes? For I am as you see me, the true bestower of 'good things,' called *stultitia* in Latin, μωρία in Greek.

But was there any need to tell you even as much as that, as if I

8. This list of mock encomia is very similar to that of the letter-preface, on which see note 5, pp. 5–6. Phalaris was a tyrant of the sixth century BC, noted for roasting his victims inside a hollow bronze bull, whose encomium was written by Lucian.

9. This proverb, in Greek in the Latin text, is included in the *Adages*. Folly is referring to an affectation of literary facility very common both in antiquity and in the Renaissance. The notation 'from the country' at the end of the letter-preface is a common and recognizable variant of the same pose. Folly's encomium of herself is in fact a very carefully composed oration and, in spite of her disclaimer in the next sentence, she did in fact follow the classical paradigms for encomiastic oratory.

didn't make it perfectly clear who I am from the look on my face, as they say? Anyone who argued that I was Minerva or Wisdom could easily be convinced of his mistake simply by the sight of me, even if I never spoke a word, though speech is the least deceptive mirror of the mind. I've no use for cosmetics, my face doesn't pretend to be anything different from my innermost feelings. I am myself wherever I am, and no one can pretend I'm not – especially those who lay special claim to be called the personification of wisdom, even though they strut about 'like apes in purple' and 'asses in lion-skins'.[10] However hard they try to keep up the illusion, their ears stick up and betray the Midas in them. There's an ungrateful lot of folk for you – members of my party if anyone is, and yet so ashamed of my name in public that they cast it freely at others as a term of strong abuse. They're 'complete fools' in fact, and yet each of them would like to pass for a wise man and a Thales; so wouldn't the best name for them all be *morosophoi* or foolish-wise?[11]

10. The Greek word for 'good things' is taken from Homer (*Odyssey*, 8, 325) and Folly's assertion that 'the look on her face' makes things clear alludes to Cicero's letters (*To Atticus*, 14, 13). The proverbs about 'apes in purple' and 'asses in lion-skins' are both the subject of commentary in the *Adages*. Minerva was the Italian goddess of handicrafts frequently identified with Athene and hence with wisdom.

Folly's assertion that she looks what she is has a special importance since Erasmus (followed here, as so often, by Rabelais) made much of the Silenus figure, whose point was that he appeared foolish and ugly while being wise and admirable. In the *Sileni Alcibiadis* of 1515 Erasmus names Christ together with Socrates and Epictetus among the Silenus figures. The *Enchiridion* contains a reference to the scriptures that 'like the Silenus of Alcibiades, conceal their real divinity beneath a surface that is crude and almost laughable'. Folly has just called herself the true bestower of all good things, perhaps implying some similarity with the Christ of the *Enchiridion*, of whom the same was said and whose wisdom the world thought folly. Folly's truth to her own appearance therefore becomes ambivalent. She is what the world considers foolish, which might mean that she has wise things to say.

11. Thales was one of the seven sages, astronomer, geographer, geometer and philosopher.

Folly is saying that those of her faction who reject the name of fools and pretend to be wise are not only 'complete fools' in fact, but are wise to be so. They ought therefore really to be called hybrid wise-fools. The 'complete

For at this point too I think I should copy the rhetoricians of today who fancy themselves practically gods on earth if they can show themselves twin-tongued, like horse leeches, and think it a splendid feat if they can work a few silly little Greek words, like pieces of mosaic, into their Latin speeches, however out of place these are. Then, if they still need something out of the ordinary, they dig four or five obsolete words out of mouldy manuscripts with which to cloud the meaning for the reader. The idea is, I suppose, that those who can understand are better pleased with themselves, and those who can't are all the more lost in admiration the less they understand. Indeed there's a special sort of refined pleasure which all my followers take in paying their highest regard to any particular exotic import from foreign parts, and the more pretentious among them have to laugh and clap their hands and 'twitch their ears' like a donkey does to show the others how well they can understand. 'So much for that.'[12]

Now I return to my subject. Well, you have my name,

---

fools' or *morotatoi* who pretend to be wise are also the subject of commentary in the *Adages* and the word is used by More in *Utopia*. They are, however, also *morosophers*, which means at the same time both wise and foolish. Lucian uses the term of the wise who pretend to be foolish (*Alexander*, 40) and Rabelais uses it of Triboullet (*Tiers Livre*, chapter 46). Erasmus is playing ironically with the wisdom in Folly's eyes of being foolish. Just possibly, he is also hinting openly at the possibility that Folly and her friends are not so foolish as they pretend to be. At any rate, the purely burlesque pose drops for a minute to reveal the potential seriousness of what Folly will go on to say. The complex thought of Erasmus suggests that, while the followers of Folly pretend to be wise, they have the wisdom to be foolish. At the end of her declamation Folly links this idea with the Pauline folly of the Cross. It should also be related to Erasmus's own exploitation of the Silenus figure.

12. The reference to leeches may derive from Pliny (*Historia naturalis* xi, 40). Erasmus is having a joke at his own expense. Just as Folly's declamation is anything but improvised, so it goes to some lengths to drag in Greek proverbs. Folly's attack on literary pretentiousness ends with two Greek proverbs. In the 1529 colloquy *The Cyclops*, Erasmus makes a similarly ironic comment on his own activity.

Here Folly, having presented herself probably in jester's garb, has pursued the introduction to the encomium of herself with a take-off of most of the classical introductory procedures. We have had an exordium, consisting of a greeting and a narration. Instead of the scholastic partition, Folly has refused

gentlemen – but how shall I address you? As 'most foolish'?
What more honourable title could the goddess Folly use in
addressing her devotees? But first of all, with the help of the
Muses, I'll try to explain my ancestry to you, which not very
many people know. I didn't have Chaos, Orcus, Saturn, Japetus,
or any other of those out-of-date mouldy old gods for a father,
but 'Plutus', god of riches himself, the sole 'father of gods and
men' whatever Homer and Hesiod and even Jupiter may say.[13]
He has only to nod his head, today as ever before, for everything
to be thrown topsy-turvy, whether sacred or profane. War,
peace, governments, councils, lawcourts, assemblies, marriage
ties, contracts, treaties, laws, arts, gaieties, gravities (I'm out of
breath) – in a word, the affairs of men, public and private, are all
managed according to his will. Without his help the entire race
of poets' divinities, or if I may be so bold, the chosen Olympian
gods themselves either wouldn't keep alive at all, or would
certainly fare very badly on the food they get 'at home'.[14] If a
man annoys Plutus not even Pallas Athene herself can save him.

---

to explain herself 'by definition, still less by division', but has presented
herself without cosmetics and with immediate effect. Erasmus implies a
contrast between the immediate religious experience mediated by the reading
of the scriptures, and the theological subtleties of the scholastics buttressing
the 'religion of works'. We now move into a discussion of Folly's birth,
parodying the genealogical section of the Greek paradigm for encomia,
prior to identifying Folly's companions and moving on to the gifts she
bestows. Folly will eventually abandon her ironic role as a fool and, having forgotten who she is and what she is doing, will not bother about a
peroration.

13. Chaos, according to Hesiod, was at the origin of the world. Orcus,
the Italian god often identified with Pluto or Hades, was one of the three
sons of Kronos and god of the lower world. Saturn was the Roman god
often identified with Kronos, father of Jupiter, Neptune and Pluto. Japetus
was one of the Titans, son of heaven and earth and the father of Atlas. Plutus
was the god of wealth and Hesiod was the Greek author of uncertain date
whose *Theogony* tried to bring the traditions concerning the gods into a
consistent system. It also established their genealogy. Jupiter is of course the
Roman sky-god and equivalent of Zeus. Homer and Hesiod frequently refer
to Zeus as the 'father of gods and men'.

14. The 'chosen Olympian gods' were normally said to be twelve in
number, although Varro says twenty. St Augustine discusses the issue in the

But anyone who wins his approval can tell mighty Jupiter to go hang himself, thunderbolt and all. 'It's my proud claim that he is my father.' And he didn't make me spring from his brain, as Jupiter did that sour and stern Athene, but gave me Freshness for a mother, the loveliest of all the nymphs and the gayest too. Nor was he tied to her in dreary wedlock like the parents of that limping blacksmith, but 'lay with her in love,' as Homer puts it, something much more delightful.[15] Moreover, my father was not the Plutus in Aristophanes (make no mistake about that), half-blind, with one foot in the grave, but Plutus as he used to be, sound and hot-blooded with youth — and not only youth, but still more with the nectar he'd just been drinking, as it happened, neat and in generous cupfuls at a banquet of the gods.[16]

If you also want to know my birthplace, as people think it matters a lot in judging noble birth nowadays where an infant uttered its first cries, I wasn't born on wandering Delos or out of the waves of the sea or 'in hollow caves', but on the very Islands of the Blest, where everything grows 'unsown, untilled'.[17] Toil, old age, and sickness are unknown there. There's no asphodel, mallow, onions, vetch, and beans or any other such worthless stuff to be seen in the fields, but everywhere there's

City of God (Book 7, chapter 2, 3, 33). Lucian says in his work on sacrifices that, without the food and drink from sacrifices, the gods would have a thin time at home on nectar and ambrosia.

15. 'Go hang himself' is the literal translation of the phrase from Juvenal (10, 53) to which Folly alludes. Folly here solemnly claims godly birth in the Homeric phrase which she quotes in Greek. The principal myth concerning Athene is that she had no mother but sprang fully armed out of Zeus' head when it was split with an axe by Hephaestus. Erasmus invents a new name for the nymph Youthfulness, normally called Hebe, the daughter of Hera and Zeus. She was the cup-bearer of the gods, here supposed to have conceived Folly by the young, vigorous and somewhat inebriated Plutus whom she served at table. Lijster says that Erasmus is implying that Folly is the product of the union between youth and riches. The limping blacksmith is Vulcan, god of fire, legitimate son of Jupiter and Juno, and the term 'hot-blooded' implies a reference to Horace (Odes, 3, 14, 27).

16. Aristophanes was the Athenian author of comedies whose Plutus was staged in 388 BC. Aristophanes makes Plutus impotent.

17. According to legend (see Ovid, Metamorphoses, 6, 333), Leto was delivered of Apollo after nine days' labour on the island of Delos. The

moly, panacea, nepenthe, marjoram, ambrosia, and lotus, roses, violets, and hyacinths, and gardens of Adonis to refresh the eye and nose.[18] Born as I was amidst these delights I didn't start life crying, but smiled sweetly at my mother straight away.

And I certainly don't envy the 'mighty son of Kronos' his she-goat nurse, for two charming nymphs fed me at their breasts, Drunkenness, daughter of Bacchus, and Ignorance, daughter of Pan.[19] You can see them both here along with the rest of my attendants and followers, but if you want to know all their

---

island, previously afloat, was anchored by Zeus to provide a birthplace for the twins Apollo and Artemis. Aphrodite, goddess of fertility, love and beauty, was born 'out of the waves' according to later Greek tradition while, according to Homer (*Odyssey*, 4, 403), Thetis and her sister Nereids were born in hollow caves. The 'Islands of the Blest', originally the winterless home of the happy dead for Homer, Hesiod and Pindar, are mentioned by Pliny and described by Horace. Folly also refers to Homer in the words 'unsown, untilled'. The islands were fertile without being cultivated, and free from illness, extremes of temperature and all forms of disease and blight. Everything was in abundant supply.

In the Renaissance the myth of the Islands of the Blest was frequently used as a vehicle either for satire or, as in More's *Utopia*, as a tentative means of exploring personal and social aspirations, in which form it later blended with the idea of Arcadia and become embedded in the pastoral tradition.

18. The list of worthless plants is compounded from various passages of Hesiod and Horace, although it looks as if Erasmus mistook a reference in Horace to sea-onions for an allusion to the common vegetable. Asphodel is mentioned as a poor man's vegetable by Hesiod (*Works and Days*, 42) and by Pliny (*Historia naturalis*, 21, 108).

In the second list some of the plants are aphrodisiacs. Moly is the wonderful herb (*Odyssey*, 10, 305) given by Hermes to Odysseus to preserve him from Circe's seductions, Panacea (Pliny, *Historia naturalis*, 25, 11) cures all ills. Nepenthe drives away care. Marjoram is the aromatic herb and ambrosia, the food of the gods, is also the name given to a fragrant herb in Dioscorides and Pliny. The lotus was the food of the Lotophagi which made the eater forget his own country and desire to live in Lotus-land (*Odyssey*, 9, 82 ff.). The gardens of Adonis, god of vegetation and fertility, mentioned by Erasmus in the *Adages* were pots filled with short-lived seasonal plants at his spring festival.

19. The mighty son of Kronos is Homer's description of Zeus, quoted by Folly in Greek (*Iliad*, 2, 403). Zeus was hidden away in Crete by his mother Rhea to save him from being swallowed by his father. In Crete Zeus was reared on the milk of the she-goat Amalthea. Erasmus invents Greek names for Drunkenness and Ignorance. The connexion between Bacchus and his

names, you'll have to hear them from me in Greek. This one you see with her eyebrows raised is, of course, '*Philautia*', Self-love. The one clapping her hands with laughter in her eyes is '*Kolakia*', Flattery. The sleepy one who looks only half-awake is '*Lethe*', Forgetfulness, and this one leaning on her elbow with her hands folded is '*Misoponia*', Idleness. This one wearing a wreath of roses and drenched in scent is '*Hedone*', Pleasure. The one here with the rolling eyes she can't keep still is '*Anoia*', Madness, and this plump one with the well-fed look is called '*Tryphe*', Sensuality. You can see there are also two gods amongst the girls; one is called '*Comus*', Revelry, and the other '*Negretos Hypnos*', Sound Sleep. This, then, is the household which serves me loyally in bringing the whole world under my sway, so that even great rulers have to bow to my rule.[20]

You've heard of my birth, upbringing, and companions. Now I don't want it to seem that I claim the name of goddess without good reason, so please pay attention and learn what great advantages I bring to gods and men alike, and how far my divinity extends. For if being a god means helping mortals, as someone sensibly

---

daughter Drunkenness is clear. Pan, the father of Ignorance, was the half-goat Arcadian god, frightening, angry and haunter of wildernesses.

Although Folly boasts here that she was nursed by Drunkenness and Ignorance, it is important not to forget that the intoxication induced by Bacchus became in Renaissance authors like Rabelais and Pontus de Tyard a figure of the divine 'furor' of the Platonist tradition which, in Marsilio Ficino, was the beginning of the soul's reunification in its ascent to beatitude. In the same way, ignorance is at this date an equivocal concept, since some at least of the evangelical humanists were heavily indebted to the idea of a 'learned ignorance' used by Nicolas of Cusa in his *de docta ignorantia* to describe human receptivity to divine knowledge. Postel, Bigot and Rabelais were to make Pan, here the father of Ignorance, into a figure of Christ, the Good Shepherd, an identification suggested by Paul Marsus's commentary on Ovid's *Fasti*. It is difficult to know whether Erasmus intended the ambivalence in Folly's nurses. The importance of the Plotinian mysticism of Ficino for Erasmus is still disputed.

20. This section marks the end of that part of the declamation which deals with Folly's birth and education. She will now proceed to the body of the encomium dealing with achievements and attributes.

The list of her companions is a variation on the list of deadly sins. Only Philautia plays any significant part in the subsequent declamation. Kolakia is

wrote; and if those who introduced mortals to wine or grain, or some other commodity, deserved their admission to the council of the gods, why shouldn't I rightly be recognized and named the 'Alpha' of all gods, when I dispense every benefit to all alike?[21]

First of all, what can be sweeter or more precious than life itself? And to whom is it generally agreed life owes its beginning if not to me? For it certainly isn't the spear of 'mighty-fathered' Pallas or the shield of 'cloud-gathering' Jupiter which fathers and propagates the human race. Even the father of the gods and king of men who makes the whole of Olympus tremble when he bows his head has to lay aside that triple-forked thunderbolt of his and that grim Titanic visage with which he can terrify all the gods whenever he chooses, and humble himself to put on a different mask, like an actor, if he ever wants to do what he always is doing, that is, 'to make a child'. And the stoics, as we know, claim to be most like the gods.[22] But give me a man who is a stoic three or four or if you like six hundred times over, and he too, even if he keeps his beard as a mark of wisdom, though he shares it with the goat, will have to swallow his pride, smooth out his frown, shake off his rigid principles, and be fond and foolish for a while. In fact, if the philosopher ever wants to be a father it's me he has to call on – yes, me.

a name coined by Erasmus. Lethe is the underworld river of mythology from which the shades of the dead drank and then forgot their earthly existence. Misoponia is a term for laziness used by Lucian. Hedone, Anoia and Tryphe are the Greek words for pleasure, madness and sensuality. Comus is the god of revelry and *Negretos Hypnos* is an Homeric expression for deep sleep (*Odyssey*, 13, 79). Folly's list of companions by whose help she rules might, if it were less humanist in form, have come from some medieval sermon or allegory.

21. The statement that it is the function of the gods to help men comes from Pliny (*Historia naturalis*, 2, 5). In Revelation, i, 8, God reveals himself as the 'Alpha and the Omega', that is the beginning and end of all things signified by the first and last letters of the Greek alphabet.

This main section of Folly's declamation dealing with her powers takes up very nearly half its total length and leads on to the consideration of Folly's followers.

22. It is Homer who refers to Athene, daughter of Zeus, as 'mighty-fathered' (*Iliad*, 5, 747) and to Zeus himself, 'father of gods and men' as 'cloud-gathering' (*Iliad*, 1, 160 and 470). The reference is to his thunderbolts.

And I may as well speak more frankly to you in my usual way. What is it, I ask you, which begets gods or men – the head, the face, the breast, hand, or ear, all thought of as respectable parts of the body? No, it's not. The propagator of the human race is that part which is so foolish and absurd that it can't be named without raising a laugh. There is the true sacred fount from which everything draws its being, not the quarternion of Pythagoras.[23] Just tell me, please, what man would be willing to offer his neck to the halter of matrimony if he applied the usual practice of the wise man and first weighed up its disadvantages as a way of life? Or what woman would ever agree to take a husband if she knew or thought about the pains and dangers of childbirth and the trouble of bringing up children? So if you

It is Virgil (*Aeneid*, 9, 106) who talks of the terror he inspires and Ovid who mentions his three-forked lightning (*Metamorphoses*, 2, 848). The mention of the Titanic visage implies a reference to Lucian (e.g. *Icaromenippus*, 23) who used the phrase on several occasions. The word for 'making a child', in Greek in the Latin text, is a coinage of Erasmus.

The ethical doctrines of the stoics, which they regarded as based on a rigorously deductive system, centred on the suppression of passion and the following of reason and nature. Since, however, some early Christian writers like Clement of Alexandria, drawing on neoplatonist as well as on stoic ideas, held that the suppression of passion demanded the total hegemony in man of spirit over matter, the stoic sage was therefore endowed with the spiritual elevation, measured in terms of freedom from matter and rationality of behaviour, of God himself. The idea that the sage is the equal of God was to be defended by some sixteenth-century Christian stoics such as Justus Lipsius and attacked as impious by representatives of a more rigorously Augustinian tradition of Christian spirituality. Erasmus himself was to exploit certain stoic themes and ideas, particularly those which, unlike this one, derived from Epictetus, as that our true good is in our power.

23. The stoics, like the cynics, wore a characteristic uniform of beard, cloak and stick. The first four whole numbers were the basis for the cosmic system of the Pythagoreans, and so the 'sacred fount' of all nature.

During the Renaissance there was a serious discussion about the seat of the soul and its affections in the various parts of the body and, in the *Enchiridion*, Erasmus had adopted a modification of the Platonist view, giving desire to the lower part of the body. Here, however, as when she refers to the stoics, Folly is in lighter mood. She goes on after Juvenal (6, 43), to talk of the 'halter of matrimony', although Erasmus elsewhere treats that subject seriously, too.

owe your existence to wedlock, you owe the fact of wedlock to madness, my attendant '*Anoia*', and can see how much in fact you owe to me. And if a woman has once had this experience, would she be willing to repeat it without the divine aid of '*Lethe*', who helps her to forget? Venus herself, whatever Lucretius says, would never deny that she would be weakened and shorn of her power if my own divinity didn't come to her aid. Thus from that game of mine, drunken and absurd as it is, spring haughty philosophers and their present-day successors who are popularly called monks, kings in their purple, pious priests, and thrice-holy pontiffs; and finally, the whole assembly of the poets' gods, now so numerous that Olympus itself, for all its spaciousness, can scarcely hold such a crowd.[24]

But I shouldn't claim much by saying that I'm the seed and source of existence unless I could also prove that whatever advantages there are all throughout life are all provided by me. What would this life be, or would it seem worth calling life at all, if its pleasure was taken away? I hear your applause, and in fact I've always felt sure that none of you was so wise or rather so foolish – no, I mean so wise – as to think it could.[25] Even the stoics don't despise pleasure, though they are careful to conceal their real feelings, and tear it to pieces in public with their incessant outcry, so that once they have frightened everyone else off they can enjoy it more freely themselves. I'd just like them to tell me if there's any part of life which isn't dreary, unpleasant, graceless, stupid, and tedious unless you add pleasure, the

24. Lucretius, author of the *de rerum natura*, starts his poem with an invocation to Venus, goddess of love. 'Kings in their purple' refers to Horace (*Odes*, 1, 35, 12). The parenthesis on 'those popularly called monks' foreshadows the sustained later attack. Monks, as Erasmus was fond of pointing out, were not instituted by Christ.

25. Folly has by now come near to laying down her ironic pose by appearing to argue sensibly. Erasmus here recalls us, and himself, too, to the convention he has established inside which foolishness is sense for Folly. However, Folly immediately goes on to argue seriously, so that Erasmus has put the reader in a situation in which he can no longer be sure what is serious and what is not. The stage is now set both for Erasmus's attack on aspects of sixteenth-century society and for his defence that they are only the outpourings of Folly.

seasoning of folly. I've proof enough in Sophocles, a poet who can never be adequately praised, who pays me a really splendid tribute in the line

'For ignorance provides the happiest life.'[26]

But now let's take the facts one by one.

First of all, everyone knows that by far the happiest and universally enjoyable age of man is the first. What is there about babies which makes us hug and kiss and fondle them, so that even an enemy would give them help at that age? Surely it's the charm of folly, which thoughtful Nature has taken care to bestow on the newly born so that they can offer some reward of pleasure to mitigate the hard work of bringing them up and win the liking of those who look after them. Then follows adolescence, which everyone finds delightful, openly supports, and warmly encourages, eagerly offering a helping hand. Now whence comes the charm of youth if not from me? I've seen to it that youth has so little wisdom and hence so few frowns. It's a fact that as soon as the young grow up and develop the sort of mature sense which comes through experience and education, the bloom of youthful beauty begins to fade at once, enthusiasm wanes, gaiety cools down, and energy slackens. The further anyone withdraws from me the less and less he's alive, until 'painful age' comes on, that is, 'old age with its troubles' unwelcome not only to others but just as much to itself.[27] This too would be intolerable to man if I weren't at his elbow out of pity

26. The line of Sophocles from his *Ajax* (5, 554) is referred to, like so many of the other allusions and quotations, in the *Adages*. Technically it is true to say that the stoics, or some of them, did not despise the pleasure which was not a passion but a 'rational affection'. Erasmus, as usual, is making learned fun and perhaps remembering that, for Seneca, the 'pleasure' which is the final end of human endeavour is for the Epicurean identified with the 'virtue' which the stoics cultivate (*de beata vita*, 13).

27. This section contains verbal reminiscences of Virgil, Seneca and Horace. The Greek phrase for 'painful age' is taken from Homer (*Iliad*, 8, 103) while that for 'second childhood' a little later comes from Lucian (*Saturn*, 9). Erasmus comments on it in the *Adages*, as he also does on the proverb from Apuleius which Folly goes on to quote, 'I hate a small child too wise for his years.'

for all he has to bear. Just as the gods of fiction often come to the aid of the dying with some metamorphosis, so do I recall people who are on the brink of the grave, as far as possible, to childhood once again. Hence the aptitude of the popular expression, 'second childhood'. And if any of you are interested in my method of transformation, I'm quite willing to tell you. The spring belonging to my nymph *Lethe* has its source in the Islands of the Blest, and what flows through the underworld is only a trickle of a stream. There I take them, so that once they have drunk deep draughts of forgetfulness the cares of the mind are gradually washed away and they recover their youth. I know they're called silly and foolish, as indeed they are, but that is exactly what it means to become a child again.

What else is childhood but silliness and foolishness? Its utter lack of sense is what we find so delightful. Everybody hates a prodigy, detests an old head on young shoulders; witness the oft-repeated saying 'I hate a small child who's too wise for his years.' And who could carry on doing business or having dealings with an old man if his vast experience of affairs was still matched by a vigorous mind and keen judgement?

So I see to it that the old man is witless, and this sets him free meanwhile from all those wretched anxieties which torment the man in his senses. He is also pleasant company for a drink, and doesn't feel the boredom with life which a more robust age can scarcely endure. There are times when, like the old man in Plautus, he goes back to those three special letters AMO, but he'd be anything but happy if he still had his wits.[28] Meanwhile, thanks to what I do for him, he's happy, popular with his friends, even a welcome guest to bring life to a party. In Homer, the speech of old Nestor flows from his lips sweeter than honey, while that of Achilles is bitter, and the old men sitting on the walls of Troy speak in 'lily-sweet' voices. On this reckoning old age surpasses even childhood, for that is pleasant but inarticulate, and lacks the chief amusement in life – talk and still more talk. Add the fact that old people are always particularly delighted by children, and children by them –

28. The reference here is to senile Jove in Plautus' *Mercator* (2, 2, 33) and the letters of course mean 'I love' AMO.

For thus the god always brings like to like

– and there really is no difference between them except the old man's wrinkles and the number of birthdays he has counted.[29] Otherwise they are exactly alike: white hair, toothless mouth, short stature, liking for milk, babbling, chattering, silliness, forgetfulness, thoughtlessness, everything in fact. The nearer people approach old age the closer they return to a semblance of childhood, until the time comes for them to depart this life, again like children, neither tired of living nor aware of death.

Anyone who likes can go and compare this service of mine with the changes made by the other gods. What they did in anger, I'd rather not recount, but even when they're particularly well-disposed to people, they have a habit of turning them into a tree, a bird, a grasshopper, or even a snake – as if becoming something else were not just the same as dying.[30] Now I restore a man unchanged to the best and happiest time of his life. But if mortals would henceforth have no truck with wisdom and spend all their time with me, there would be no more old age and they could be happy enjoying eternal youth.

You must have seen those soured individuals who are so wrapped up in their philosophic studies or some other serious, exacting affairs that they are old before they were ever young; I suppose it's because their preoccupations and the unremitting

29. See the *Iliad*, 1, 249 and 3, 152 for the references to Nestor and 'lily-sweet' voices. The verse comes from the *Odyssey*, 17, 218.

30. The first allusion is probably to Daphne, changed into a laurel tree after asking for help while being pursued by an amorous Apollo (Ovid, *Metamorphoses*, 1, 452 ff.). Ceyx and his wife Alcyone were punished for calling themselves Zeus and Hera. Ceyx was drowned and Alcyone threw herself into the sea after him. Both were changed into birds by the pity of the gods (Ovid, *Metamorphoses*, 11, 410 ff.). Tithonus, Priam's brother, was given by Zeus the gift of immortality but not that of eternal youth, for which Eos, goddess of the dawn, forgot to ask. When he became old and garrulous she finally shut him up in a room or, in the version of the legend deriving from Hellanicus, he was changed into a chirping grasshopper. Cadmus, the son of Agenor, built the Cadmea, citadel of Thebes, and introduced writing into Greece. In old age he and his wife Harmonia, daughter of Ares and Aphrodite, were turned into snakes in Illyria (Ovid, *Metamorphoses*, 4, 571 ff.).

strain of their keen concentration gradually sap their spirit and vitality. By contrast my morons are plump, sleek, and glossy, typical 'Acarnanian porkers', as they say, and never likely to know any of the disadvantages of old age unless they pick up some infection from the wise. However, man isn't permitted to be happy every bit of his life.[31]

Then there's further good evidence in the common saying which is often quoted: 'Folly is the one thing which can halt fleeting youth and ward off the relentless advance of old age.' And there's good reason for what is generally said about the natives of Brabant, that increasing age brings other men wisdom, but they grow more and more foolish the nearer they approach old age. At the same time there are no people so cheerful in company or so little affected by the misery of growing old. Close to them as neighbours and also in their way of life are my Hollanders – for why shouldn't I call them mine? They're my devoted followers, so much so that they've earned a popular epithet of which they're not at all ashamed, indeed they make a special boast of it.[32]

Off you go, you foolish mortals, find a Medea, Circe, Venus and Aurora, and some sort of a spring you can use to give you back your youth! But I alone can provide this power and do so. My hands hold the magic philtre with which Memnon's daughter prolonged the youth of her grandfather Tithonus. I am the Venus by whose favour Phaon became young again to be loved

31. 'Plump', 'sleek' and 'glossy' are words used by Horace of himself (*Epistles*, 1, 4, 15–16) when he presents himself as a pig from the herd of Epicurus. The Acarnanian pigs are also mentioned in the *Adages*.

In the Renaissance Epicurus was usually taxed with denying the immortality of the soul and his followers were not unusually referred to as pigs from his herd. His view that man's final end was pleasure could be taken in a severe and almost stoic sense, as Seneca interpreted it, or as something altogether less lofty, which explains something of the ambiguity of the Renaissance attitude towards him. In the seventeenth century, Gassendi produced a full-scale Christian version of his philosophy.

32. The 'special boast' is the Dutch proverb that the older a Dutchman is, the stupider he is,

Hoe ouder, hoe botter Hollander.

By claiming a special relationship with the Dutch, Folly is of course being ironic at Erasmus's expense.

so much by Sappho.[33] Mine are the herbs, if there are any, mine the supplications received, mine the spring which can not only restore lost youth but (better still) preserve it for evermore. And if you all share the view that nothing is better than youth, nothing so hateful as old age, I think you must see how much you owe to me for maintaining such a blessing and driving such an evil away.

But why am I still talking about mortals? Search the heavens, and then anyone who likes can taunt me with my name if he finds a single one of the gods who wouldn't be disagreeable and disliked if he weren't graced by my divine powers. Why is Bacchus always a boy with long flowing hair? Surely because he's irresponsible and drunk, and spends all his life at banquets and dances, singing and revelling, and never has any dealings with Pallas. In fact he's so far from asking to be thought wise that he's happy to be worshipped with merriment and fun. Nor does he take offence when given a name which means 'foolish' in the Greek saying 'more foolish than Morychus'.[34] His name was

33. Medea is said (Ovid, *Metamorphoses*, 7, 162 ff.) to have renewed the youth of Aeson, Jason's father, by boiling him with herbs. Circe is the witch in Homer who turns Odysseus' men into swine (*Odyssey*, 10, 137 ff.). Venus is the goddess of love, and Aurora, the Roman goddess of the dawn identified with the Greek Eos, is noted for the lovers she abducted. It was the granddaughter of Aurora who obtained from Jupiter the transformation of Tithonus into a grasshopper (Ovid, *Metamorphoses*, 19, 576 ff. and see note 30, p. 24. Phaon, the old boatman of Lesbos, was rejuvenated by Venus. Sappho fell in love with him and jumped off the Leucadian rock for his sake.

34. Virgil describes the cult of Bacchus in the *Georgics* (2, 380 ff.). Bacchus is the Lydian name of Dionysus, and as this became more popular, the older, bearded figure of the god gave place to the youthful, almost effeminate figure of later Greek sculpture. The proverb concerning Morychus is discussed by Erasmus in the *Adages*. It apparently refers to one who neglects the places where important things are going on and alludes to a Sicilian statue of Bacchus which was outside his temple. Athenaeus tells us that Bacchus was known as Morychus. Folly goes on to refer to Bacchus' birth from the thigh of Jupiter. His mother Semele, tricked by a jealous Hera, had her request granted by Jupiter that he should come to her, as to Hera, in his full glory, which resulted in her death from his thunderbolts. Jupiter put the premature child into his thigh, whence in due course he was born. The 'Old Comedy' refers to Aristophanes' *The Frogs*.

changed to Morychus because the country people in their revels used wine-must and fresh figs to smear the statue sitting at the door of his temple. Then think of the insults flung at him in Old Comedy! 'Stupid god', they would say, 'just the sort to be born from a thigh.' Yet who wouldn't choose to be this light-hearted fool who is always young and merry and brings pleasure and gaiety to all, rather than 'crooked-counselled' Jupiter who is universally feared, or old Pan who confounds everything with his sudden alarms, ash-grimed Vulcan, always filthy from his work in the smithy, or even Pallas herself who strikes terror with her Gorgon and spear and 'fixed grim stare'? Why is Cupid always a boy? Simply because he's a joker and never shows 'sound sense' in word or thought. Why does the beauty of golden Venus never lose its bloom of youth? Surely because she's related to me and gets the colour of her complexion from my father. That's why Homer calls her 'golden Aphrodite'. And besides, she's always smiling, if we are to believe the poets or the sculptors who copy them. What deity did the Romans ever worship more devoutly than Flora, the mother of all delights?[35] And if anyone cares to ask some searching questions of Homer and the other poets about the lives even of the sterner gods, he'll find folly everywhere. I don't think I need go into the behaviour of the others, as you're well aware of the love-affairs and goings-on of Jupiter the thunderer himself, and how even that chaste Diana who ignored her sex and devoted herself to hunting could still lose her heart to Endymion.

I only wish they could still hear their conduct ridiculed by Momus, as they often used to do at one time, but it isn't long since they lost their tempers and threw him and Até headlong

35. 'Crooked-counselled' is a word applied by Homer to Zeus and by Hesiod to Prometheus. Pan, the god of woods, was known for the terror ('panic') with which he inspired travellers. On Vulcan the smith, see note 15, p. 16. Pallas Athene as goddess of war is frequently depicted with shield, lance, helmet and her goatskin cloak fringed with serpents and with the Gorgon's head in the centre. The 'fixed grim stare' is a reference to Sophocles (*Ajax*, 452). On Cupid, Folly refers to the *Iliad* (8, 524) and on Venus to the *Odyssey* (8, 337). Aphrodite was the classical Greek name for Venus. Flora is the goddess of flowering plants whose spring festival was renowned for its licentiousness.

down to earth because he disturbed the gods' carefree happiness with his pertinent interruptions.[36] And not a single mortal thinks of offering hospitality to the exile, far from it – there's no room for him in the halls of princes where my 'Kolakia' holds first place; she can no more get on with Momus than the wolf with the lamb. So now that they've got rid of him the gods can have their fun with much more gaiety and freedom, 'living an easy life' in fact, as Homer says, with no one to keep a sharp eye on them. What joke will that fig-wood Priapus not play? And Mercury is up to all sort of tricks with his thefts and sleight-of-hand. Vulcan too has always acted the 'buffoon' at the banquets of the gods, and delighted the company by his limping or his taunts or the funny things he says. Then there's that amorous old Silenus who is always obscenely dancing the *'cordax'* along with Polyphemus stamping his *'ratatan'*, and the nymphs dancing a 'barefoot ballet'. The half-goat satyrs play Atellan farces, Pan makes everyone laugh with his hopeless efforts at singing, and the gods would rather listen to him than to the Muses themselves, especially when the nectar has started to flow freely. But I needn't say here what the gods are up to when they've drunk well and the banquet's over – absurdities like these often make me feel I can't stop laughing myself. It would really be better at this point to remember Harpocrates and keep silent in case some

36. Jupiter's love-affairs were notorious. Hesiod enumerates his seven wives, and there were of course numerous affairs with mortals. Diana, goddess of the moon, who fell in love with the beautiful sleeping hunter Endymion, had his sleep indefinitely prolonged by Jupiter in order to be able to embrace him every night without his knowledge. The Endymion legend is usually referred to Selene or Artemis. But Selene was the moon goddess and Artemis, the chaste goddess of the hunt, was the sister of the sun god Apollo. The Romans identified her with Diana, their moon goddess, so that Diana took over Artemis' functions as virgin hunter to give the legend as Folly refers to it.

Momus, although mentioned by Hesiod, is a literary rather than a mythological character. He is the fault-finder who mocks at his fellow-gods, normally depicted taking off his mask and associated with folly and stinging satire. Erasmus writes of him in the *Adages*. Atè, the personification of blindness and infatuation, caused so much trouble among the gods, notably by leading Juno to deceive Jupiter, that Jupiter threw her down to earth, where she is responsible for discord and disaster (*Iliad*, 19, 91 ff.).

Corycian god may hear us say things which even Momus couldn't get away with.[37]

But now it's time we left the gods in heaven and came down to earth for a spell, as Homer does. There too we shall see there's nothing happy and gay unless I've made it so. In particular, you observe how wisely mother Nature, the parent and creator of the human race, has seen to it that some spice of folly shall nowhere be lacking. By stoic definition wisdom means nothing else but being ruled by reason; and folly, by contrast, is being swayed by the dictates of the passions. So Jupiter, not wanting man's life to be wholly gloomy and grim, has bestowed far more passion than reason – you could reckon the ratio as twenty-four to one. Moreover, he confined reason to a cramped corner of the

37. Homer refers, in slightly different terms, to the 'easy life' of the gods in the *Iliad* (6, 138). Priapus, god of fertility, shrank to the garden-god and was depicted as grotesque rather than serious or impressive. Horace puts into his mouth that he was once a (useless) piece of fig-wood (*Satires*, 1, 8, 1). Mercury, the god of commerce and subsequently of theft, was responsible for stealing Apollo's cattle and, while being reproached for it, his quiver. Lucian tells us that Mercury stole Vulcan's tongs and in the Ode of Horace to which Folly refers (1, 10), Mercury's intervention to protect Priam on his midnight journey to recover the body of Hector is also mentioned. Homer recounts how Vulcan or Hephaestus clowned at the feasts of the gods, moving them to laughter at his limp or by his scoffing (*Iliad*, 1, 568 and 18, 397).

Silenus was the drunken and misshapen companion of Bacchus, and the 'cordax' an obscene dance which existed before the Old Comedy and was illustrative of the effects of debauchery.

Polyphemus is one of the Homeric Cyclopes, who destroyed with a rock his rival Acis for the love of the nymph Galatea. The reference to the 'barefoot ballet' comes from Lucian's *de saltatione* (chapter 12). The satyrs were sylvan creatures, half-goat, half-man, and the Atellan farces, with stock characters and ritualized action, were noted for their obscenity. Pan was always considered to be musical, but his instrument was the shepherd's pipe.

Harpocrates, mentioned in the *Adages*, is the god of silence, depicted as a chubby child with his index finger covering his lips. The Corycian cave on Mount Parnassus, also mentioned in the *Adages*, is associated with unsuccessful attempts to conceal what one is doing.

Folly's new reference to Momus underlines the irreverence with which she is discoursing on such apparently serious topics as the goings-on of the gods and paves the way for her equal irreverence later about contemporary ecclesiastics and their affairs.

head and left all the rest of the body to the passions. Then he set up two raging tyrants in opposition to reason's solitary power: anger, which holds sway in the breast and so controls the heart, the very source of life, and lust, whose empire spreads far and wide, right down to the genitals. How far reason can prevail against the combined forces of these two the common life of man makes quite clear. She does the only thing she can, and shouts herself hoarse repeating formulas of virtue, while the other two bid her go hang herself and are increasingly noisy and offensive until at last their ruler is exhausted, gives up, and surrenders.[38]

But since man was born to manage affairs he had to be given a modicum, just a sprinkling, of reason; and in order to do her best for him in this matter Nature called on me for counsel here as she had on other occasions. I was ready with a piece of advice worthy of myself: she should give him a woman, admittedly a stupid and foolish sort of creature but amusing and pleasant company all the same, and she could share his life, and season and sweeten his harsh nature by her folly. For Plato's apparent doubt whether to place woman in the category of rational animal or brute beast is intended to point out the remarkable folly of her sex. If ever a woman wanted to be thought wise she

38. Erasmus's reference to 'mother Nature' is a reminiscence of Cicero (de natura deorum, 1, 8). The proportion of twenty-four to one is Lijster's interpretation of Erasmus's quantities. On the stoic opposition between reason and passion, see note 22, p. 20, and on the attribution of the passions to the various parts of the body, note 23, p. 20. The reference here is to Plato's Timaeus (69d). The Phaedrus had contained the parable of the charioteer (reason) with his two horses (the noble and obedient passions and the wild, disobedient ones). The Timaeus goes on to ascribe the rational part of the soul to the head, the faculty of courage and anger to the part of the body near the heart, and desire to the lower part of the body.

This was the doctrine, popularized by Cicero, which Erasmus quoted from Plato in the Enchiridion Militis Christiani. Plato himself, who regarded ethical activity as determined by rational judgement, ascribed desire to the liver, and by widening the 'lower part of the body' to include the sexual organs, Erasmus retained plausibility for Plato's ascription of the soul's faculties to the three regions of the body. It is only under the influence of St Augustine that the later Renaissance authors will reverse Plato's doctrine and put love into the heart.

only succeeded in being doubly foolish, just as if one enters an ox for a wrestling match, they say, one can't hope for the approval and support of Minerva. The defect is multiplied when anyone tries to lay on a veneer of virtue and deflect a character from its natural bent. As the Greek proverb puts it, an ape is always an ape even if clad in purple: and a woman is always a woman, that is, a fool, whatever mask she wears.[39]

But I don't think the female sex is so foolish as to be angry with me for attributing folly to them, seeing that I *am* Folly, and a woman myself. If they look at the matter in the right way they must see that it's entirely due to folly that they are better off than men in many respects. In the first place they have the gift of beauty, which they rightly value above everything else, for it ensures their power to tyrannize over tyrants themselves. Besides, that unkempt look, rough skin, bushy beard, and all the marks of old age in a man can only come from the corrupting influence of wisdom, seeing that a woman always has smooth cheeks, gentle voice, soft skin, and a look of perpetual youth. Next, what else do women desire in this life but to give maximum pleasure to men? Isn't this the purpose of all their attention to their persons, all that make-up, bathing, hair-dressing, and all those ointments and perfumes, as well as so many arts of arranging, painting, and disguising face, eyes, and skin? Now, does anything count more in winning them men's favour than their folly? There's nothing men won't permit to women, and for no other return than pleasure, but it's women's folly which makes them delight men. No one will deny the truth of this who considers the nonsense a man talks with a woman and the silly things he does whenever he wants to enjoy the pleasure she gives. So there you have the source of life's first and foremost delight.

39. Folly's reference to Plato's doubts about whether women were human or animal (*Timaeus*, 90e) does not give a fair idea of what either Plato or Erasmus thought. Rabelais borrows this reference for the *Tiers Livre* (chapter 32). The two proverbs in this paragraph are both commented on in the *Adages*. That concerning Minerva refers to the attempt to teach something to someone who cannot understand.

The idea that women's folly sweetens the harsh nature of men comes from Aulus Gellius (15, 25, 2).

However, there are some men, especially old men, who are more given to wine than to women, and find their greatest pleasure in drinking parties. Now whether a party can have much success without a woman present I must ask others to decide, but one thing is certain, no party is any fun unless seasoned with folly. In fact, if there's no one there to raise a laugh with his folly, genuine or assumed, they have to bring on a 'jester', one who's paid for the job, or invite some absurd hanger-on whose laughable, that is, foolish, remarks will banish silence and gloom from the company. What was the point of loading the stomach with all those delicacies, fancy dishes, and titbits if the eyes and ears and the whole mind can't be fed as well on laughter, jokes, and wit? But when it comes to that sort of confectionery, I'm the only mistress of the art. And all the usual rituals of banquets, drawing lots for a king, throwing dice, drinking healths, 'passing round the cup', singing with a myrtle branch, dancing, miming – none of them was discovered for the benefit of the human race by the Seven Sages of Greece, but by me.[40] The very nature of all things of this sort is that the more folly they have, the more they enrich man's life, for if that is joyless it seems scarcely worth calling life at all. But it can't fail to end up joyless unless you can find diversions of this kind to remove the boredom inseparable from it.

But there will perhaps be some who have no use for this kind of pleasure, and find their satisfaction in the affection and companionship of their friends. Friendship, they're always saying, must come before everything. It is something even more essential than air, fire, and water, so delightful that if it were removed from their midst it would be like losing the sun, and finally, so respected (if this is at all relevant) that even the philosophers do not hesitate to mention it amongst the greatest of blessings. Here again I can show that of that greatest blessing I am both poop

40. The banquet rituals include choosing a 'king' or president, to prescribe who will sing, how much he must drink and in general to direct the festivities (see Horace, *Odes*, 1, 4, 18). 'Drinking healths' refers to a sort of friendly competition. 'Singing with a myrtle branch' is a proverb considered in the *Adages* and refers to the habit of passing round a stick of myrtle, held by the singer and given by him to the guest whom he wished to sing next.

and prow. And I'll demonstrate it not by the Crocodile's Syllogism, or the Heap, or the Horns, or any other dialectical subtlety of that kind – no, with what is called sound common sense I can put my finger on the spot.[41] Just think: winking at your friend's faults, passing over them, turning a blind eye, building up illusions, treating obvious faults as virtues which call for love and admiration – isn't all that related to folly? One man showers kisses on his mistress's mole, another is charmed by the polyp in his dear lamb's nose, a father talks about the wink in his son's squinting eye – what's that, please, but folly pure and simple? Let's have it repeated, three and four times over, it is folly, and the same folly, which alone makes friendships and keeps friends together. I'm talking of ordinary mortals, none of whom is born faultless, and the best among them is the one with fewest faults. But amongst those stoic philosopher-gods either no friendship forms at all, or else it is a sour and ungracious sort of relationship which exists only with very few men – I hesitate to say with none at all, for most men have their foolish moments, or rather, everyone is irrational in various ways, and friendship joins like to like. But if ever some mutual goodwill does arise amongst these

41. The reference to 'poop and prow' is proverbial and is noted in the *Adages*. The Crocodile's Syllogism is mentioned by Quintilian and is a trick. The example normally given is that of a crocodile promising to return to its mother a child he has snatched, providing she can correctly forecast what he will do. If she says he will return it, she is wrong. If she says he will not, she is right, but only if he in fact does not. The Horned Sorites is also in Quintilian and is best illustrated by dilemmas of the type posed by the question 'Have you stopped beating your wife?'

Among the philosophers who praise the joys of friendship are the stoics and Cicero. The tradition passed through St Ambrose into Christian writings and was strongly taken up both in the middle ages and in the Renaissance, when friendship came to be considered as essentially disinterested, a union of wills divorced from desire and sensual inclination. The neoplatonist context of so much Renaissance writing on the affections made friendship non-instinctive and, in spite of earlier gropings, it was not until the late-sixteenth century that morally elevating friendship came to be considered even to be compatible with instinctively based affection.

Erasmus, like the other humanists, reacted very strongly against the educational system largely focused round a knowledge of the complex rules of minor logic.

austere characters it certainly can't be stable and is unlikely to last long, seeing that they're so captious and far keener-eyed to pick out their friends' faults than the eagle or the Epidaurian snake. Of course they're blind to their own faults and simply don't see the packs hanging from their backs.[42] It's in man's nature for every sort of character to be prone to serious faults. In addition, there are wide variations of temperament and interests, as well as all the lapses and mistakes and accidents of mortal life. Consequently the delights of friendship couldn't last a single hour among such Argus-eyed folk without the addition of what the Greeks aptly named '*εὐήθεια*', a word we can translate either as "folly" or as "easy-going ways". Besides, isn't Cupid himself, who is responsible for creating all relationships, totally blind, so that to him 'ugliness looks like beauty'? And so he sees to it that each one of you finds beauty in what he has, and the old man loves his old woman as the boy loves his girl. This happens everywhere and meets with smiles, but nevertheless it's the sort of absurdity which is the binding force in society and brings happiness to life.[43]

42. Most of this paragraph so far is a reminiscence of Horace, from whom it quotes and whom it paraphrases (*Satires*, 1, 3). The eagle's eye is proverbially acute. The Epidaurian snake mentioned by Horace Is' Asclepius, Greek hero and god of healing, whose symbol was a snake, often coiled on a staff, and who originally came into prominence at Epidaurus, the site of his first and principal shrine. He is said to have come to Rome in the form of a snake.

43. Argus had eyes in the back of his head. The Greek word for 'good nature' is taken from Plato's *Republic* (401e). Cupid is represented as blind both because the lover sees no defects in the object of his love and on account of the ill-assorted relationships over which he presides. The Greek phrase for 'ugliness looks like beauty' comes from Theocritus (6, 19) and the proverbial expression 'the old man loves his old woman' is treated in the *Adages*.

At the end of this paragraph, Folly suggests that love, however absurd, is the binding force of society. This is an allusion to the celebrated neoplatonist notion of love as the 'vinculum Mundi'. The Renaissance neoplatonists, following Plotinus, saw the 'vinculum Mundi' in terms of God's love for men and men's love for one another and for God, so that love was circular, beginning and ending in God. Panurge, in the mock encomium of the early chapters of Rabelais' *Tiers Livre* will facetiously hold that debt is the bond of society.

What I've said about friendship is much more applicable to marriage, which is nothing other than an inseparable union for life. Goodness me, what divorces or worse than divorces there would be everywhere if the domestic relations of man and wife were not propped up and sustained by the flattery, joking, complaisance, illusions, and deceptions provided by my followers! Why, not many marriages would ever be made if the bridegroom made prudent inquiries about the tricks that little virgin who now seems so chaste and innocent was up to long before the wedding. And once entered on, even fewer marriages would last unless most of a wife's goings-on escaped notice through the indifference or stupidity of her husband. All this can properly be attributed to Folly, for it's she who sees that a wife is attractive to her husband and a husband to his wife, that peace reigns in the home and their relationship continues. A husband is laughed at, called a cuckold and a cuckoo and who knows what else when he kisses away the tears of his unfaithful wife, but how much happier it is for him to be thus deceived than to wear himself out with unremitting jealousy, strike a tragic attitude, and ruin everything!

In short, no association or alliance can be happy or stable without me. People can't tolerate a ruler, nor can a master his servant, a maid her mistress, a teacher his pupil, a friend his friend nor a wife her husband, a landlord his tenant, a soldier his comrade nor a party-goer his companion, unless they sometimes have illusions about each other, make use of flattery, and have the sense to turn a blind eye and sweeten life for themselves with the honey of folly. I dare say you think this is the last word on the subject, but there are more important things to come.

Now tell me: can a man love anyone who hates himself? Can he be in harmony with someone else if he's divided in himself, or bring anyone pleasure if he's only a disagreeable nuisance to himself? No one, I fancy, would say he can unless there's someone more foolish than Folly. Remove me, and no one could put up with his neighbour, indeed, he'd stink in his own nostrils and find everything about himself loathsome and disgusting. The reason is that Nature, more of a stepmother than a mother in several ways,[44] has sown a seed of evil in the hearts of mortals, especially in the more thoughtful men, which makes them dissatisfied with their own lot and envious of another's. Consequently, all the blessings of life, which should give it grace and charm, are damaged and destroyed. What good is beauty, the greatest gift of the gods, if it is tainted by the canker of decay? Or youth, if it is soured and spoiled by the misery of advancing age? And finally, is there any duty throughout life which you can perform gracefully as regards yourself or others (for the importance of decorum extends beyond mere skill and covers every action) unless you have Self-love at hand to help you, Self-love who is so prompt to take my place on all occasions that she is rightly called my sister? What is so foolish as self-satisfaction and self-admiration? But then what agreeable, pleasant, or graceful act can you perform if you aren't self-satisfied? Take away this salt of life and immediately the orator and his gestures will be a bore, the musician will please no one with his tunes, the actor and his posturings will be hissed off the stage, the poet be a laughing-stock along with his Muses, the painter and his works deemed valueless, and the doctor starve amidst his remedies. Finally, you'll look like Thersites and Nestor instead of Nireus and Phaon, a pig rather than Minerva, and a speechless child and a boor instead of an eloquent and civilized man; which shows how necessary it is for a man to have a good opinion of himself, give himself a bit of a boost to win his own self-esteem before he can win that of others.

And since for the most part happiness consists in being willing to be what you are, my Self-love has provided a short cut to it by ensuring that no one is dissatisfied with his own looks, character, race, position, country, and way of life. And so no Irishman would want to change places with an Italian, nor Thracian with an Athenian, nor Scythian with an inhabitant of the Islands of the Blest. What remarkable foresight of Nature it was, to level out all these variations and make all alike! Where she has withheld some of her gifts she generally adds a tiny bit

44. The idea that nature is only a stepmother is a well-known Renaissance topos originating in Quintilian.

more Self-love – but it's silly of me to say this, seeing that Self-love is her greatest gift. Just let me add that no great deed was ever performed without my prompting and no new art discovered unless I was responsible.[45]

And of all deeds which win praise, isn't war the seed and source? But what is more foolish than to embark on a struggle of this kind for some reason or other when it does more harm than good to either side? For those who fall in battle, like the men of Megara, are 'of no account'. When the mail-clad ranks confront each other and the trumpets "blare out their harsh note", what use, I ask you, are those wise men who are worn out with their studies and can scarcely draw breath now their blood is thin and cold? The need is for stout and sturdy fellows with all the daring possible and the minimum of brain. Of course some may prefer a soldier like Demosthenes, who took Archilochus' advice and had scarcely glimpsed the enemy before he threw away his shield and fled, as cowardly in battle as he was skilled in speech-making. People say that judgement matters most in war, and so it does for a general, I agree, but it's a soldier's judgement, not a philosopher's. Otherwise it's the spongers, pimps, robbers, murderers, peasants, morons, debtors, and that sort of scum of the earth who provide the glories of war, not the philosophers and their midnight oil.[46] As an example of just how useless these

45. Nireus, according to Homer, was the most handsome of the Greeks after Achilles, but a weakling (*Iliad*, 2, 671) and Thersites was the ugliest (*Iliad*, 2, 212). Nestor is said by Ovid to have lived to be more than two hundred years old (*Metamorphoses*, 12, 187, ff.) while Phaon was rejuvenated by Venus (see note 33, p. 26). The comparison between Nireus and Thersites occurs in Ovid and the allusion to Minerva corresponds to a reference in the *Adages*.

Folly quotes Martial on being willing to be what you are (10, 47, 12).

46. The men of Megara also figure in the *Adages*. This is a proverbial expression for people of no account. The harsh note of the trumpets alludes to Virgil (*Aeneid*, 8, 2). The incidents concerning the Athenian orator Demosthenes and the advice of Archilochus the Ionic poet are both mentioned in Plutarch.

Erasmus was withering in his satire on the futility of war, inheriting his view from Colet and the tradition of neoplatonist evangelism. He shared it with More and, even more, with Rabelais. Among Erasmus's own writings against war are the famous *Dulce bellum inexpertis* from the 1515 *Adages* and the 1517 *Querela pacis*, a 'complaint' put into the mouth of Peace.

philosophers are for any practice in life there is Socrates himself, the one and only wise man, according to the Delphic oracle. It showed little enough wisdom in its judgement, for once when he tried to do something in public he had to break off amid general laughter. Yet on one point the man was sensible enough – he refused to accept the epithet 'wise' but attributed it to the god. He also held the view that the wise man should steer clear of taking part in politics, though maybe he should have gone further and advised anyone who wants to be counted a man to keep well away from wisdom. What drove him to drink the hemlock after his trial if not his wisdom? For while he was philosophizing about clouds and ideas, measuring a flea's foot, and marvelling at a midge's humming, he learned nothing about the affairs of ordinary life. And at the master's side in his hour of peril stands his pupil Plato, a splendid advocate, I must say, when he was so overwhelmed by the clamour of the crowd that he could hardly get out half a sentence. Then what shall I say about Theophrastus? When he stepped forward to speak he was immediately struck dumb as if he'd suddenly seen a wolf. Who could have fired the military-minded in the time of war? Not Isocrates, who was so timid by nature that he never ventured to open his mouth. Cicero, the father of Roman eloquence, always rose to speak in an unseemly state of agitation like a child with hiccups. Quintilian explains this as a mark of an intelligent orator conscious of the risks he ran, but in saying so, doesn't he openly admit that wisdom is an obstacle to successful performance? If people are half-dead of fear when they have to fight only with words, what will they do if the issue must be settled by the sword?[47]

And on top of all this, please heaven, that famous saying of

47. The passage on Socrates draws on several Platonic dialogues, and notably the *Apology*. There is also a reference to Aristophanes on the midges' humming (*Clouds*, 146 and 157). The anecdote about Plato's reaction to the crowd is from Diogenes Laertius (2, 41). The incident involving Theophrastus; the disciple of Aristotle, is of unknown origin. The effect of wolves is proverbial and is mentioned in the *Adages*. The mention of Isocrates, the Athenian orator, alludes to Cicero (*de oratore*, 2, 3, 10). Cicero himself writes of his own nervousness when he spoke in public (*pro Roscio Amerino*, 4, 9). The reference to Quintilian is to the *Institutio oratoria*, 11, 1, 43.

Plato's is always quoted: "Happy the states where either philosophers are kings or kings are philosophers!" But if you look at
history you'll find that no state has been so plagued by its rulers
as when power has fallen into the hands of some dabbler in
philosophy or literary addict. The two Catos are sufficient proof
of this, I think, when one of them was a disturber of the peace of
the republic with his crazy denunciations, and the other showed
his wisdom by defending the liberty of the Roman people, and
in doing so completely destroyed it. Then there are the families
of Brutus and Cassius, the Gracchi brothers and even Cicero
himself, who was just as much a scourge to the republic of
Rome as Demosthenes was to Athens. As for Marcus Aurelius,
we have to admit that he was a good emperor, but I could still
deny him this distinction on the grounds that he was unpopular
and disliked amongst his subjects for the very reason that he was
so much of a philosopher. And even admitted that he was good,
he undoubtedly did more harm to Rome by leaving it such a
son as his than he ever benefited it by his administration. In fact
this type of man, who is devoted to the study of wisdom, is
always most unlucky in everything and particularly when it
comes to procreating children; I imagine this is because Nature
wants to ensure that the evil of wisdom shall not spread further
throughout mankind. ⟨So it's well known that Cicero had a
degenerate son, and the children of the great sage Socrates
himself took after their mother rather than their father, as
someone put it rather well: meaning, they were fools.⟩[48]
One could put up with it somehow if these folks would be the
'ass playing the lyre' only in public affairs, and not be so utterly

48. Plato's statement about philosopher-kings is from the *Republic* (5,
473d). Rabelais borrows this allusion for *Gargantua* (chapter 45). The Cato
who is blamed by Folly for his denunciations is Cato the Censor (234–149
BC) who attacked the Scipios, became consul, and was noted for conservatism
in a somewhat puritan tradition. The second Cato is Cato of Utica (95–46
BC), moderate but unamiable, who joined cause with Pompey in 52 BC and
who governed Utica in Pompey's interest during the civil war which
Pompey lost to Caesar. Brutus and Cassius, outlawed by Octavian, lost the
famous Battle of Philippi to Antony and Octavian. The Gracchi brothers
were both reformers who attempted to undermine the authority of the
senate by allying the rich business class with the plebs. Cicero was an

incompetent in every single thing in life. Ask a wise man to dinner and he'll upset everyone by his gloomy silence or tiresome questions. Invite him to a dance and you'll have a camel prancing about. Haul him off to a public entertainment and his face will be enough to spoil the people's enjoyment. He'll have to leave the theatre like Cato the Wise when he couldn't lay aside his scowl. If he joins in a conversation, all of a sudden there's the wolf in the fable. If there's anything to be bought or an arrangement to be made, in fact if any one of those things has to be done without which our daily life can't be carried on, you'll call your wise man a blockhead, not a man. It's quite impossible for him to be of any use to himself, his country, or his family because he's ignorant of ordinary matters and far removed from any normal way of thinking and current practice. And so inevitably he is also disliked, doubtless because of the great dissimilarity in mentality and way of life. For nothing happens in this world which isn't full of folly, performed by fools amongst fools. If any individual wants to make a stand against the rest, I'd recommend him to take his lead from Timon and move off to some wilderness where he can enjoy his own wisdom in solitude.[49]

But to return to my subject. Take those wild men sprung from hard rocks and oak trees – what power brought them together into a civilized society if not flattery? This is all that's meant by the lyre of Amphion and Orpheus. What was it which recalled the Roman mob to harmony in the state when it was plotting violence – a philosopher's speech? Not a bit of it. It was a silly, childish fable made up about the belly and other parts of

intermittent enemy of Caesar and supporter of Pompey. Modern scholars would generally accept Folly's criticism of Marcus Aurelius. His son Commodus, sole emperor from AD 180 to 192, ruled by favourites and was much influenced by his concubine Marcia. He was obsessed by power and deeply antagonistic to the senate. Cicero's son, also Marcus Tullius, born in 65 BC is said to have been idle, extravagant and devoted to the bottle.

49. The proverbial 'ass with the lyre' figures in the *Adages*, as do the prancing camel and the sudden silence caused by the wolf in the fable. Cato the Censor's serious frown is a commonplace of Latin literature. Lucian's dialogue *Timon* was translated by Erasmus in 1506. Timon of Athens cut himself wholly off from the world and would see no one but Alcibiades.

the body. A similar sort of story told by Themistocles about a fox and a hedgehog had the same effect. No sage's speech could ever have achieved so much as that fictitious white hind of Sertorius, or the ridiculous anecdote invented about the famous Spartan with his two dogs, and the one told by Sertorius about pulling the hairs out of a horse's tail, to say nothing of Minos and Numa who both ruled the foolish mob by means of fantastic trumped-up tales. It's absurdities like these that sway the huge powerful monster which is the common people. But what society ever took its laws from Plato or Aristotle or the teachings of Socrates?[50]

Again, what made the house of Decius choose to dedicate their lives to the gods of the underworld and brought Quintus Curtius to the abyss if not the vain hope of fame, the sweetest of all sirens, though damned by your wise men to a remarkable

50. Amphion and Orpheus both come from the well-known Renaissance list of musicians whose music produced extraordinary or magical effects. Amphion was given a lyre by Jupiter and, together with his brother, constructed the walls of Thebes by drawing the stones into position with his music. Orpheus, too, charmed beasts, trees and stones with Apollo's lyre (see Horace, *Ars poetica*, 391 ff.). The legendary fable of the Belly and the Limbs which calmed the Roman mob and brought them back to Rome was reputedly told them by Menenius Agrippa in the fifth century BC (see Livy, 2, 32). Themistocles, the Athenian statesman, is said by Plutarch to have dissuaded the Athenians from throwing off the yoke of taxation by a fable in which a fox will not have the blood-sucking flies removed by a hedgehog on the grounds that they would only be replaced by other unsatisfied ones. According to Plutarch, Sertorius persuaded the Spaniards that the white hind signified that he was in communication with the gods, and the anecdote about the Spartan, also from Plutarch, concerned Lycurgus who demonstrated to the Spartans the importance of education by showing them the difference between a trained and an untrained dog. The reference to the hairs from the horse's tail comes from an anecdote in Valerius Maximus (7, 3, 6) in which Sertorius showed his barbarian army the futility of trying to overcome the Romans in one great battle by demonstrating that the only way to pluck a horse's tail was one hair at a time. Minos was believed by his people to retire every nine years to Jupiter's grotto to be inspired by the god. Numa Pompilius, the second king of Rome, is said by Plutarch to have made his followers believe he was advised by the nymph Egeria in a wood near Rome.

Folly's reference to the gullibility of the common people is a common Renaissance topos. It is historically important as it indicates the new and

degree? Nothing is so foolish, they say, as for a man to stand for office and woo the crowd to win its vote, buy its support with presents, court the applause of all those fools and feel self-satisfied when they cry their approval, and then in his hour of triumph to be carried round like an effigy for the public to stare at, and end up cast in bronze to stand in the market-place.[51] Then there are changes of names and surnames, divine honours awarded to a nobody, official ceremonies devised to raise even the most criminal of tyrants to the level of the gods. All this is utterly foolish, and more than one Democritus is needed for these absurdities, everyone agrees. Yet from this source spring the deeds of valiant heroes to be lauded to the skies in the writings of so many eloquent men. This same folly creates societies and maintains empires, officialdom, religion, law courts, and councils – in fact the whole of human life is nothing but a sport of folly.

Now let us turn to the arts. What else has fired men's natural talents to devise and hand on to posterity so many disciplines which they think remarkable if not their thirst for fame? With all their toil and sweat and sleepless nights men have thought to gain some sort of reputation, emptiest of acquisitions, and thereby showed themselves complete fools. Meanwhile it's Folly to whom you owe so many of life's major blessings, and the nicest thing of all is that you have someone else's madness to thank for your enjoyment.

Well, now I've proved that I must be given credit for courage and industry, shall I go on to lay claim to prudence? You might

---

exciting nature of the insights into social and personal possibilities among those who experienced them. Erasmus was to explore the natural rectitude of moral aspirations but, like Rabelais and the Pléiade poets, he could only plausibly do so on the presupposition that he was dealing with the naturally well-endowed. High birth was a condition of entry into *Thélème*. But there are classical precedents, and both Horace and Plato regard the common people as a monster.

51. The reference to the house of Decius draws its point from the deaths of three of its members at war for their country. The young knight Marcus Curtius, according to legend, rode his horse into an abyss which opened in the forum after the auguries had said that it could be closed only when Rome's greatest treasure was thrown into it (Livy, 7, 6, 5). The phrase 'cast in bronze' alludes to Horace (*Satires*, 2, 3, 183).

as well mix fire and water, I can hear someone say. But here again I believe I can succeed, if you'll continue to give me your ears and attention as before.

First of all, if prudence develops through experience, does I ⟨the honour of⟩ possessing a claim to it rightly belong to the wise man who attempts nothing, partly through his sense of propriety, partly through his natural timidity, or to the fool who isn't deterred from anything either by the propriety which he hasn't got or the dangers which he doesn't think about? The wise man seeks refuge in his books of antiquity and learns from them the pure subtleties of what the ancients say. The fool tries everything, meets his dangers at first hand, and thereby acquires what I'm sure is genuine prudence. That is something Homer appears to have seen, despite his blindness, when he says 'even the fool is wise after the event'. For the two main obstacles to learning by experience are a sense of propriety which clouds the judgement and fear which advises against an undertaking once danger is apparent. Folly offers a splendid liberation from both of them. Few mortals realize how many other advantages follow from being free from scruples and ready to venture anything.[52]

But if people prefer the sort of prudence which comes from forming judgements on life, please hear how far those who pride themselves on that account are from having it. In the first place, it's well known that all human affairs are like the figures of Silenus described by Alcibiades and have two completely opposite faces, so that what is death at first sight, as they say, is life if you look within, and vice versa, life is death. The same applies to beauty and ugliness, riches and poverty, obscurity and fame, learning and ignorance, strength and weakness, the noble and the baseborn, happy and sad, good and bad fortune, friend and foe, healthy and harmful – in fact you'll find everything suddenly reversed if you open the Silenus. Maybe some of you will think I've expressed this too philosophically; well, I'll speak bluntly, as they say, to make myself clear. We all agree a king is rich and

52. 'Mixing fire and water' is one of Erasmus's *Adages*, as is the saying of Homer that the fool is wise after the event (*Iliad*, 17, 32) and the reference to clouding the judgement. The advantages claimed by Folly for folly have again become serious ones.

powerful, but if he lacks all spiritual goods and can never be satisfied, then he's surely the poorest of men. And if he's addicted to a large number of vices he's no more than a cheap slave. We could philosophize about others in the same way, but one example will suffice.[53] What's the point of this, someone will say. Hear how we'll develop the argument. If anyone tries to take the masks off the actors when they're playing a scene on the stage and show their true, natural faces to the audience, he'll certainly spoil the whole play and deserve to be stoned and thrown out of the theatre for a maniac. For a new situation will suddenly arise in which a woman on the stage turns into a man, a youth is now old, and the king of a moment ago is suddenly Dama, while a god is shown up as a common little man.[54] To destroy the illusion is to ruin the whole play, for it's really the illusion and make-up which hold the audience's eye. Now, what else is the whole life of man but a sort of play? Actors come on wearing their different masks and all play their parts until the producer orders them off the stage, and he can often tell the same man to appear in different costume, so that now he plays a king in purple and now a humble slave in rags. It's all a sort of pretence, but it's the only way to act out this farce.

At this point let us suppose some wise man dropped from heaven confronts me and insists that the man whom all look up to as god and master is not even human, as he is ruled by his passions, like an animal, and is no more than the lowest slave for serving so many evil masters of his own accord. Or again, he might tell someone else who is mourning his father to laugh

53. On the Silenus figure, see note 10, p. 13. In his essay *Silent Alcibiadis* for the 1515 *Adages*, Erasmus writes, '. . . For it seems that the Sileni were small images divided in half, and so constructed that they could be opened out and displayed; when closed they represented some ridiculous, ugly flute-player, but when they opened they suddenly revealed the figure of a god!' (Translated Margaret Mann Phillips, *Erasmus on His Times: A Shortened Version of the Adages of Erasmus*, Cambridge University Press, 1967, p. 77.)

The phrase for 'speaking bluntly' also occurs in the *Adages*. The Latin contains an allusion to Minerva, identified with Athene as goddess of wisdom, and implies that lofty discourse can obscure the simplest things.

54. Dama is the name given by Horace to a Syrian slave (*Satires*, 2, 5, 18; 2, 7, 54). The phrase 'true natural faces' appears in the *Adages*.

because the dead man is only just beginning to live, seeing that this life of ours is nothing but a sort of death. Another man who boasts of his ancestry he might call low-born and bastard because he is so far removed from virtue, which is the sole source of nobility. If he had the same sort of thing to say about everyone else, what would happen? We should think him a crazy madman. Nothing is so foolish as mistimed wisdom, and nothing less sensible than misplaced sense. A man's conduct is misplaced if he doesn't adapt himself to things as they are, has no eye for the main chance, won't even remember that convivial maxim 'drink or depart', and asks for the play to stop being a play.[55] On the other hand, it's a true sign of prudence not to want wisdom which extends beyond your share as an ordinary mortal, to be willing to overlook things along with the rest of the world or to wear your illusions with a good grace. People say that this is really a sign of folly, ⟨and I'm not setting out to deny it – so long as they'll admit on their side that this is the way to play the comedy of life.⟩

As for my next point – immortal gods, shall I speak out or keep silence? But why keep silent when it's something truer than truth? Though perhaps it would be better for a matter of such importance to summon the Muses from Helicon, seeing that poets are always calling on them for help over the merest trifles. Come, then, for a while, daughters of Jove, while I show that no one can approach that perfect wisdom which the wise call the citadel of bliss unless Folly shows the way.

First of all, it's admitted that all the emotions belong to Folly, and this is what marks the wise man off from the fool; he is ruled by reason, the fool by his emotions. That is why the stoics segregate all passions from the wise man, as if they were diseases. But in fact these emotions not only act as guides to those hastening towards the haven of wisdom, but also wherever virtue is put into practice they are always present to act like spurs and goads as incentives towards good deeds. Yet this is hotly denied by that double-dyed stoic Seneca who strips his wise man

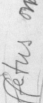

55. The phrases for 'an eye for the main chance' and 'drink or depart' are both in the *Adages*.

of every emotion. In doing so he leaves nothing at all of the man, and has to 'fabricate' in his place a new sort of god who never was and never will be in existence anywhere. Indeed, if I may be frank, what he created was a kind of marble statue of a man, devoid of sense and any sort of human feeling.[56] Well, if that's what they like, they can enjoy their wise man, love him without a rival, live with him in Plato's Republic or in the kingdom of Ideas, if they prefer, or else in the gardens of Tantalus. Who wouldn't flee in terror from a man like that as a monstrous apparition, deaf as he is to all natural feelings, and no more moved by love or pity or any emotions

than if hard flint or Parian crag stands fixed?

He misses nothing, he is never deceived, but like Lynceus he sees all clear, weighs up everything precisely, and finds nothing to excuse. Self-sufficient, self-satisfied, the only man to be rich and healthy, a king and free – unique in fact in everything, but only in his own unique opinion – he feels no need of friends and is a friend to no one, he doesn't hesitate to bid the gods themselves go hang, and everything that happens in real life he treats as crazy with ridicule and contempt.[57] But this is the sort of animal who is the perfect wise man. I ask you, if it were put to the vote, what state would elect such a man to office, what army would want him for a general? Still less would any woman want or

56. The reference to the muses on Helicon alludes to Virgil (*Aeneid*, 7, 641).

There was some confusion between the later stoics who held only that man should overcome his passions and the sceptics like Pyrrho who held that they should not even feel pleasure or pain. Folly is rather harsh on Seneca, although some of his somewhat rhetorical formulations could be quoted in support of her view.

57. Lucian said of Plato's *Republic* that Plato was the only person to live in it (which implies a deliberate misunderstanding of its literary *genre*). Like Utopia, which means nowhere, the gardens of Tantalus did not exist. Erasmus comments on the phrase in the *Adages*. The line quoted is from Virgil (*Aeneid*, 6, 471). Parian marble was much esteemed for its durability. The Argonaut Lynceus, brother of Idas, had preternaturally sharp sight and is mentioned by Pindar and Horace as well as occurring in the *Adages*. The final sentence is very reminiscent of Horace (*Satires*, 1, 3, 124–5), and its description of the sage is a summary of one of the principal stoic 'paradoxes'.

endure that sort of husband, or host that guest, or servant a master with a character like his. Anybody would prefer someone from the ordinary run of fools, someone who can manage fools or obey them as a fool himself, and can please those like himself, that is, most men. And he would be pleasant to his wife and agreeable to his friends, a congenial guest for a meal and good company for a drink, a man in fact who thinks every human interest is his concern.[58] The wise man's a bore, I had enough of him long ago; and so my speech will move on to more profitable themes.

Now suppose someone could look down on the life of a man from a great height, as the poets say Jove sometimes does, how many disasters would he see in store for it! Man's birth is painful and sordid, his upbringing wearisome, his childhood fraught with dangers, and his youth hard-won with toil. Old age is a burden and death a harsh necessity; armies of disease close their ranks around him, misfortunes lie in wait, ill luck is always ready to attack. There's nothing without its tinge of acute bitterness, quite apart from all the evil things man does to man, such as the infliction of poverty, imprisonment, slander, dishonour, torture, treachery, betrayal, insult, litigation, and fraud. But now I'm clearly trying to 'measure grains of sand'. What man has done to deserve all this or what angry god has caused him to be born for these miseries is not for me to say at the moment, yet anyone who reflects on the question will surely approve the example set by the maidens of Miletus, however deplorable it was. But who are the people whose death was so often self-sought through weariness of life? Weren't they closely connected with wisdom? I'll say nothing at this point about people like Diogenes, Xenocrates, Cato, Cassius, and Brutus, but there's the famous centaur Chiron, who could have been immortal if he hadn't preferred to choose death. This will show you, I fancy, what would happen if wisdom spread throughout mankind: we'd soon need some more clay and a

58. Lijster seems to have missed the obvious reference to Terence's famous comment '*homo sum, humani nil a me alienum puto*' (there is no human interest which is not my concern, *Heautontimorumenos*, 77). The phrase 'being pleasant to his wife' is an allusion to Horace (*Epistles*, 2, 2, 133).

second Prometheus to model it.[59] However, I am here, and with a mixture of ignorance and thoughtlessness, often with forgetfulness when things are bad, or sometimes hope of better things, with a sprinkling too of honeyed pleasures, I bring help in miseries like these. And I do so with such effect that men are reluctant to leave life even when their thread of destiny has run out and life has long been leaving them. The less reason they have for staying alive, the more they enjoy living – so far are they from feeling at all weary of life.

Thanks to me you can see old men everywhere who have reached Nestor's age and scarcely still look human, mumbling, senile, toothless, white-haired, or bald – or rather, in the words of Aristophanes, 'dirty, bent, wretched, wrinkled, hairless, toothless, sexless'. Yet they're still so pleased with life and eager 'to be young' that one dyes his white hair, another covers up his baldness with a wig, another wears borrowed teeth taken from some pig perhaps, while another is crazy about a girl and outdoes any young man in his amorous silliness. For any real old drybones with a foot in the grave can take some tender young girl for a wife today, even if she has no dowry and is ready for others to enjoy her – it's common practice, almost something to boast about.

Yet it's even more fun to see the old women who can scarcely carry their weight of years and look like corpses that seem to have risen from the dead. They still go around saying 'Life is good', still on heat, καπρῶν 'longing for a mate', as the Greeks say, and hiring some young Phaon by paying out large sums of

59. It is Homer who refers to Zeus as contemplating from above men and their doings (*Iliad*, 8, 51). Folly here elaborates the well-worn theme of the miseries of human life. Miletus was one of the great Ionian seaports, and, according to Aulus Gellius (15, 10, 1), there was a spate of suicides among its young women stopped only by the emergency ruling that their bodies should be displayed naked at their funerals. Folly's list of suicides is well known. Diogenes the Cynic and Xenocrates are sometimes said (as by Diogenes Laertius) to have committed suicide. Cato of Utica is perhaps the most famous of all the antique suicides (along with Socrates and Seneca) for Renaissance authors. Both Cassius and Brutus killed themselves in 42 BC after Antony's victory at Philippi; Chiron, accidentally wounded by Hercules, preferred to die although he was immortal.

money. They're forever smearing their faces with make-up, always looking in the mirror, and taking tweezers to their pubic hairs, exposing their sagging withered breasts and trying to rouse failing desire with their quavery whining voices, while they drink, dance among the girls, and scribble their little love-letters.[60] All this raises a general laugh for what it is – absolute foolishness; but meanwhile they're pleased with themselves, lead a life of supreme delight suffused with sweet fantasy, and owe all their happiness to me. Those who find this too ridiculous should please consider whether they'd rather spend a life sweetened with folly like this or go and look for the proverbial beam to hang from.

The fact that such conduct is generally frowned on means nothing to my fools, for either they don't realize anything is wrong, or if they do, they find it easy to take no notice. If a rock falls on your head it does positive harm, but shame, disgrace, reproaches, and insults are damaging only in so far as you're conscious of them. If you're not, you feel no hurt at all. What's the harm in the whole audience hissing you if you clap yourself? And Folly alone makes this possible.[61]

60. The words of Aristophanes were used by him to describe Plutus, and there is a further allusion to Aristophanes in the phrase 'longing for a mate'. The reference to pubic hair alludes to Martial (10, 90) while the 'sagging and withered breasts' come from Horace (Epistles, 8, 7) as does the 'rousing of desire' (Odes, 4, 13, 5). This section contains a further reference to Horace in the phrase 'clap yourself' (Satires, 1, 1, 66), and a further adage about 'the beam to hang from'.

61. Folly's specious arguments are ironic inversions of perfectly serious humanist contentions, and there is a strong element of self-parody running through Erasmus's text. The idea that non-physical evils do harm only in so far as one is conscious of them, for instance, is a caricature of the stoic view that, while there are legitimate affective reactions to present goods, future goods and future evils, there is no rational affective reaction to present evils, which exist only in the imagination. There is no rational grief as nothing which happens externally is a source of grief for the sage.

Erasmus himself, strongly committed with all the humanists to a belief in man's power of autonomous self-determination, develops the view with which Epictetus' Manual opens, that our true good is in our power. It follows that all those things we cannot change, the fortuitous events of the external world, cannot constitute true goods or true evils. In the evangelical humanists generally, and particularly in Erasmus, Budé and Rabelais, the

Now I believe I can hear the philosophers protesting that it can only be misery to live in folly, illusion, deception, and ignorance. But it isn't – it's human. I don't see why they call it a misery when you're all born, formed, and fashioned in this pattern, and it's the common lot of all mankind. There's no misery about remaining true to type, unless maybe someone thinks man is to be pitied because he can't fly with the birds or go on all fours like the other animals and isn't armed with horns like a bull. In the same way the finest horse could be called unfortunate because it knows no grammar and doesn't eat cake, and a bull unhappy because it's useless in the gymnasium. But a horse who knows nothing of grammar isn't unhappy, and a foolish man is not unfortunate, because this is in keeping with his nature.

Then these verbal wizards produce another argument. Man, they say, is especially gifted with understanding of the branches of learning so that they can help him to compensate by his wits for what nature has denied him. But does it seem likely that nature would be so alert and careful about things like midges and grasses and flowers and yet be caught napping over man alone, so that he needs the kinds of learning which the notorious Thoth, the evil genius of the human race, devised to be its greatest curse?[62] These are quite useless as regards happiness, they

---

stoic principles of Epictetus were developed in the interest of supporting man's power of self-determination. As a result the common medieval idea of contempt for adversity is given a new significance. Erasmus wrote to Marguerite de Valois, soon to be Queen of Navarre, after the disastrous battle of Pavia in 1525, to congratulate her on her contempt for adversity, and this is the quality which defines Pantagruelism in the prologue to Rabelais' quart livre. In 1521 Budé published his three books *de contemptu rerum fortuitarum* and Erasmus's own early *de contemptu mundi* was published in the same year and republished in the 1529 edition of his great work on education *de pueris instituendis*.

62. Thoth, the Egyptian god, is said to have invented numbers and letters and in Plato's *Phaedrus* (274) the Theban king Thamus demonstrates the malignity of his influence. The Latin word for 'verbal wizards' also contains an allusion to the *Phaedrus* (266c).

Folly continues to caricature the humanist arguments and to exploit them in an anti-humanist sense. For the scholastics as for the fifteenth-century

are in fact an obstacle to the very thing for which they were specially invented, as that sensible king in Plato neatly proves in discussing the invention of letters. And so the branches of learning crept in along with all the other banes of human life, introduced by the same evil spirits who are responsible for every wickedness, namely the 'demons' who were given their name because it means "those who know" in Greek.[63] But the innocent folk of the Golden Age had no learning to provide for them and lived under the guidance of nothing but natural instinct. What need had they of grammar when all spoke the same language, and the sole purpose of speech was to make communication possible? They had no use for dialectic when there was no battle of conflicting opinions, no place for rhetoric where no one was out to make trouble for his neighbour, no demand for jurisprudence when there were no bad habits, which are the undoubted antecedents of good laws. They were also too pious in their beliefs to develop an irreverent curiosity for probing the secrets of nature, measuring the stars, calculating their movements and influence, and seeking the hidden causes of the universe. They thought it sacrilege for mortal man to attempt to acquire knowledge outside his allotted portion. The madness of inquiring into what is beyond the heavens never even entered their heads. But as the innocence of the Golden Age gradually fell away, the branches

Florentine Platonist Marsilio Ficino, man's nature occupied a fixed position in the hierarchy of being, between the spiritual and the material creation, and much of medieval spirituality and ethics centres on his need to live in accordance with his place in the hierarchy. 'Truth to type' was a serious ethical and spiritual principle although, in Erasmus's immediate predecessor, Pico della Mirandola, man had already become detached from the fixed hierarchy and was capable of self-determination in such a way as to be able to achieve parity of stature with the angels or degradation to the status of the irrational beasts (see the Introduction, p. xxviii). The argument that man should be guided by reason rather than by instinct was another serious ethical principle parodied here by Folly, with deliberate allusion to the Sermon on the Mount. But this is still self-parody rather than any serious attack on the spirit of scientific inquiry.

63. See Plato's *Cratylus* (396b). The etymological derivation of the demons, originally the manifestations of supernatural power, from the Greek word for knowing or teaching seems most unlikely.

of learning were invented by those evil spirits, as I said. These were few at first and taken up by few, but later on the superstition of the Chaldeans and the idle frivolity of the Greeks added hundreds more simply to torment the wits of man – indeed, it only takes a single system of grammar to provide continuous torture for life.[64]

The most highly valued amongst these learned disciplines, however, are those which come closest to common sense, or rather, to folly. Theologians go hungry, scientists are cold-shouldered, astrologers laughed at, and dialecticians ignored; only 'the doctor is a man worth many men'. And the more ignorant, reckless, and thoughtless a doctor is the higher his reputation soars even amongst powerful princes. In fact medicine ⟨as it is practised now by so many⟩ is really only one aspect of flattery, ⟨just as rhetoric is⟩. Next to doctors the petty lawyers take second place. Maybe they ought to be first, but the philosophers are all agreed that theirs is a profession for asses and are always laughing at them, and I don't want to do the same. Yet these asses can settle matters large and small if they give the word, and their estates multiply, while the theologian who has combed through

64. The myth of the Golden Age is in some ways similar to that of the Islands of the Blest (see note 17, p. 16). It was originally an early paradise ruled by Saturn, a period of peace and prosperity without wars or violence and in which laws were superfluous. The earth was fertile without being cultivated and even the animals lived peacefully with one another. See especially Ovid, *Metamorphoses*, 1, 89 ff. Macrobius points out that good laws derive from evil habits (*Saturnalia*, 3, 17, 10).

The Golden Age was an influential myth in the Renaissance, but the most important feature of Folly's account, however, is the glossing over of the problem of original sin. The early sixteenth century went some way towards attempting to replace the authority of Augustine, gloomily conscious of human sinfulness, with that of Origen, who minimizes the effects of original sin on fallen nature. Erasmus himself in the 1516 *Paraclesis* goes so far as to regard the philosophy of Christ and Christian rebirth as the 'establishment of well-formed human nature', just as Folly here asserts the innocence of natural instinct. This is perhaps the heart of evangelical humanism. Erasmus always defended the view that human perfection, even religious perfection, was achieved in accordance with natural needs and moral aspirations, while the scholastics of the early sixteenth century thought of religious perfection in practice as something extrinsic to human needs and not empirically verifiable in human experience.

his bookcases in order to master the whole of divinity nibbles at a dry bean and carries on a non-stop war with bugs and lice.

Thus the happier branches of knowledge are those which are more nearly related to folly, and by far the happiest men are those who have no traffic at all with any kind of learning and follow Nature for their only guide. We shall never find her wanting unless we take it into our heads to overstep the limits of our mortal lot. Nature hates any counterfeit and everything turns out much more happily when it's unspoilt by artifice.[65] Well then, can't you see that of all the rest of living creatures the happiest in life are those which have least to do with any formal learning and have Nature alone for a teacher? Bees do not even have all natural instincts, yet they are the happiest and most marvellous of insects. No architect could match them in building structures nor could any philosopher set up a state like theirs. Contrast the horse, which is almost human in its instincts, and since it has taken to sharing the life of man, it also has to share man's misfortunes. It feels ashamed if it loses a race, so quite often it ends up broken-winded, and while it seeks glory on the battlefield it is run through and "bites the dust" along with its rider.[66] I needn't go into details – the sharp-toothed bit, pricking spurs, prison-like stable, whips, sticks, bridle, rider, the whole tragedy of the voluntary servitude the horse chose to undergo when he imitated man's fortitude and was all eagerness to take vengeance on the foe. Far more to be desired is the life of flies and little birds who live for the moment solely by natural instinct,

65. The Greek phrase about doctors comes from Homer (*Iliad*, 11, 514). The reference to flattery alludes to Socrates' discourse in Plato's *Gorgias* (463a). Since rhetoric was considered to be the art of moving an audience, so that Aristotle treats the passions of the soul in his *Rhetoric*, the affinity between rhetoric and flattery was natural.

Doctors and lawyers were a favourite subject for satire well beyond the Renaissance, and Folly's reference to the contrast between nature and art takes up another subject which was important in the Renaissance but which was endlessly to occupy educational and poetic theorists for very much longer. Goethe and Schiller were still engaged in this debate.

66. The happiness of bees in spite of their lack of any sexual instinct (Virgil, *Georgics* 4, 198–9), was something of a classical topos, and is to be found, for instance, in Virgil, Ovid and Pliny. Folly remembers the *Aeneid* in the phrase 'bites the dust' (11, 418). The Latin term for 'broken-winded' comes from Horace (*Epistles*, 1, 1, 9).

so far as the snares laid by men permit. Once they are shut in cages and taught to imitate the human voice all their natural brightness is dulled, for in every way Nature's creations are more cheerful than the falsifications of art.

And so I could never have enough praise for the famous cock who was really Pythagoras. When he had been everything in turn, philosopher, man, woman; king, commoner, fish, horse, frog, even a sponge, I believe, he decided that man was the most unfortunate of animals, simply because all the others were content with their natural limitations while man alone tries to step outside those allotted to him.[67] Again, amongst men in many ways he preferred the ignorant to the learned and great. ⟨Gryllus was considerably wiser than 'many-counselled Odysseus' when he chose to grunt in his sty rather than share the risks of so many dangerous hazards.⟩ Homer, the father of fables, seems to take the same view when he calls all mortals 'wretched' and 'long-suffering', and often describes Ulysses, his model of wisdom, as 'unfortunate', though he never does this to Paris or Ajax or Achilles. The reason for this is clear: that cunning master of craftiness never did a thing without Pallas to advise him, and became far too wise as he moved further and further away from Nature's guidance.

So amongst mortal men those who strive after wisdom are the furthest from happiness; they are in fact doubly stupid simply because they ignore the fact that they were born men, try to adopt the life of the immortal gods, and like the giants would rebel against Nature, with the sciences for their engines of war.[68] Conversely, the least unhappy are those who come nearest to the instinctive folly of dumb animals and attempt nothing beyond the capacities of man. Now let's see if we can't prove our point by means of a simple illustration – no need to bother with your stoic syllogisms. Heavens above, doesn't the happiest group of people comprise those

67. The cock is Lucian's *Gallus* in Erasmus's translation. Aristotle and Pliny thought the sponge was an animal.

68. On Gryllus, see note 5, p. 6. 'Many-counselled' is a Homeric epithet for Odysseus. Homer often calls mortals 'wretched', but as a matter of fact never 'long-suffering'. Odysseus, Latinized as Ulysses, is called 'unfortunate' in the *Odyssey* (e.g. 5, 436). The allusion to the giants who rebel against nature comes from Cicero (*de senectute*, 2, 5).

popularly called idiots, fools, nitwits, simpletons – all splendid names according to my way of thinking? Perhaps what I'm saying seems foolish and absurd at first sight, but really it's a profound truth.

To begin with, these people have no fear of death, and that surely frees them from no small evil. They're also free from pangs of conscience. Tales of the dead hold no terrors for them, and they've no fear of ghosts and spectres. They are neither tortured by dread of impending disaster nor under the strain of hopes of future bliss. In short, they are untroubled by the thousand cares to which our life is subject. They don't feel shame, fear, ambition, envy, or love. Finally, if they come still closer to dumb animals in their lack of reasoning power, the theologians assure us they can't even sin.[69] Now, foolish sage, please count up for me all the nights and days when your soul is tortured by anxieties – heap all your life's troubles in one pile, and then at last you'll realize what the evils are from which I've saved my fools. Add the fact that they're always cheerful, playing, singing, and laughing themselves, and bring pleasure and merriment, fun and laughter to everyone else wherever they go as well, as if the gods had granted them the gift of relieving the sadness of human life. Consequently, though other folk may be at odds, they are always accepted, sought out, fed, tended, embraced, helped at time of need, and allowed to say or do anything with impunity. No one would dream of hurting them – even wild beasts have some natural perception of their innocence and do them no harm. They are indeed under the protection of the gods and most of all under mine; and for this reason they are rightly held in honour by all.

They are moreover the favourites of kings, so much so that many great rulers can't eat a mouthful or take a step or last an hour without them, and they value their fools a long way above the crabbed wiseacres they continue to maintain for the sake of appearance. The reason for their preference is obvious, I think,

69. The word used by Folly for the stoic 'syllogisms' is pejorative, denoting a suggestion which is not backed up by a logically cogent argument.

The moral theologians traditionally grouped together the categories of the young and the mad ('*infans et amens*') as incapable of the moral self-determination implied by sin.

and shouldn't cause surprise. Wise men have nothing but misery to offer their prince; they are confident in their learning and sometimes aren't afraid to speak harsh truths, which will grate on his delicate ear, whereas clowns can provide the very thing the prince is looking for – jokes, laughter, merriment, and fun. And, let me tell you, fools have another gift which is not to be despised. They're the only ones who speak frankly and tell the truth, and what is more praiseworthy than truth? For although Plato makes Alcibiades quote the proverb which says that truth belongs to wine and children the credit really should be mine; witness Euripides and that famous line of his about me: 'for the fool speaks folly'. Whatever the fool has in his mind shows in his face and comes out in his speech, but the wise man has two tongues, as Euripides also says, one to speak the truth with, the other for saying what he thinks fits the occasion. He makes a habit of changing black into white and blowing hot and cold in the same breath, and there's all the difference between the thoughts he keeps to himself and what he puts into words.[70] And so for all their good fortune princes seem to me to be particularly unfortunate in having no one to tell them the truth and being obliged to have flatterers for friends.

It might be said that the ears of princes shun the truth, and that they steer clear of wise men for the simple reason that they fear there may be someone outspoken enough to risk saying what is true rather than pleasant to hear. The fact is, kings do dislike the truth, but the outcome of this is extraordinary for my

70. The reference to a 'delicate ear' is from Persius (*Satires*, I, 107). The proverb 'truth belongs to wine', discussed in the *Adages*, is important here, because it demonstrates that Erasmus was using the Ficino translation of Plato, whose mistranslation Folly adopts. Erasmus quotes at some length from the Ficino translation of the same work in the *Enchiridion*. The text is from the *Symposium* (217e). The reference to Euripides is to the *Bacchae* (369). The reference to the wise man's two tongues is not to an authentic text of Euripides (*Rhesus*, 394). Juvenal (*Satires*, 3, 30) mentions changing black into white. The phrase 'blowing hot and cold' alludes to one of Aesop's fables.

Folly's allusion to the jesters of kings points to a custom which, familiar from Shakespeare, was already widespread in the early sixteenth century, when there were real 'fools' renowned for their wisdom.

fools. They can speak truth and even open insults and be heard with positive pleasure; indeed, the words which would cost a wise man his life are surprisingly enjoyable when uttered by a clown. For truth has a genuine power to please if it manages not to give offence, but this is something the gods have granted only to fools.

It is also the reason why these people give so much pleasure to women, who are naturally more inclined to amusement and frivolity. Besides, however much women carry on with fools, even when things take a serious turn, as they often do, it can always be passed off as joking and fun. The feminine sex is artful, especially at covering up its own doings.

To return to the happiness of fools. After living a life full of enjoyment, with no fear or awareness of death, they move straight off to the Elysian fields where their tricks can amuse pious souls who have come to rest.

Let's now compare the lot of a wise man with that of this clown. Imagine some paragon of wisdom to set up against him, a man who has frittered away all his boyhood and youth in acquiring learning, has lost the happiest part of his life in endless wakeful nights, toil, and care, and never tastes a drop of pleasure even in what's left to him. He's always thrifty, impoverished, miserable, grumpy, harsh and unjust to himself, disagreeable and unpopular with his fellows, pale and thin, sickly and blear-eyed, prematurely white-haired and senile, worn-out and dying before his time. Though what difference does it make when a man like that does die? He's never been alive. There you have a splendid picture of a wise man.[71]

Here the 'stoic frogs' start croaking at me again. Nothing, they say, is so pitiable as insanity, and exceptional folly is near-insanity, or could even be called the real thing. Insanity only means wandering in your mind; but these frogs wander right off

71. The portrait of the wise man is uncomfortably like a grotesque caricature of Erasmus himself, whose self-parody cuts particularly deep in this section. Erasmus did 'fritter away' his youth in acquiring learning. He also worked extremely hard, was thrifty, intermittently impoverished and exceptionally waspish. He was also sickly almost to the point of hypochondria.

the track. So let's demolish their argument, if the Muses will lend their support, subtle though it is. In Plato Socrates shows how a single Venus and a single Cupid are divided into two, and so these masters of dialectic should really have distinguished between two forms of insanity, if they wanted to appear sane themselves. For not every form of insanity is a disaster, or Horace would not have asked, "Or is it fond insanity deceiving me?" And Plato would not have counted the frenzy of poets, seers, and lovers amongst life's chief blessings, nor would the sybil have called the great undertaking of Aeneas insane.[72]

The nature of insanity is surely twofold. One kind is sent from hell by the vengeful furies whenever they let loose their snakes and assail the hearts of men with lust for war, insatiable thirst for gold, the disgrace of forbidden love, parricide, incest, sacrilege, or some other sort of evil, or when they pursue the guilty, conscience-stricken soul with their avenging spirits and flaming brands of terror. The other is quite different, desirable above everything, and is known to come from me. It occurs whenever

72. The reference to Horace is to the *Odes* (3, 4, 5) and that to Aeneas to the *Aeneid* (6, 135).

In Plato's *Symposium* (180), Pausanias proposes the division of love which is common and includes that for a woman's body, and that which is divine and seeks satisfaction only in the union of the souls. From this division result the double Venus and the double Cupid. Marsilio Ficino's famous 'commentary' is at its most powerful at this point and in a letter Ficino himself coined the term 'Platonic love' to describe the higher and morally perfective affection. But unlike some of his followers, and Erasmus himself in the *Enchiridion*, Ficino holds the compatibility of the two loves. The doctrine of the four *furores*, poetic, Bacchic, prophetic and erotic, the forms of divine frenzy which move the soul to its reunification in the ascent of its love through the four circles of creation to beatitude is elaborated in Ficino from the doctrine of Socrates in the *Phaedrus* (244). The poetic *furor* in particular was an important Renaissance concept. It was used, for instance, to explain the religious and moral significance which Sébillet and the Pléiade attributed to poetic activity, and allowed them to insist on the need for the poet to be moved emotionally when he wrote. By 1546 Richard Le Blanc in his preface to the translation of Plato's *Ion* could go so far as explicitly to identify the poetic *furor* with divine grace.

Rabelais makes much play of Ficino, whose Plotinian philosophy he caricatures, especially on the erotic and Bacchic frenzies. On Erasmus and Ficino, see the Introduction.

some happy mental aberration frees the soul from its anxious cares and at the same time restores it by the addition of manifold delights. This is the sort of delusion Cicero longs for as a great gift of the gods in a letter to Atticus, for it would have the power to free him from awareness of his great trouble. Horace's Argive too was on to the right thing. His insanity was only sufficient to keep him sitting whole days alone in the theatre, laughing and clapping and enjoying himself because he believed marvellous plays were being acted on the stage, when in fact there was nothing at all. In all his duties in life he behaved well:

> Pleasant to his friends,
> Kind to his wife, a man who could forgive
> His slaves, and at a bottle's broken seal
> Not mad with rage.

When his relatives intervened and gave him remedies to cure him, and he was wholly restored to his senses, he protested like this to his friends:

> 'My friends,' he said,
> 'This is not saving; it's killing me to snatch
> My pleasure, take by force what I enjoyed –
> My mind's delusion.'

He was quite right too. They were deluded themselves and more in need of hellebore than he was for thinking that such a pleasurable and happy form of insanity was an evil to be dispelled by potions.[73]

But I've not yet made up my mind whether every vagary or mental aberration should be given the name of insanity. A purblind man who takes a donkey for a mule or one who praises an ill-written poem as an excellent one certainly won't be thought insane. But someone who is wrong in his mental judgement as well as in his perception, especially if this is continuous and goes beyond accepted practice, will surely be put down as a borderline case. Take, for example, a man who hears a donkey

73. The reference to Cicero alludes to the *Letters to Atticus* (3, 13, 2). The quotations from Horace come from the *Epistles* (2, 2, 133 ff). Hellebore was supposed to cure madness.

bray and thinks he hears a marvellous symphony, or some wretched humbly born pauper who imagines he's Croesus, king of Lydia. But often enough this kind of insanity is pleasurable and affords considerable enjoyment both to those who suffer from it and those who witness it but aren't mad in the same way, for in this form it is far more widespread than the common man believes. One madman laughs at another, and each provides entertainment for the other; and you'll often see the madder one laughing the louder at the one who's not so mad.[74] In Folly's opinion then, the more variety there is in a man's madness the happier he is, so long as he sticks to the form of insanity which is my own preserve; and which indeed is so widespread that I doubt if a single individual could be found from the whole of mankind who is wise every hour of his life and doesn't suffer from some form of insanity. The only difference is one of degree. A man who sees a gourd and takes it for a woman is called insane because this happens to very few people. But when a husband swears that the wife he shares with her many lovers outdoes faithful Penelope, and congratulates himself on what is a happy delusion, no one calls him insane, because this is seen happening in marriages everywhere.[75]

In the same category belong those who care for nothing but hunting wild game, and declare they take unbelievable pleasure in the hideous blast of the hunting horn and baying of the hounds. Dogs' dung smells sweet as cinnamon to them, I suppose, and what delicious satisfaction when the beast is to be dismembered! Common folk can cut up an ox or a sheep of course, but only a gentleman has the right to carve wild game. Bareheaded, on bended knee, with a special sword for the purpose (it would be sacrilege to use any other), with ritual gestures in a ritual

74. The reference to taking a donkey for a mule is an allusion to Theognis (996) and the proverb 'rich as Croesus' is discussed in the *Adages*.

From this point on Folly abandons for the time being her classical examples and moves on to contemporary social criticism. Needless to say, she sees early sixteenth-century society through the eyes of Erasmus even when, as in the following section, she is clearly remembering Horace.

75. The view that no one is wise every hour of his life comes from Pliny (*Historia Naturalis*, 7, 41). Penelope's fidelity to Odysseus is the framework of the *Odyssey*'s narrative.

order he cuts the ritual number of pieces in due solemnity, while the crowd stands round in silence and admires the spectacle it has witnessed a thousand times and more as if it was some new rite. And then if anyone's lucky enough to get a taste of the creature, he fancies he's stepped up a bit in the world. All they achieve by this incessant hunting and eating wild game is their own degeneration – they're practically wild beasts themselves, though all the time they imagine they lead a life fit for kings.

Much the same is the class of people who are consumed with an insatiable passion for building, forever changing round to square and square to round without limit or proportion, until they're reduced to utter destitution with nowhere to live and nothing to eat. What does that matter? They've spent several years enjoying themselves to the full.

Next to them I think I'll put those who are always working to change the face of nature by new and secret devices and searching land and sea for some sort of a fifth element. Led on by sweet hope so that they never grudge labour and expense, they show wonderful ingenuity in always thinking up something whereby to deceive themselves afresh. They go on enjoying their self-deception until they've spent every penny and can't even afford to set up a small furnace. Even so they continue to dream pleasant dreams and do their best to fire others to enjoy the same happiness. When at last all hope is gone they've still got a saying to give them great comfort:

> The intent suffices in a great design.

And then they blame the shortness of life, which wasn't enough for the magnitude of their task.[76]

Now there are the gamblers. I'm a bit doubtful about

---

76. Seneca had argued in his *de brevitate vitae* that life is long enough if it is well spent. The verse comes from Propertius (2, 10, 6). Lijster suggests that the hunter's rites described by Folly are partly inspired by Erasmus's experiences in England.

The reference to builders comes from Horace (*Epistles*, i, I, 100). Erasmus was always ironical about alchemy, magic, astrology and superstition, so Folly naturally claims as her own the seekers after the fifth essence. Rabelais published his two books under the name of 'M. Alcofribas, abstracteur de quinte essence'.

admitting them to our fellowship, though a lot of them put on a foolish show to make us laugh. They're so addicted to the game that their hearts leap and pulses quicken at the mere sound of the rattling dice. When their hopes of winning have lured them on to make shipwreck of their entire resources, ⟨their ship has run on to the rock of the dice, which is no less fearsome than Cape Malea,⟩ and they've managed to climb out of the water without a shirt on their backs, they'll take to cheating anyone – except the winner; they don't want people to suppose they're not men of honour. Now they're old and can scarcely see, but they carry on playing in spectacles, and when well-earned gout has crippled their joints they end up paying a substitute to put the dice in the box for them. It would all be delightful if this sort of game didn't so often turn into a furious quarrel, and then it is the Furies' concern, not mine.[77]

But there's no doubt that those folk are all men of my kidney who delight in miracles and fictitious marvels, whether hearing or telling about them. They can never have enough of such tales when there are any wonders to relate about ghosts, spectres, phantoms, and the dead, and all the countless miracles there are of this kind. The further these are from truth, the more eagerly they are believed and the more agreeably they titillate the ear. Such things not only serve remarkably well for whiling away a tedious hour but can also be profitable, especially for preachers and demagogues.[78]

77. Cape Malea, the southeast promontory of Laconia, was notorious for its shipwrecks and is mentioned as a pun on the Latin word for dice, *alea*.

78. Folly, having claimed various forms of indubitably foolish behaviour as her own, here tendentiously goes on to establish rights over forms of religious behaviour which could not easily be criticized with impunity, but about which Erasmus felt as strongly as Luther.

The phrase for being 'of my kidney' (literally 'flour') comes from Persius (*Satires*, 5, 115). Much of Lucian's sceptical irreverence about the doings of the ancient gods is here applied to the contemporary Christian scene, with an important emphasis on clerical venality. In particular this paragraph appears to allude to the *Philopseudes* translated by More. The evangelical humanists were often bitterly opposed by the friars who had a virtual and lucrative preaching monopoly, and it is certain that the exploitation of the fear of death in later medieval religious practice was partly nourished by the economic needs of the clergy.

Closely related to them are the people who've adopted the foolish but pleasurable belief that if they see some carving or painting of that towering Polyphemus, Christopher, they're sure not to die that day, or if anyone addresses a statue of Barbara in the set formula he'll return unhurt from battle, or a man will soon become rich if he approaches Erasmus on the proper days with the proper bits of candle and the proper scraps of prayer. They've already got a second Hippolytus, but in George they've found another Hercules too. They piously deck out his horse with trappings and amulets and practically worship it. Its favours are sought with some new small offering, and an oath sworn by the saint's bronze helmet is fit for a king.[79]

Now what am I to say about those who enjoy deluding

79. Erasmus frequently returned to the subject of the superstitious practices which had grown up round the cults of saints. Several of the saints in the present section figure also in the *Enchiridion* and in the Colloquies *A Pilgrimage for Religion's Sake* and *On the Eating of Fish*. This section of the encomium is to some extent an elaboration of parts of the *Enchiridion*.

St Christopher, the third-century martyr, was according to legend enormous in stature. The medieval paintings and statues are on that account often of generous dimensions, whence the comparison with the giant Polyphemus. A series of Latin rhymes testifies to the belief that no one would die on any day on which he saw a picture or carving of the saint.

St Barbara, the third-century virgin martyr, was executed by her own father who, it is said, was struck dead by lightning as he finished his task. St Barbara subsequently became the patron of gunners and, in consequence, also the protectress of warriors. The allusion to the need to get the formula right is typical of the extrinsicism of much popular late medieval devotion.

St Erasmus, martyred in the early fourth century, was usually invoked in certain illnesses and by sailors. Exactly why his intercession should be especially powerful in the production of wealth is uncertain.

St Hippolytus is said to have been martyred by being dragged behind two horses because Hippolytus, the mythological son of Theseus, was dragged to death behind his chariot when Poseidon at Theseus's request sent a sea-monster to frighten his horses.

St George is celebrated in legend for his conquest of the dragon, as Hercules conquered the Hydra of Lerna. During the Renaissance, Hercules often appears as a figure of Christian saints and even Christ himself. His labours, for instance, are depicted on the façade of the Colleoni Chapel in Bergamo (as well as at Lyons and on the Campanile in Florence) alongside Old Testament scenes. The *Hercule Chrétien* is one of Ronsard's most celebrated *Hymnes*.

themselves with imaginary pardons for their sins? They measure the length of their time in Purgatory as if by water-clock, counting centuries, years, months, days, and hours as though there were a mathematical table to calculate them accurately. Then there are people who rely on certain magic signs and prayers thought up by some pious imposter for his own amusement or for gain – they promise themselves everything: wealth, honours, pleasure, plenty, continual good health, long life, a vigorous old age, and finally a seat next to Christ in heaven. However, that's a blessing they don't want until the last possible minute, that is, when the pleasures of this life have left their tenacious and reluctant grasp to make way for the heavenly joys to come.[80] Take for example some merchant, soldier, or judge who believes he has only to give up a single tiny coin from his pile of plunder to purify once and for all the entire Lernean morass he has made of his life. All his perjury, lust, drunkenness, quarrels, killings, frauds, perfidy, and treachery he believes can be somehow paid off by agreement, and paid off in such a way that he's now free to start afresh on a new round of sin.

But could anything be so foolish – or, I suppose, so happy – as

80. The word used by Folly for 'pardons' is a non-technical term which, while it suggests the forgiveness of sins, does not explicitly affirm anything beyond the much-disputed remissions not of guilt but of the residual 'temporal debt' due to sin which were known as indulgences. The 'temporal debt' remained after the sin itself had been repudiated and its guilt therefore remitted, and it is about this limited and residual effect of sin that the dispute raged. Indulgences were granted in particular for onerous works or for alms-donated to specific causes (like the building of St Peter's in Rome or the prosecution of wars against the Turks). They could be applied to the souls of the defunct, thereby hastening or obtaining their release from Purgatory, the state of final purification from the effects of sin which was conceived as extending for definite but varying periods of time. In effect, therefore, if it was not possible to buy forgiveness from sin, it was possible to buy the souls of the dead out of Purgatory and into heaven, and to buy off the residual effects of one's own repented sins. Folly's remarks are carefully limited to counterfeit indulgences, just as her remarks about magic signs and prayers are carefully confined to those of venal impostors.

Erasmus frequently expresses himself about indulgences, the chief subject of Luther's Wittenberg theses of 1517, most notably in the *Enchiridion* and the *Exomologesis*, always taking the view that all religious practice should be the expression of an inner moral conversion.

those who promise themselves supreme bliss for repeating daily those seven short verses of the holy Psalms – the magic verses which some demon is believed to have pointed out to St Bernard? He was a joker no doubt, but silly rather than witty, as the poor fellow was caught in his own trap. Things like this are so foolish that I almost blush for them myself, yet they win general approval, and not just among the mob but also among those who make profession of religion.

It is much the same when separate districts lay claim to their own particular saints. Each one of these is assigned his special powers and has his own special cult, so that one gives relief from toothache, another stands by women in childbirth, a third returns stolen objects, a fourth will appear as a saviour for shipwrecks, another protect the flocks, and so on – it would take too long to go through the whole list. There are some whose influence extends to several things, notably the Virgin, Mother of God, for the common ignorant man comes near to attributing more to her than to her son.[81]

But what do men seek from these saints except what belongs to folly? Amongst all the votive offerings you see covering the walls of certain churches right up to the very roof, have you ever seen one put up for an escape from folly or for the slightest gain in wisdom? One man escaped drowning, another was run

81. The Lernean morass was the legendary marsh where Hercules killed the hydra. Legend has it that a devil told St Bernard that he knew of seven verses from the Psalms which, if repeated daily, would ensure salvation. When he would not reveal which they were, the saint is said to have replied that, since he recited daily the whole psalter, he must anyway include the seven magic verses.

The list of superstitious practices concerned with local cults, special patrons and assured salvation was a long one, and it lived long enough for Pascal to attack it in his *Provincial Letters*.

It was one of the principles of the evangelical humanists to restore the redemptive work of Christ to the centre of religious attention, and among the undoubted aberrations of late medieval piety was a cult of the virgin Mary which detracted from the proper place of Jesus in Christian devotion.

During the whole of this section Lijster's notes back-pedal heavily as he explains throughout that it is only abuses to which Folly is drawing attention, and that she does not wish to attack authentic indulgences, the legitimate cult of saints or non-superstitious practices.

through by his enemy and survived, another boldly (and equally fortunately) fled from battle and left his fellows to continue the fight. Another fell down from the gallows, thanks to some saint who befriends thieves, and went on to relieve a good many people of their burden of wealth. This one broke out of prison, that one recovered from a fever, to the annoyance of his doctors; yet another swallowed poison, but it acted as a purge and did him good instead of killing him – a waste of effort and money for his wife, who was not at all pleased. Another upset his wagon but drove his horses home unhurt, another escaped with his life when his house collapsed, and another was caught in the act by a husband but got away. Not one of them gives thanks for being rid of folly, and it's so pleasant not to be wise that mortals would prefer to pray for deliverance from anything rather than from me.

But I don't know why I'm wading through this sea of superstition:

> Had I a hundred tongues, a hundred mouths,
> A voice of iron, I could not count the types
> Of fool, nor yet enumerate the names
> Of every kind of folly.[82]

The ordinary life of Christians everywhere abounds in these varieties of silliness, and they are readily permitted and encouraged by priests who are not unaware of the profit to be made thereby. Meanwhile, if some disagreeable wiseacre were to get up and interrupt with a statement of the true facts: "You won't do badly when you die if you've been good in your lifetime. You'll redeem your sins only by adding hatred for wrong-doing, tears, vigils, prayers, fasts, and a change in your whole way of living to the small sum you've already paid. The saint will protect you if you'll try to imitate his life" – if, I repeat, your

---

82. The story of the man who swallowed poison and, to the displeasure of his wife, survived, comes from Ausonius (*Epigrams*, 10). The adulterous wife, wishing to kill her husband, gave him two poisons together, of which either alone would have killed him but of which one was the antidote to the other.

The lines of verse are taken, with slight changes, from the *Aeneid* (6, 625–7).

wise man starts blurting out these uncomfortable truths, you can see how he'll soon destroy the world's peace of mind and plunge it into confusion.

In the same company belong those who lay down such precise instructions in their lifetime for the funeral ceremonies they want that they even list in detail the number of candles, black cloaks, singers, and hired mourners they wish to be there, as if it were possible for some awareness of this spectacle to return to them, or the dead would be ashamed if their corpses didn't have a splendid burial. They might be newly elected officials planning a public show or banquet, such is their zeal.[83]

I must press on, and yet I can't pass over without a mention those who are no better than the humblest worker but take extraordinary pride in an empty title of nobility, one tracing his family back to Aeneas, another to Brutus, a third to Arcturus.[84] They display the statues and portraits of their ancestors everywhere, tot up their great-grandfathers and great-great-grandfathers, know all the old family names by heart, though they're not far off being dumb statues themselves and could well be worse than the statuary they display. And yet, thanks to sweet Self-love, they lead happy lives; and there are always plenty of fools like themselves to look up to this sort of brute as if he were a god.

But I needn't cite one instance after another like this when ⟨everywhere⟩ there are countless people made marvellously happy by Self-love. Here's a man uglier than an ape who rivals Nireus in his own eyes, and another who has only to trace three

83. Folly's irony at the expense of those who are over-concerned with providing for their own funerals is inspired by Seneca's *de brevitate vitae*, chapter 20.

84. The mention of the 'humblest worker' and the inclusion of Aeneas and Brutus in the list of desirable ancestors are reminiscences of Juvenal (*Satires*, 8, 181–2). The reference to Arcturus has sometimes been taken as an elliptical reference to the claim of the Tudor kings to descend from King Arthur. It most probably alludes to Cicero's *de natura deorum* (2, 42, 110). Arcturus, killed by drunken shepherds, was put in the heavens by Jupiter and became the constellation Boötes, while his daughter Erigone, who had killed herself at the news of her father's death, became Virgo. Their dog, who led Erigone to her dead father, became Canicula.

arcs with a compass to imagine himself Euclid. And the 'ass playing the lyre' with a voice worse than a squawking cock when he pecks his hen believes he sings like a second Hermogenes. But by far the most enjoyable form of insanity is that which makes many people boast about any talent in their household as if it were their own. An example of this is the doubly fortunate rich man in Seneca. He kept servants at hand to whisper the names whenever he had a tale to tell, and though he was so frail he was hardly alive, he was quite ready to take up a challenge of fisticuffs, secure in the knowledge that he had plenty of stout fellows at home.[85]

As for those who teach and practise the arts – what shall I say about them? They all have their special form of Self-love, and you're more likely to find one who'll give up his family plot of land than one who'll yield an inch where his ability is in question. This is especially true of actors, singers, orators, and poets; the more ignorant one of them is, the more immoderate his self-satisfaction, boastfulness, and conceit. They can always find like to meet their like, in fact anything wins more admiration the sillier it is. The worst always pleases the most people, since the majority of men, as I said before, are prone to folly. Besides, if an artist is all the more pleased with himself and the more generally admired the less skilled he is, why should he choose to undergo a proper course of instruction? It'll cost him a lot in the first place, then make him more nervous and self-conscious, and he'll end up pleasing far fewer people.

Now, just as Nature has implanted his personal self-love in each individual person, I can see she has put a sort of communal variety in every nation and city. Consequently the British think they have a monopoly, amongst other things, of good looks, musical talent, and fine food. The Scots pride themselves on their nobility and the distinction of their royal connections as much as on their subtlety in dialectic. The French lay claim to polite

85. On Nireus, see note 45, p. 37. Euclid was of course the great geometer of the fourth century BC and Hermogenes was a famous singer from Sardia protected by Augustus and mentioned by Horace (*Satires*, 1, 3, 129). The rich man with the bad memory, called Calvisius Sabinus, is mentioned in Seneca's letters (27, 5).

manners and the Parisians demand special recognition for their theological acumen, which they think exceeds nearly everyone else's. The Italians usurp culture and eloquence, and hence they're all happy congratulating themselves on being the only civilized race of men. In this kind of happiness the Romans take first place, still blissfully dreaming of the past glories of Rome, while the Venetians have their own opinion of their noble descent to keep them happy. Meanwhile the Greeks, as originators of the arts, imagine they should still share the honours of the illustrious heroes of their past; while the Turks and all the real barbarian riff-raff actually demand recognition for their religion and pour scorn on Christians for their superstition. The Jews go even further, still faithfully awaiting their Messiah and clinging tooth and nail to their Moses to this very day. The Spaniards admit no rival in the glories of war, while the Germans boast of their height and their knowledge of the magic arts. I'm sure you can see without my going into further details how much pleasure Self-love brings to men, both individually and collectively, and her sister Flattery does almost as much.[86]

Philautia is only flattery of yourself, and if you do the same to someone else it becomes 'Kolakia'. Fawning on people has fallen into disrepute today, but only amongst those who are less concerned with facts than the names applied to them. They think

86. Folly is here drawing on popular caricatures and proverbial national characteristics, most of which occur elsewhere in Erasmus's writings, but which have little to do with Erasmus's personal views about the countries he mentions. Apart from the gratifying remarks about England, where Erasmus spent some of what must have been the happiest years of his life, the most noteworthy comments concern the Scots, the French and the Italians.

In the early sixteenth century many Scotsmen taught philosophy at Paris, which was undoubtedly the intellectual capital of northern Europe and whose theology faculty was totally intent on the preservation of medieval orthodoxy, concerned neither with pastoral needs nor even, as a body, with monastic reform. Both the English and the French owed much to the new learning and new values which they found south of the Alps, but the French especially were at the same time concerned to vindicate the superiority and antiquity of their own culture, for which they invented a glorious history. Anti-Italian jokes appear early in sixteenth-century France and are a by-product of the new national consciousness, often based on an attempt to revive twelfth-century glories.

it's incompatible with sincerity, but examples from dumb animals could prove them quite wrong. No animal fawns so much as a dog, and none is so faithful. Nothing has such winning ways as a squirrel, and where could you find a greater friend to man? Unless perhaps you think savage lions, fierce tigers, or dangerous leopards contribute more to the life of man. There *is* a kind of flattery which is wholly noxious, and a good many treacherous persons use it in mockery in order to destroy their unfortunate victims. But the form I use stems from a sort of ingenuous goodness of heart and is far nearer being a virtue than the critical asperity which is its opposite: what Horace calls a harsh and disagreeable surliness. Mine raises downcast spirits, comforts the sad, rouses the apathetic, stirs up the stolid, cheers the sick, restrains the headstrong, brings lovers together, and keeps them united. It attracts children to pursue the study of letters, makes old men happy, and offers advice and counsel to princes in the form of praise which doesn't give offence. In short, it makes everyone more agreeable and likeable to himself, and this is the main ingredient in happiness. What shows such willingness to please as the way mules scratch each other? For the moment I'll say nothing about the large part flattery plays in your celebrated eloquence, a larger one in medicine, and its largest in poetry, but will sum up by saying that it is what sweetens and gives savour to every human relationship.[87]

But it's sad, people say, to be deceived. Not at all, it's far sadder *not* to be deceived. They're quite wrong if they think man's happiness depends on actual facts; it depends on his opinions. For human affairs are so complex and obscure that nothing

87. On Kolakia, see note 20, p. 18. After ironically praising self-love, Folly here goes on in the same style to praise flattery, a vice which, in the guise of servility to princes, Erasmus found both odious and dangerous. Erasmus however does not primarily object to flattery simply because it is insincere, and Folly makes little of that objection. The use of animal behaviour as an example to shame men is traditional and became very popular in later Renaissance authors like Montaigne. The allusion to Horace, who favours a mean between insincere adulation and forthright criticism, refers to *Epistles* (1, 18, 508). The mules who scratch one another are proverbial and occur in the *Adages*. The argument that praise makes life tolerable is borrowed from Plato (*Gorgias*, 463a).

can be known of them for certain, as has been rightly stated by my Academicians, the least assuming of the philosophers. Alternatively, if anything can be known, more often than not it is something which interferes with the pleasure of life. Finally, man's mind is so formed that it is far more susceptible to falsehood than to truth. If anyone wants an immediate, clear example of this he has only to go to church at sermon time, where everyone is asleep or yawning or feeling queasy whenever some serious argument is expounded, but if the preacher starts to rant (I beg your pardon, I mean orate) on some old wives' tale, as they often do, his audience sits up and takes notice openmouthed. And again, if there's some legendary saint somewhat celebrated in fable (you can put George or Christopher or Barbara in that category if you need an example) you'll see that he receives far more devout attention than Peter or Paul or even Christ himself. But this is not the point for the moment.[88]

Now this gain in happiness costs very little, whereas real facts often take a lot of trouble to acquire, even when they are quite unimportant, like grammar. An opinion, on the other hand, is very easily formed, and it is equally conducive to happiness, or even more so. Just suppose that a man is eating rotten salt fish, and they taste like ambrosia to him though another man can't stand the stink; does that affect his happiness? Whereas if the taste of sturgeon makes someone sick, what can it add to the blessings of life? If anyone has a particularly ugly wife who has the power to rival Venus in her husband's eyes, isn't it just the same as if she were genuinely beautiful? The possessor of a dreadful daub in

88. This paragraph begins with an allusion to the stoic view that man's true good depends not on what happens to him but on his own state of mind, which remains in his power. Historically this view was the ethical consequence of the sceptical contention, to which Folly goes on to refer, that we cannot know the true world. Although there is a clear distinction between the stoics and the academicians or sceptics, the sixteenth century very often confused the two, powerfully assisted by Cicero who makes Pyrrho, the most important sceptic, sound like an exaggerated stoic. Folly is here drawing on Cicero's *De Oratore* (I, 10). On the subject of the saints mentioned here, see note 79, p. 63. Folly is careful not to go so far as to say that they were not saints – it was to be four and a half centuries before they were dropped from the calendar.

red and yellow paint who gazes at it in admiration, convinced that it is a painting by Apelles or Zeuxis, would surely be happier than someone who has paid a high price for a genuine work by one of these artists but perhaps gets less pleasure from looking at it. I know someone of my name who made his new bride a present of some jewels which were copies, and as he had a ready tongue for a joke, persuaded her that they were not only real and genuine but also of unique and incalculable value. Now, if the young woman was just as happy feasting her eyes and thoughts on coloured glass, what did it matter to her that she was keeping such trinkets hidden carefully away in her room as if they were some rare treasure? Meanwhile her husband saved expense, enjoyed his wife's illusion, and kept her as closely bound in gratitude to him as if he'd given her something which had cost him a fortune. What difference is there, do you think, between those in Plato's cave who can only marvel at the shadows and images of various objects, provided they are content and don't know what they miss, and the philosopher who has emerged from the cave and sees the real things? If Mycillus in Lucian had been allowed to go on dreaming that golden dream of riches for evermore, he'd have had no reason to desire any other state of happiness.

And so there's nothing to choose between the two conditions, or if there is, the fools are better off, first because their happiness costs them so little, in fact only a grain of persuasion, secondly because they share their enjoyment of it with the majority of men.[89] Indeed, no benefit gives pleasure unless it is enjoyed in company. Yet we all know how few sages there are, always

89. Folly's views about the unimportance of grammar reflect Erasmus's impatience with those humanists whose grammatical interests deflected them from absorbing the values and attitudes contained in classical literature.

Apelles and Zeuxis are both famous Greek painters mentioned by Pliny. 'Someone of my name' seems to refer to Thomas More who had married in 1505. Plato's image of men as cave-dwellers who take the shadows they see for the only reality occurs at the beginning of Book 7 of the *Republic*. Erasmus frequently refers to this image for those who take shadows for reality, and he had used it in the *Enchiridion*. At the beginning of Lucian's *The Dream or the Cock*, a dialogue translated by Erasmus, Mycillus complains that he cannot even escape from his poverty in beautiful dreams at night without being awakened by the cock.

supposing there's one at all. Out of all those centuries the Greeks can count seven sages at the most, and if anyone looks at them more closely I swear he'll not find so much as a half-wise man or even a third of a wise man among them. Next, among the many things to Bacchus' credit must be counted what is his chief claim to fame – his ability to free our minds from care. Of course the effect lasts only a short time, for as soon as you've slept off your drink your troubles come racing back in triumph, as the saying goes.[90] Isn't the blessing I confer much more generous and effective? I fill the mind with a kind of perpetual intoxication, with transports of rejoicing and delight, all without any effort, and I don't leave a single mortal without a share in my bounty, though the gifts of the other deities are unevenly bestowed. Not every region produces the mellow wine of good quality which can banish care and flow with rich hopes. Few have a lovely face, the gift of Venus, and still fewer the eloquence Mercury grants. Not many owe their wealth to Hercules, and Homer's Jupiter doesn't allow authority to all comers. Often enough Mars remains neutral in battle, and a lot of people return disconsolate from Apollo's oracle. Saturn's son can often flash lightning and Phoebus shoot plague with his arrows, while Neptune destroys more lives than he spares. As for those underworld Jupiters, Plutos, Discords, Punishments, Fevers, and all that lot, I don't call them gods, but murderers. I, Folly, am the only one who extends my ever-ready generosity to all alike.[91]

I don't expect prayers, and I don't lose my temper and demand expiation for some detail of ceremony which has been overlooked. Nor do I confound heaven and earth if someone has sent invitations to all the other gods and left me out, so that

90. The phrase 'come racing back', literally 'with four white horses' comes from Plautus, *Asinaria*, 279 and Horace (*Satires*, 1, 7, 8). It is discussed in the *Adages*.

91. The regions flowing 'with rich hopes' are a reminiscence of Horace (*Epistles*, 1, 15, 19). The reference to Hercules comes from Persius (2, 11). The Latin text uses for Mars the primitive 'Mavors' also used by Virgil. Phoebus is the cause of plague in the *Iliad* (1, 10 and 51). The word used for 'Jupiters' is *Vejoves*, the plural form of a hostile god and, in its singular form, given by Ovid to the youthful Jupiter (*Fasti*, 3, 429 ff.). The word for 'Discords' is *Atas*, plural form of the goddess of discord, Até, on whom see note 36, p. 28.

I'm not admitted to a sniff of the steaming victims.[92] The rest of the gods are so particular about these matters that you'd almost find it better and even safer to leave them alone instead of worshipping them. There are several men who are just the same, so hard to please and easily offended that it's wiser to have nothing at all to do with them than treat them as friends.

But no one offers sacrifice to Folly, people say, or sets up a temple. Well, I'm quite surprised myself, as I said before, at such ingratitude, but I'm easy-going and take it all in good part. Besides, I can't say this is really what I want. Why should I need a whiff of incense, a sacrificial meal, a goat, or a pig? Mortals all over the world worship me in a manner which is highly approved, even by the theologians. Ought I to envy Diana because she is propitiated by human blood? I hold the view that I'm worshipped with truest devotion when all men everywhere take me to their hearts, express me in their habits, and reflect me in their way of life – as in fact they do. This form of worship even of the saints and among Christian believers is quite rare. Think of the many who set up a candle to the Virgin, Mother of God, and at midday too, when it isn't needed, and of the few who care about emulating her chastity of life, her modesty, and her love of heavenly things. Yet that is surely the true way to worship and by far the most acceptable to heaven. Besides, what should I want with a temple? The entire world is my temple, and a very fine one too, if I'm not mistaken, and I'll never lack priests to serve it as long as there are men. And I'm not yet so foolish as to demand statues carved in stone and coloured with paint, which can often do harm to the cult of us gods, when the stupid and thick-headed give their devotion to images instead of

92. Eris is the mother of Até and also the goddess of discord, a title she earned by avenging the failure to invite her to the marriage of Peleus and Thetis by throwing into the midst of the guests the golden apple marked 'for the most beautiful', a gesture which led to the judgement of Paris and the Trojan war. Folly's reference to 'steaming victims' alludes also to Diana, who avenged herself on Calydon whose King Oeneus made offerings to all the gods except her (Ovid, *Metamorphoses*, 8, 276). The reference to human sacrifices a few lines lower is explained by the identification of the goddess to whom the shipwrecked foreigners on Tauris were sacrificed with Diana (Ovid, *Epistulae ex Ponto*, 3, 2, 53 and *Tristia*, 4, 4, 63).

to the divinities they represent, and we suffer the fate of being supplanted by our substitutes. I fancy I can count as many statues set up to me as there are men who wear my living image in their faces, whether willingly or not. And so I've no reason to be envious of the other gods because they're each worshipped in their own corner of the earth on fixed days, like Apollo, for example, in Rhodes, Venus in Cyprus, Juno at Argos, Minerva at Athens, Jupiter at Olympus, Neptune at Tarentum, and Priapus at Lampsacus. To me the whole world offers far more precious victims, without ceasing and with one accord.[93]

In case anyone thinks I'm presuming too far and not speaking the truth, let's take a brief look at the way men live, and it will then become clear how much they owe me and how they appreciate me, whether great men or humble.

We won't go into every kind of life, it would take too long, but will pick out some outstanding examples from which it will be easy to judge the rest, and there's no point in mentioning the vulgar crowd and humble folk who all belong to me without question. They abound in so many forms of folly and devise so many new ones every day that a thousand Democrituses wouldn't be enough to laugh at them, and we'd always have to call in one Democritus more. It's hardly believable how much laughter, sport, and fun you poor mortals can provide the gods every day. For they allocate their sober morning hours to settling altercations and listening to prayers, but once the nectar is flowing freely they want a change from serious business, and that is when they settle

93. This passage concludes the section dealing with Folly's powers. The next section opens the famous description by Folly of her followers. But in this section Folly drops her mask. She has claimed for herself the theologians who defend rites and superstition, but she now enlists among her devotees those who worship her in their hearts and express her in their habits. The irony is not totally consistent. After the theologians, Folly claims for her own those whose religion is interior and evangelical.

The worship of the sun-god Apollo at Rhodes is associated with the cloudless sky above that city. Horace remarks on the cult of Venus at Cyprus (*Odes*, 1, 3, 1), of Juno at Argos (*Odes*, 1, 7, 8–9), of Minerva or Pallas, the eponymous goddess of Athens (*Odes*, 1, 7, 5) and of Neptune in the town founded by his son Taras (*Odes*, 1, 28, 29). Olympus is Greece's highest mountain, seat of the king of the gods. Virgil (*Georgics*, 4, 3) mentions the association between Priapus and Lampsacus where he was born.

down on some promontory of heaven and lean over to watch the goings-on of mankind, a show they enjoy more than anything.

Heavens, what a farce it is, what a motley crowd of fools! I often take a seat myself amongst the ⟨poets'⟩ gods. Here's a man who has lost his heart to a young woman, the more hopelessly in love the less he's loved in return. Another marries a dowry, not a wife, and while one man prostitutes his bride, another is watching his as jealous-eyed as Argus. Here's one in mourning, and dear me, what foolish things he says and does, hiring mourners like actors to play a comedy of grief. There's another shedding tears at his stepmother's tomb. This one gives everything he can scrape together to his belly, but soon he'll go hungry again, and that one finds his happiness in idleness and sleep. There are men who spend their time bustling about on other people's affairs to the neglect of their own. One thinks himself rich on loans and credit though he'll soon be bankrupt, and another enjoys nothing so much as living like a pauper in order to enrich his heir. This one scours the seas for a meagre and uncertain profit, entrusting to wind and wave his life, which no money can replace, while that one prefers to seek his fortune in war to living in peace and safety ⟨at home⟩. Others fancy they've found an easy road to wealth by cultivating childless old men, and there are plenty of people too who court the affection of rich old women with the same end in view. Both groups provide special entertainment to the audience of gods when they end by being duped by the guile of the very people they set out to ensnare. Most foolish of all, and the meanest, is the whole tribe of merchants, for they handle the meanest sort of business by the meanest methods, and although their lies, perjury, thefts, frauds, and deceptions are everywhere to be found, they still reckon themselves a cut above everyone else simply because their fingers sport gold rings. There are plenty of sycophantic friars too who will sing their praises and publicly address them as honourable, doubtless hoping that a morsel of these ill-gotten gains will come their way.[94] Elsewhere

94. Folly here adopts the perspective of the gods in viewing human affairs, and derives from Lucian's *Icaromenippus*, Chapter 15, translated by Erasmus in 1512. Menippus comments from heaven on the behaviour of the

you'll see certain Pythagoreans whose belief in communism of property goes to such lengths that they pick up anything lying about unguarded, and make off with it without a qualm of conscience as if it had come to them by law. Some too are rich only in their prayers, and live on pleasant dreams, which they find enough for happiness. Several enjoy a reputation for wealth abroad while they conscientiously starve at home. One man hurries to squander every penny he has, another hoards everything by fair means or foul; one goes canvassing for public office, another takes his pleasure by his own fireside. A good many engage in interminable litigation, but their efforts to outdo each other all end in enriching the judge who defers judgement and the advocate who acts in collusion with his opposite number. One man is eager for revolution, another toils on with some vast project. Yet another leaves wife and children at home, and goes off to Jerusalem or Rome or St James's shrine, where he has no call to be. To sum up, if you could look down from the moon, as Menippus once did, on the countless hordes of mortals, you'd think you saw a swarm of flies or gnats quarrelling amongst themselves, fighting, plotting, stealing, playing, making love, being born, growing old, and dying. It's hard to believe how much trouble and tragedy this tiny little creature can stir up, shortlived as he is, for sometimes a brief war or an outbreak of plague can carry off and destroy many thousands at once.[95]

---

gods and their views of men. The shedding of tears at a stepmother's funeral is a proverbial image of feigned grief which appears in the *Adages*. The man whose belly counts for all comes from Horace (*Epistles*, 1, 15, 32) and many of the attitudes censured by Folly had been satirized by Persius, Juvenal or Horace.

Folly remembers the patristic strictures on trading and ends the paragraph with an attack on merchants, no doubt with reference to the contemporary scene. For Erasmus the greed and self-interest of merchants was socially counter-productive.

95. The Pythagorean belief in the community of goods which, Folly says, allows people to make off with unguarded property, was none the less an ideal taken seriously by Erasmus, who devotes the first proverb of the *Adages* to discussing it, and by More, who makes it the basis for his *Utopia*. The early Fathers had been reluctantly concessive in allowing the legitimacy

But it would be very foolish of me and certainly call for some of Democritus' outbursts of laughter if I tried to enumerate all the types of folly and madness among the people. Let's look at those who have some reputation for wisdom amongst mortals and seek the golden bough, as the saying goes.

Among them the schoolmasters hold first place. They would surely be the most unfortunate and wretched class of men and the one most hateful to the gods if I didn't mitigate the hardships of their miserable profession by a pleasant kind of madness. For they're exposed not merely to the 'five curses', that is, the five calamities mentioned in the Greek epigram, but to six hundred, always famished and dirty as they are amidst their hordes of boys in their schools; though what I call schools should rather be their 'thinking-shop', or better still, their treadmill and torture chamber. There they grow old with toil and deaf with the clamour, wasting away in the stench and filth. Yet, thanks to me, in their own eyes they are first among men, and enjoy considerable satisfaction when they terrify the trembling crowd with threatening voice and looks, thrashing their wretched pupils with cane, birch, and strap, venting their fury in any way they please like the famous ass of Cumae. Meanwhile the squalor they live in is sheer elegance to them, the stink smells sweet as marjoram, and their pitiful servitude seems like sovereignty, so that they wouldn't change their tyranny for all the power of Phalaris or Dionysius.[96]

of private property, and Erasmus points out in the discussion of his first adage that the ideal which he takes from Plato could not be more Christian. The pilgrimage to the popular shrine of St James at Compostella was as important in the middle ages as that to Rome or Jerusalem. Erasmus did himself compose a liturgy for the pilgrimage shrine of the Virgin Mother of Loreto in 1523 without, however, alluding in it to the miraculous translation of the house said to have taken place in the thirteenth century but first recognized by a Bull of 1470.

96. In late antiquity, Democritus was known as 'the laughing philosopher' on account of his attitude to the folly of the world. The 'five curses' are enumerated in an epigram of Palladas, listing the misfortunes alluded to in the first five lines of the *Iliad*, a text to which of course all 'grammarians' were exposed. The ass of Cumae probably refers to Aesop's ass in the lion's skin (which figures in the *Adages*). On Phalaris, see note 8, p. 12. Dionysius

Yet they get even more happiness out of their remarkable belief in their own learning. There they are, most of them filling boys' heads with arrant nonsense, but setting themselves above any Palaemon or Donatus! And by some sort of confidence-trick they do remarkably well at persuading foolish mothers and ignorant fathers to accept them at their own valuation. Then there's this further type of pleasure. Whenever one of them digs out of some mouldy manuscript the name of Anchises' mother or some trivial word the ordinary man doesn't know, such as neatherd, tergiversator, cutpurse, or if anyone unearths a scrap of old stone with a fragmentary inscription, O Jupiter, what a triumph! What rejoicing, what eulogies! They might have conquered Africa or captured Babylon.[97] And again, when they keep on bringing out their feeble verses, their own hopeless efforts, and find no lack of admirers, of course they believe the spirit of Virgil is reborn in themselves. But the funniest thing of all is when there's an exchange of compliments and appreciation, a mutual back-scratching. Yet if someone else slips up on a single word and his sharper-eyed fellow happens to pounce on it, 'Hercules', what dramas, what fights to the death, accusations, and abuse! The whole world of grammarians may turn on me if I lie. 'I know one 'jack-of-all-trades', scholar of Greek and Latin, mathematician, philosopher, doctor, all in princely style, a man already in his sixties, who has thrown up everything else

---

was a famous tyrant of Syracuse. Folly's description of schoolmasters owes something to Juvenal's seventh satire and takes up a traditional butt of satirical attack. The grammarians or schoolmasters whom Folly treats so harshly were also elsewhere attacked by Erasmus, who believed in an educational system that was humane as well as humanist. He abhorred the harsh discipline and physical discomfort of the Parisian colleges, and especially the Collège de Montaigu under the reforming Standonck which he had attended in 1495–6. He was later to lampoon Montaigu in the colloquy *On the Eating of Fish* in 1526, by which time it had become the focal point of the scholastic opposition to evangelical humanism.

97. Palaemon was the first Roman grammarian to write a fully comprehensive grammatical treatise. He was known also for his arrogance and notorious morals, and lived under Tiberius and Claudius. Donatus lived in the fourth century AD and taught St Jerome. His grammar was the standard textbook throughout the middle ages. In his seventh satire Juvenal mentions

and spent twenty years vexing and tormenting himself over grammar. He supposes he'd be perfectly happy if he were allowed to live long enough to define precisely how the eight parts of speech should be distinguished, something in which no one writing in Greek or Latin has ever managed to be entirely successful. And then if anyone treats a conjunction as a word with the force of an adverb, it's a thing to go to war about. To this end, though there are as many grammars as grammarians – or rather, more, since my friend Aldus[98] alone has brought out more than five – there isn't one, however ignorantly or tediously written, which our man will pass over without scrutinizing it from cover to cover. Nor is there anyone, however inept his efforts in this field, who won't arouse his jealousy, for he's pitiably afraid that someone will win the prize before him, and that all his labours of so many years will be wasted⟩. Would you rather call this madness or folly? It doesn't really make much difference to me, as long as you admit that it's entirely due to me that a creature who'd otherwise be quite the most unfortunate can be carried away to such a pitch of happiness that he wouldn't want to change places with the kings of Persia.

Poets aren't so much in my debt, though they're admittedly members of my party, as they're a free race, as the saying goes, whose sole interest lies in delighting the ears of the foolish with pure nonsense and silly tales. Yet strange to say, they rely on these for the immortality and godlike life they assure themselves, and they make similar promises to others. 'Self-love and Flattery' are their special friends, and no other race of men worships me with such wholehearted devotion.

Then there are the rhetoricians; they may side with the philosophers and not want to commit themselves, but they too really belong to me – witness the fact, amongst others, that the trivialities they've written about include so many painstaking passages on the theory of joking. And so whoever it was who dedicated his *Art of Rhetoric* to Herennius lists folly amongst the

---

the 'name of Anchises' nurse' as an instance of the unknowable things grammarians quarrel about. The conquest of Africa and the capture of Babylon were proverbial expressions for the achievement of the impossible.

types of witticism, while Quintilian, the prince of orators by a long way, has a chapter on laughter which is even longer than the *Iliad*. They pay high tribute to folly in believing that what can't be refuted by argument can often be parried by laughter; unless anyone supposes that raising a laugh by witticisms according to plan has nothing to do with folly.[99]

Of the same kidney are those who court immortal fame by writing books. They all owe a great deal to me, especially any who blot their pages with unadulterated rubbish. But people who use their erudition to write for a learned minority and are anxious to have either Persius or Laelius[100] pass judgement don't

---

98. The passage about the 'jack-of-all-trades' was inserted in 1516 and refers to Thomas Linacre (c. 1460–1524), who was a fellow of All Souls, Oxford, from 1484, and from 1487 to 1499 was in Italy, where he studied Greek and medicine. He became tutor to Prince Arthur and in 1509 doctor to Henry VIII.

Aldus Manutius, the famous humanist and printer, opened his press at Venice in 1485. Linacre was among those who helped him. By 1500 his house had become the centre of a small academy of Greek scholars, and the famous Roman small typeface, said to be copied from the hand of Petrarch, was known to humanists throughout Europe. Erasmus came to call in 1507 and stayed to see the *Adages* through the Aldine press in 1508. He writes of Aldus in the 1508 adage *Festina lente* and again, waspishly defending himself against attack after Aldus's death, in the 1531 colloquy *Opulentia Sordida*. Alberto Pio, a pupil of Aldus who from 1525 was convinced that Erasmus was a Lutheran in disguise, felt it necessary to defend Aldus against what he erroneously took to be an attack on him in this passage on grammarians. Erasmus's reply makes it clear that no offence was intended or could reasonably be taken, but his reminiscences of Venice in the colloquy were coloured by his need to defend himself against accusations that he had acted as a paid proofreader for Aldus and risen drunk from his table. In 1513 Erasmus had published a book on the right parts of speech.

99. That 'poets are a free race' is a proverb quoted by Lucian and used in the *Adages*. The theme of poetic immortality touched on by Folly is a commonplace associated especially with Horace. The popular rhetorical handbook *Ad Herennium* was once thought to be by Cicero, but this attribution was questioned from the fifteenth century. The reference to Folly is in I, 6, 1. Quintilian deals with laughter in a famous chapter (book 6, chapter 3) of the *Institutio oratoria* which he published towards the end of the first century AD.

100. Persius and Laelius come from Cicero's *de Oratore* (2, 6, 25) where they signify the very learned and not so learned for reasons which are historically obscure.

seem to me favoured by fortune but rather to be pitied for their continuous self-torture. They add, change, remove, lay aside, take up, rephrase, show to their friends, keep for nine years, and are never satisfied. And their futile reward, a word of praise from a handful of people, they win at such a cost – so many late nights, such loss of sleep, sweetest of all things, and so much sweat and anguish.[101] Then their health deteriorates, their looks are destroyed, they suffer partial or total blindness, poverty, ill will, denial of pleasure, premature old age, and early death, and any other such disasters there may be. Yet the wise man believes he is compensated for everything if he wins the approval of one or another purblind scholar.

The writer who belongs to me is far happier in his crazy fashion. He never loses sleep as he sets down at once whatever takes his fancy and comes to his pen, even his dreams, and it costs him little beyond the price of his paper. He knows well enough that the more trivial the trifles he writes about the wider the audience which will appreciate them, made up as it is of all the ignoramuses and fools. What does it matter if three scholars can be found to damn his efforts, always supposing they've read them? How can the estimation of a mere handful of savants prevail against such a crowd of admirers?

Even better sense is shown by those who publish other men's work as their own, with a few verbal changes, in order to transfer to themselves the fame someone else has worked hard to acquire. They buoy themselves up with the thought that even if they're convicted of plagiarism they'll have profited meanwhile by whatever time is gained. Their self-satisfaction's a sight worth seeing whenever they're praised in public and pointed out in a crowd ('That's him, the great man himself!'), or when they're on show in the bookshops, every title-page displaying their three names, which are mostly foreign and evidently intended to be spellbinding, though heaven knows these are nothing more than names. How few people will hear of them, if you consider the vast size of the world, and fewer still will give them a word of

101. The reference to nine years comes from Horace, *Ars Poetica*, 388. The sweetness of sleep is referred to in the *Odyssey* 7, 289.

Desiderius Erasmus Rotterdamus, Three names

praise, since even the ignorant must have their preferences! Then too, those names are invented more often than not, or borrowed from the works of the ancients, so that a man can call himself Telemachus, Stelenus, or Laertes. One rejoices in the name of Polycrates, another of Thrasymachus, and it doesn't matter now-adays if you inscribe your book Chameleon or Gourd, or do as the philosophers do and sign it alpha or beta.

But the best joke of all is when they praise each other in an exchange of letters, verses, and eulogies, one ignorant fool glorify-ing another. A votes B an Alcaeus, so B votes A a Callimachus, or B thinks A superior to Cicero, so A says B is more learned than Plato. And sometimes they look for an opponent, to add to their reputation as his rivals. Then

the hesitant mob is split in opposite views

until both leaders go off victorious to celebrate their triumphs. Sensible men laugh at this, for that is supreme folly, no one will deny. But meanwhile I enable these people to lead a pleasant life, and they wouldn't exchange triumphs with the Scipios. And for getting so much pleasure from laughing at this and enjoying the madness of their fellows, the others are much in my debt, learned though they are – they can't deny it without being the most ungrateful of men.[102]

102. The Greek phrase for the 'great man himself' is a reminiscence of Horace (Odes, 4, 3, 21–3). The 'three names' of each author refer to the Roman usage in which a middle name denoted nobility. Telemachus was the son and Laertes the father of Ulysses. Stelenus is not classical and may be a mistake for the Sthenelus who was a tragic poet of the fifth century BC. Polycrates was an Athenian orator and sophist (see letter-preface note 5, p. 5). Thrasy-machus was a sophist and rhetorician from Chalcedon in the fifth century BC. Folly alludes to the Aristotelians who used letters like alpha and beta for numbers and signs. Alcaeus was a famous Greek lyric poet of the seventh century BC. The two names are mentioned together by Horace (Epistles, 2, 2, 99). The final verse about the hesitant mob is from the Aeneid (2, 39).

Folly's advice to plagiarize touches on a practice to which Erasmus became increasingly sensitive. In 1533 he added to the adage Festina lente, pointing out how ill-regulated the printing trade had become. The law had not yet caught up, and the press which had once been welcomed as the instrument for the dissemination of the great works had become, says Erasmus, the tool of commercial exploiters.

Amongst the learned the lawyers claim first place, the most self-satisfied class of people, as they roll their rock of Sisyphus and string together six hundred laws in the same breath, no matter whether relevant or not, piling up ⟨opinion on opinion and⟩ gloss on gloss to make their profession seem the most difficult of all. Anything which causes trouble has special merit in their eyes.

Let's group with them the sophists and dialecticians, a breed of men which can rattle on better than one of Dodona's copper pots. Any one of them could be a match for twenty picked women in garrulity, but they'd be happier if they were only talkative and not quarrelsome as well — they're so stubborn in their fights to the death about things like goat's wool, and they generally lose sight of the truth in the heat of the argument. However, their self-love keeps them happy, and three syllogisms arm them enough to go straight to battle on any subject and with any man. You could put Stentor up against them, but their obstinacy would see that they won the day.[103]

Next to them come the philosophers, cloaked and bearded to command respect, who insist that they alone have wisdom and all other mortals are but fleeting shadows. Theirs is certainly a pleasant form of madness, which sets them building countless universes and measuring the sun, moon, stars, and planets by rule of thumb or a bit of string, and producing reasons for thunderbolts, winds, eclipses, and other inexplicable phenomena. They never pause for a moment, as if they were private secretaries to

103. Sisyphus was condemned everlastingly to roll a large rock up a mountain only to see it fall down again just before it reached the top. The humanist lawyers like Erasmus's contemporary Budé were concerned to disinter the text of ancient legislation from under the burden of medieval glosses which had hitherto determined its interpretation. Dodona was the seat of an ancient oracle of Jupiter, whose priests interpreted the rustling of leaves and the clanging or vibrating of copper pots in the wind. Goat's wool signifies something of trivial value in the *Adages*. Stentor was the Greek in the Trojan war whose voice (*Iliad*, 5, 785) sounded like that of fifty men.

The inclusion of lawyers among the followers of Folly might seem less surprising than the omission of doctors, since later satirists spared neither, and Folly had earlier mentioned them both together (p. 52). But even the lawyers are here seen as merely garrulous rather than the venal or stupid characters for which many later writers took them. Both legal and medical studies were being renewed by Erasmus's humanist contemporaries.

Nature, architect of the universe, or had come to us straight from the council of the gods. Meanwhile Nature has a fine laugh at them and their conjectures, for their total lack of certainty is obvious enough from the endless contention amongst themselves on every single point. They know nothing at all, yet they claim to know everything. Though ignorant even of themselves and sometimes not able to see the ditch or stone lying in their path, either because most of them are half-blind or because their minds are far away, they still boast that they can see ideas, universals, separate forms, prime matters, ⟨quiddities, ecceities,⟩ things which are all so insubstantial that I doubt if even Lynceus could perceive them. And how they despise the vulgar crowd whenever they bring out their triangles, quadrilaterals, circles, and similar mathematical diagrams, piled on top of each other and intertwined like a maze, and then letters of the alphabet, which they marshal in line and deploy hither and thither in order to throw dust in the eyes of the less well-informed! Some of them too will also foretell the future by consulting the stars, promising further wonderful marvels, and they are lucky enough to find people to believe them in this too.[104]

104. *Quiddities, ecceities* was added in 1512. On the philosophers, Folly delights in cataloguing the subtle abstractions of the scholastics. All the terms listed here were used in the context of disputes about universal ideas behind which in fact were hidden totally different views about man. Generally Platonist psychological presuppositions led to the view either that universal concepts like 'tree-ness' were merely words with nothing to correspond to them in reality or that actual things were modifications of realized 'universal' ideas. Both solutions entailed theological difficulties, and there developed a more Aristotelian epistemology in which the universal concept was 'abstracted' from a perception by a process which always remained obscure.

Quiddities or essences defined the nature of particular objects whether or not they had being or existence. Ecceities were important in the Scotist reaction against Thomist realism. They designated individual natures not really but only 'formally objectively' distinct from a common or universal nature. Forms were the object of intellectual abstractions conferring reality and numerical distinction for the Aristotelian scholastics on objects whose other component was 'prime' or undifferentiated matter. See on this matter the Introduction.

The cloaks and beards which philosophers wore do not, Erasmus elsewhere assures us, themselves suffice to make a philosopher. On Lynceus, see note 57, p. 46.

Then there are the theologians, a remarkably supercilious and touchy lot.[105] I might perhaps do better to pass over them in silence without 'stirring the mud of Camarina' or grasping that noxious plant, lest they marshal their forces for an attack with innumerable conclusions and force me to eat my words. If I refuse they'll denounce me as a heretic on the spot, for this is the bolt they always loose on anyone to whom they take a dislike.

Now there are none so unwilling to recognize my good services to them, and yet they're under obligation to me on several important counts, notably for their happiness in their self-love, which enables them to dwell in a sort of third heaven, looking down from aloft, almost with pity, on all the rest of mankind as so many cattle crawling on the face of the earth. They are fortified meanwhile with an army of ⟨schoolmen's definitions⟩, conclusions, and corollaries, and propositions both explicit and implicit. They boast of so many 'bolt holes' that the meshes of Vulcan's net couldn't stop them from slipping out by means of the distinctions they draw, with which they can easily cut any knot (a double axe from Tenedos wouldn't do better), for they abound in newly coined expressions and strange-sounding words.[106]

In addition, they interpret hidden mysteries to suit themselves: how the world was created and designed; through what channels the stain of sin filtered down to posterity; by what means, in what measure, and how long Christ was formed in the Virgin's womb; how, in the Eucharist, accidents can subsist without a domicile. But this sort of question has been discussed threadbare. There are others more worthy of great and enlightened theologians (as they call themselves) which can really rouse them to

105. The Latin for 'supercilious and touchy' refers to Horace, *Epistulae* 2, 2, 102.

106. The 'mud of Camarina' refers to a swamp which, when drained against Apollo's orders, then allowed the city to be sacked by its enemies. It is proverbial for the cause of one's own ruin and is discussed in the *Adages*. The 'noxious plant' (*Anagyris foetida*, or bean trefoil, an emetic) is the subject of the following adage.

The bolt holes come from Lucian, *Eunuchus*, 10. Vulcan used an invisible net to envelop his unfaithful wife Venus and her lover Mars (*Odyssey*, 8, 270 ff.). Its mesh was close enough to immobilize them. The axe of Tenedos is

action if they come their way. What was the exact moment of divine generation? Are there several filiations in Christ? Is it a possible proposition that God the Father could hate his Son? Could God have taken on the form of a woman, a devil, a donkey, a gourd, or a flintstone? If so, how could a gourd have preached sermons, performed miracles, and been nailed to the cross? And what would Peter have consecrated ⟨if he had consecrated⟩ when the body of Christ still hung on the cross? Furthermore, at that same time could Christ have been called a man? Shall we be permitted to eat and drink after the resurrection? We're taking due precaution against hunger and thirst while there's time.[107]

---

discussed in the *Adages*. It is a weapon for wreaking swift justice and cutting through ambiguities and excuses.

Folly's long indictment of the theologians lies at the very heart of the *Praise of Folly* and of Erasmus's evangelical humanism. The ironic mask has gradually been lowered through the succession of followers from grammarians to philosophers until Folly, in this paragraph, attacks her own followers in something very like the voice of Erasmus. The form becomes freer. Bantering irony gives way more often to withering sarcasm at first and then to total seriousness in the praise of evangelical folly. Although the ironic mask is frequently resumed, it is no longer consistently worn until in the last paragraphs of all Folly grasps for it hastily and admits that she has forgotten who she is.

107. Folly's implication, of course, is that the scholastics, enmeshed in their own abstract categories, were more interested in speculative subtleties than in questions relevant to religious and moral experience. The Paris theologians, with very few exceptions, regarded themselves as above all custodians of an orthodoxy which in their view needed to have no pastoral relevance or link with human experience. It remains, however, true that some of the questions listed by Folly such as the origin of the world and the transmission of guilt were matters of obvious religious significance, that the scholastics themselves were often aware of the religious relevance of the apparently abstruse matters they discussed, and that others originated in classroom debates on issues considered trivial but which could be used to teach the techniques of theological debate.

There was in fact a serious debate about whether the world existed from eternity, which the fourth Lateran Council had failed to settle satisfactorily in 1215. The transmission of original sin was also subject to debate, but solutions to this problem were wrapped up with views about universal ideas, as it was obviously easier to understand the transmission of original sin if all

⟨There are any amount of 'quibbles' even more refined than these, about concepts, relations, instants, formalities, quiddities, and ecceities, which no one could possibly perceive unless like Lynceus he could see through blackest darkness things which don't exist. Then add those 'maxims' of theirs, which are so 'paradoxical' that in comparison the pronouncements of the stoics, which were actually known as paradoxes, seem positively commonplace and banal; for example, that it is a lesser crime to butcher a thousand men than to cobble a poor man's shoe on a single occasion on the Lord's day, and better to let the whole world perish down to the last crumb and stitch, as they say, than to tell a single tiny insignificant lie. These subtle refinements of subtleties are made still more subtle by all the different lines of scholastic argument, so that you'd extricate yourself faster from a labyrinth than from the tortuous obscurities of realists, nominalists, Thomists, Albertists, Ockhamists and Scotists and I've not mentioned all the sects, only the main ones.[108]

---

men were actual modifications of the universal 'humanity', and those who rejected this 'exaggerated' realism had to find alternative hypotheses for the transmission of sin.

The subsistence of the accidents of bread when the substance of the Eucharistic species had been changed was a serious difficulty caused by the application of Aristotelian categories to a phenomenon they were never intended to explain. Erasmus uses the classical 'domicile' ironically. The ordinary correlative of 'accident' in this sense is 'substance'. The moment of divine generation and the number of filiations in Christ had been discussed in the context of the Arian debates and the *Filioque* dispute which split eastern and western Christians, but were not important issues in the late middle ages. Erasmus mentions these issues with similar distaste in the preface to his 1523 edition of St Hilary. The 'hatred' of the Father for his Son, who had assumed the sins of the world, was a hypothesis about the theology of the redemption accepted even by so late an author as Bossuet. Discussions about the forms in which God could have become incarnate were of pedagogical utility only, although it appears from a letter to Colet of 1499 that Erasmus had had to put up with them. The possibility of consecrating the Eucharistic species before the resurrection posed real problems of sacramental causality and was a touchstone for the whole theology of the sacraments.

108. The idea that the murder of a thousand is a lesser crime than the breaking of the Sabbath derives from the exaggerated application of the

Such is the erudition and complexity they all display that I fancy the apostles themselves would need the help of another Holy Spirit if they were obliged to join issue on these topics with our new breed of theologian. Paul could provide a living example of faith, but when he says "Faith is the substance of things hoped for, the evidence of things not seen," his definition is quite unscholastic. And though he provides the finest example of charity, in his first letter to the Corinthians, chapter 13, he neither divides nor defines it according to the rules of dialectic. The apostles consecrated the Eucharist with due piety, but had they been questioned about the *terminus a quo* and the *terminus ad quem*, about transubstantiation, and how the same body can be in different places, about the difference between the body of Christ in heaven, on the cross, and at the sacrament of the Eucharist, about the exact moment when transubstantiation takes place, seeing that the prayer which effects it is a distinct quantity extended in time, they

---

scholastic principle that crimes against God have a malice not intrinsic to crimes against men. That a lie may not be told to save the world from destruction admirably illustrates the way the scholastics derived moral norms from abstract principles rather than human needs. Lies are intrinsically evil. The end does not justify the means, and no extrinsic end can therefore justify a lie. The application of abstract principle is logical, but the resulting norm takes no account of charity or compassion. Realists and nominalists were so called from the opposite positions they took up in the debate about universals.

The realists believed that the universal was in some way realized in individual objects and the nominalists that universals were merely logical categories.

Thomists were the followers of Thomas Aquinas (died 1274), now acknowledged to be the greatest of the scholastics but whose system, which automatically geared divine command to human moral aspiration, found general recognition only after the humanist reform of theology in the sixteenth century. Albertists were followers of Albertus Magnus (died 1280), teacher of Thomas Aquinas, notable for his scientific work and his openness to the new Aristotelianism. Ockhamists and Scotists were followers respectively of William of Ockham (died 1347) and Duns Scotus (died 1308), both of whom took part in the reaction against Aquinas which led to the late-medieval nominalist emphasis on the transcendence of God and the arbitrary nature of his revelation and his law.

wouldn't, in my opinion, have shown the same subtlety in their reply as the Scotists do in their dissertations and definitions. The apostles knew personally the mother of Jesus, but which of them proved how she had been kept immaculate from Adam's sin with the logic our theologians display? Peter received the keys, and received them from one who would not have entrusted them to an unworthy recipient, yet I doubt whether Peter understood (nowhere does he show signs of subtle reasoning power) how a man who has not knowledge can still hold the key to it. The apostles baptized wherever they went, yet nowhere did they teach the formal, material, efficient, and final cause of baptism, nor did they ever mention the delible and indelible marks of the sacraments. They worshipped, that is true, but in spirit, in accordance only with the words of the Gospel, "God is a spirit: and they that worship him must worship in spirit and in truth."[109] Apparently it had

---

109. Paul's description of faith comes from Hebrews ii, 1. The thorny problems of Eucharistic theology led in the early sixteenth century to a great variety of views and all the points mentioned by Folly were in fact discussed. In the attempts at reconciliation both at Ratisbon in 1541 and at Poissy in 1561 Eucharistic theology was apparently (but perhaps only apparently) the one irreconcilable doctrinal issue separating the two sides of the schism opened up by the Reformation.

The doctrine of Mary's immaculate conception to which Folly goes on to refer had been accepted by the Paris theology faculty only in 1497. Scotus had argued against Aquinas that it did not compromise the unique mediation of Christ, but his treatment of the question made the immaculate conception into a Marian privilege not clearly relevant to religious experiences, although it is of fundamental importance for an understanding of the effects of the redemption. The 'keys' mentioned in Matthew xvi, 19, signified the 'ruling' power of the Church, which is distinct from its teaching authority. The point made by Folly refers to the Scotist insistence that the power of the Church to teach does not derive from the learning of its prelates and theologians.

On baptism, the scholastics were caught up in the attempt to apply to the sacraments the four types of cause in Aristotle, formal, material, efficient and final. The 'character' of baptism is indelible, although not all the sacrament's effects are permanent. It accounts for the fact that baptism may not be received more than once.

The scriptural reference to worship 'in spirit and in truth' comes from John iv, 24.

never been revealed to them that a mediocre drawing sketched in charcoal on a wall should be worshipped in the same manner as Christ himself, provided that it had two fingers outstretched, long hair, and three rays sticking out from the halo fastened to the back of its head. Who *could* understand all this unless he has frittered away thirty-six whole years over the physics and metaphysics of Aristotle and Scotus?

Similarly, ⟨the apostles⟩ repeatedly teach grace, but nowhere do they draw the distinction between grace *gratis data* and grace *gratificans*. ⟨They encourage good works without distinguishing between *opus operans* and *opus operatum*⟩. Everywhere they teach charity, but fail to separate infused charity from what is acquired. Nor do they explain whether it is accident or substance, a thing created or uncreated. They detest sin, but on my life I'll swear they couldn't offer a scientific definition of what we call sin unless they'd been trained in the Scotist spirit.

Nothing will make me believe that Paul, from whose learning we may judge all the other apostles, would so often have condemned questions, arguments, genealogies, and what he himself called 'battles of words', if he had been well up in those niceties, especially when all the controversies and disagreements of that time would have been clumsy and unsophisticated affairs in comparison with the more than Chrysippean subtleties of the schoolmen of today.[110] Not but what these

110. The scholastic theologians distinguished between three categories of worship, applicable respectively to God, Mary and the other saints. Some at least, says Lijster, held that the images should themselves be venerated with the category of worship applicable to the subject signified, although the veneration of images apart from the subjects they signified was neither intended nor discussed. The iconographical details are those conventionally applicable to images of Christ.

On grace Erasmus uses the technical scholastic terms *gratia gratis data* and *gratia gratificans* (for which Lijster has the more usual *gratia gratum faciens*). The technical English equivalents are 'actual' and 'sanctifying' grace. Sanctifying grace produces an enduring state of soul known as justification, while 'actual' grace belongs not to the soul but to its operative faculties like intellect and will, and enables them to perform, for instance, the meritorious works which either prepare for or flow from justification. The sentence

are extremely moderate men. If anything written by the apostles lacks polish and the master's touch, they don't damn it outright but suggest a suitable interpretation, and this, I suppose, is intended as a tribute in deference to its antiquity and apostolic authorship. It would of course hardly be fair to expect such a standard from the apostles when they never heard so much as a word on these matters from their own teacher. If the same sort of thing turned up in Chrysostom, Basil, or Jerome, then they'd have good reason to mark it "not accepted".

Those apostles certainly refuted pagan philosophers and the Jews (who are by nature the most obstinate of men), but did so more by the example of their way of life and their miracles than by syllogisms, especially in the case of those who would have been intellectually quite incapable of grasping a single *quodlibet* of Scotus. Today there's no heathen ⟨or heretic⟩ who doesn't give way at once when confronted by these ultra-subtle refinements, unless he's so thick-headed that he can't follow them, or so imprudent that he shouts them down, or so well trained in the same wiles that the battle's evenly matched – as if you set magician against magician or a man with a

---

about the *opus operans* and the *opus operatum* was inserted in 1522, when Luther's attack on the theology of the sacraments, the *Opus Operatum*, had broken out. The distinction was made to emphasize that the validity of a sacramental rite (the *opus operatum*) is independent of the religious disposition of the officiating minister (the *opus operans* or *operantis*).

The distinctions of charity are parallel to those of grace. Charity is infused at the moment of the justification which it effects. But its own effects on the operative faculties can be augmented and, in this case, it is possible to talk of 'acquired' charity. The charity which is infused into the soul has to be created, but the full effect of justification cannot be explained unless in some sense God's uncreated charity is communicated to us, so that the distinction became necessary to explain the metaphysics of justification.

Whether grace achieves in us a 'substantial' or an 'accidental' modification was a question bound to arise in any discussion of the modalities of justification inside Aristotelian categories.

St Paul's condemnations of dissension and vain dispute are to be found, for instance, in 1 Timothy (i, 4; vi, 4 and 20), 2 Timothy (ii, 16 and 23) and Titus (iii, 9). Chrysippus was the subtlest of the stoic philosophers.

lucky sword fights another who has one too. This would just
be reweaving Penelope's web. And in my opinion Christians
would show sense if they dispatched these argumentative
Scotists and pigheaded Ockhamists and undefeated Albertists
along with the whole regiment of sophists to fight the Turks
and Saracens instead of sending those armies of dull-witted
soldiers with whom they've long been carrying on war with
no result. Then, I think, they'd witness a really keen battle and
a victory such as never before. For who is too cold-blooded to
be fired by their ingenuities, too stupid to be stung into action
by their attacks? And is there anyone so keen-sighted that they
can't leave him groping in the dark?[111]

You may suppose that I'm saying all this by way of a joke,
and that's not surprising, seeing that amongst the theologians
themselves there are some with superior education who are
sickened by these theological minutiae, which they look upon
as frivolous. Others too think it a damnable form of sacrilege
and the worst sort of impiety for anyone to speak of matters
so holy, which call for reverence rather than explanation, with
a profane tongue, or to argue with the pagan subtlety of the
heathen, presume to offer definitions, and pollute the majesty
of divine theology with words and sentiments which are so
trivial and even squalid.⟩

Yet those who do so are so happy in their self-satisfaction and
self-congratulation, and so busy night and day with these enjoyable tomfooleries, that they haven't even a spare moment in
which to read the Gospel or the letters of Paul even once
through. And while they're wasting their time in the schools
with this nonsense, they believe that just as in the poets Atlas

111. Before it became a literary form the *Quaestio de quodlibet* was a
scholastic exercise held twice a year. The subjects were unconnected with the
ordinary course of lectures and disputations, were often genuinely disputed
questions and often aroused much passion in the audience, which was
allowed to participate. *Quodlibet* is the name given first to these solemn
disputations and then to published treatments of theological questions suitable
for defending at one of these acts. The words 'or heretic' were added in
1515.

Penelope, the wife of Ulysses, never finished her web because she
unwove at night what she had done during the day.

holds up the sky on his shoulders, they support the entire church on the props of their syllogisms and without them it would collapse. Then you can imagine their happiness when they fashion and refashion the Holy Scriptures at will, as if these were made of wax, and when they insist that their conclusions, to which a mere handful of scholastics have subscribed, should carry more weight than the laws of Solon and be preferred to papal decrees.

⟨They also set up as the world's censors, and demand recantation of anything which doesn't exactly square with their conclusions, explicit and implicit, and make their oracular pronouncements: "This proposition is scandalous; this is irreverent; this smells of heresy; this doesn't ring true." As a result, neither baptism nor the gospel, neither Paul, Peter, St Jerome, Augustine, or even Thomas, 'the greatest' of Aristotelians', can make a man Christian unless these learned bachelors have given their approval, such is the refinement of their judgement. For who could have imagined, if the savants hadn't told him, that anyone who said that the two phrases "chamber-pot you stink" and "the chamber-pot stinks", or "the pots boil" and "that the pot boils" are equally correct can't possibly be a Christian?[112] Who could have freed the church from the dark error of its ways when no one would ever have read about these if they hadn't been published under the great seals of the schools? And aren't they perfectly happy doing all this?⟩ They are happy too while they're depicting everything in hell down to the last detail, as if they'd spent several years there, or giving free rein to their fancy in fabricating new spheres and adding the most extensive and beautiful of all in case the blessed spirits lack space to take a walk in comfort or give a dinner-party or even

112. The scholastics drew on an increasing range of censures from 'heretical' down to 'offensive to pious ears'. Folly throws in a few variations of her own.

The phrase for 'greatest of Aristotelians' is a Greek coinage of Erasmus not intended to be ironical. Folly, it should be noticed, is much harder on Scotus and his followers than on Thomas Aquinas.

The final sentence of this passage mocks at an Oxford dispute about correct Latin grammatical usage. The use of accents in the original text suggests that abstruse fun is being made of a technical dispute. Folly replaces the traditional examples with those involving 'chamber-pot'.

play a game of ball. Their heads are so stuffed and swollen with these absurdities, and thousands more like them, that I don't believe even Jupiter's brain felt so burdened when he begged for Vulcan's axe to help him give birth to Athene. And so you mustn't be surprised if you see them at public disputations with their heads carefully bound up in all those fillets – it's to keep them from bursting apart.[113]

For myself, I often have a good laugh when they particularly fancy themselves as theologians if they speak in a specially uncouth and slovenly style, and while they mumble so haltingly as to be unintelligible except to a fellow-stammerer, they refer to their powers of perception, which can't be attained by the common man. They insist that it detracts from the grandeur of sacred writing if they're obliged to obey the rules of grammar. It seems a most peculiar prerogative of theologians, to be the only people permitted to speak ungrammatically; however, they share this privilege with a lot of working men. Finally, they think themselves nearest to the gods whenever they are reverently addressed as "our masters", a title which holds as much meaning for them as the 'tetragram' does for the Jews. Consequently, they say it's unlawful to write MAGISTER NOSTER except in capital letters, and if anyone inverts the order and says "*noster magister*", he destroys the entire majesty of the theologians' title at a single blow.[114]

113. Jupiter, having swallowed the pregnant Metis in case his child should dethrone him, felt a pain in his head and asked Vulcan to split it open, whereat Pallas Athene emerged from it fully armed. There is some doubt whether Folly goes on to refer to heads swathed in bandages or doctoral bonnets.

114. Folly, like Erasmus and many of the humanists, clearly associates non-classical, careless and erroneous Latin usage with the decay of true religion, and accuses the theologians of responsibility for both.

The fun made of the MAGISTER NOSTER was to be notably exploited by the humanist Ulrich von Hutten's ironic attack on the scholastics in 1515, the *Letters to Obscure Men*, written to defend the humanist theologian Johannes Reuchlin. Reuchlin was a Hebraeist, the first of the humanists to provoke a concerted attack from the scholastics. After his death, Erasmus wrote a colloquy on his 'apotheosis' (1522). Erasmus had meanwhile quarrelled with Hutten who, having become a Lutheran, wished to turn the old Holy Roman Empire into an all-German kingdom and do away with any connexion with Rome. Against him Erasmus wrote his *Sponge* of 1523.

The happiness of these people is most nearly approached by those who are popularly called 'religious' or 'monks'. Both names are false, since most of them are a long way removed from religion, and wherever you go these so-called solitaries are the people you're likely to meet. I don't believe any life would be more wretched than theirs if I didn't come to their aid in many ways. The whole tribe is so universally loathed that even a chance meeting is thought to be ill-omened – and yet they are gloriously self-satisfied. In the first place, they believe it's the highest form of piety to be so uneducated that they can't even read. Then when they bray like donkeys in church, repeating by rote the psalms they haven't understood, they imagine they are charming the ears of their heavenly audience with infinite delight. Many of them too make a good living out of their squalor and beggary, bellowing for bread from door to door, ⟨and indeed making a nuisance of themselves in every inn, carriage, or boat⟩, to the great loss of all the other beggars. This is the way in which these smooth individuals, in all their filth and ignorance, their boorish and shameless behaviour, claim to bring back the apostles into our midst![115]

But nothing could be more amusing than their practice of doing everything to rule, as if they were following mathematical calculations which it would be a sin to ignore. They work out

---

The tetragram consisted of the four Hebrew consonants in the name of God, I H W H. Out of respect the word was never written out in full or pronounced. 'Jehovah' combines the consonants with the vowels from the Hebrew for 'lord'. In the next paragraph, the first sentence alludes to the derivation of the word 'monk' from the Greek for 'solitary'.

115. Usage has become blurred with time, but monks are properly members of the monastic orders, exempt from episcopal (diocesan) jurisdiction, normally constrained to reside in their monasteries. Their principal activity consisted in singing the divine office, divided into the canonical hours of matins, lauds, prime, terce, sext, none, vespers, and compline. The whole psalter filled a weekly cycle, but there were complex seasonal variations. In the middle ages the 'mendicant' orders of friars were founded, not constrained to reside in any one house of their order but still exempt from diocesan jurisdiction. Later a large number of smaller 'congregations' were founded. By the sixteenth century many of the foundations had outlived their original purposes, without finding acceptable new social roles.

the number of knots for a shoestring, the colour and number of variations of a single habit, the material and width to a hair's breadth of a girdle, the shape and capacity (in sacksful) of a cowl, the length (in fingers) of a haircut, the number of hours prescribed for sleep. But this equality applied to such a diversity of persons and temperaments will only result in inequality, as anyone can see. Even so, these trivialities not only make them feel superior to other men but also contemptuous of each other, and these professors of apostolic charity will create extraordinary scenes and disturbances on account of a habit with a different girdle ⟨or one which is rather too dark in colour⟩. Some you'll see are so strict in their observances that they will wear an outer garment which has to be made of Cilician goat's hair and one of Milesian wool next to the skin, while others have linen on top and wool underneath. There are others again who shrink from the touch of money as if it were deadly poison, but are less restrained when it comes to wine or contact with women. In short, they all take remarkable pains to be different in their rules of life. ⟨They aren't interested in being like Christ but in being unlike each other.⟩

Consequently, a great deal of their happiness depends on their name. Some, for instance, delight in calling themselves Cordeliers, ⟨and they are subdivided into the Colletines, the Minors, the Minims and the Bullists.⟩ Then there are the Benedictines and the Bernardines, ⟨the Brigittines, Augustinians, Williamites and Jacobins⟩, as if it weren't enough to be called Christians.[116] ⟨Most of them rely so much on their ceremonies and

116. Cilician goat's hair is rough and Milesian wool exceptionally fine.

'Cordeliers' was a generic name for all Franciscans or friars minor. Folly deliberately chooses some lesser known orders and lesser known names for well known orders.

By the time Erasmus came to write the *Praise of Folly*, serious attempts at monastic reforms were being made. But it is true that some orders, notably the Franciscans, were extremely distrustful of learning, and especially the humanist learning which they regarded as leading to heresy. When Rabelais was a Franciscan, his Greek books were confiscated. The earliest French humanists were themselves favourable to the monastic vows. Some indeed were monks. But the Parisian humanists favourable to monks were inclined to feel that if only priests understood Latin all would be well again. This was the view of Josse Clichtove, an early humanist who defended the monastic

petty man-made traditions that they suppose heaven alone will hardly be enough to reward merit such as theirs. They never think of the time to come when Christ will scorn all this and enforce his own rule, that of charity. One monk will display his wretched belly, swollen with every kind of fish. Another will pour out a hundred sacksful of psalms, while another adds up his myriads of fasts and accounts for his stomach near to bursting by the single midday meal, which is all he usually has. Yet another will produce such a pile of church ceremonies that seven ships could scarcely carry them. One will boast that for sixty years he has never touched money without protecting his fingers with two pairs of gloves, while another wears a cowl so thick with dirt that not even a sailor would want it near his person. Then one will relate how for over fifty years he has led the life of a sponge, always stuck in the same place; others will show off a voice made hoarse by incessant chanting, or the inertia brought on by living alone, or a tongue stiff with disuse under the rule of silence. But Christ would interrupt the unending flow of these self-glorifications to ask: 'Where has this new race of Jews sprung from? I recognize only one commandment as truly mine, but it is the only one not mentioned. Long ago in the sight of all, without wrapping up my words in parables, I promised my father's kingdom, not for wearing a cowl or chanting petty prayers or practising abstinence, but for performing the duties of ⟨faith and⟩ charity. I do not acknowledge men who acknowledge their

---

vows, worked for the reform of the monasteries and was strongly anti-Lutheran. He typifies a party of humanists less reactionary than the rest of the Paris theology faculty, but less radical than Erasmus, whom Clichtove attacked soon after the publication of the *Praise of Folly*.

Stories of debauched, drunken and lecherous monks may be exaggerated, but totally irreligious behaviour was scandalous and widespread. Folly gets the mentality with pitiless accuracy when she points to the mixture of excessive punctiliousness in rule-keeping with wide-ranging breaches of the spirit and letter of the vows. Her most important criticism is that directed against the imposition of uniformity on people of different gifts and temperaments. This was the kernel of the moderate humanist criticism of the religious orders and is frequently found in Erasmus.

own deeds so noisily. Those who also want to appear holier than I am can go off and live in the heavens of the Abraxasians, if they like, or give orders for a new heaven to be built for them by the men whose foolish teaching they have set above my own commands.' When they hear these words and see common sailors and waggoners preferred to themselves, what sort of looks do you think they'll give each other?

But for the moment they're happy in their expectations, not without help from me.⟩[117] And although they are segregated from civil life, no one can afford to belittle them, least of all the mendicants, who know all about everyone's secrets from the confessional, as they call it. They know it's forbidden to publish these abroad, unless they happen to be drinking and want to be amused with enthralling stories, but then no names are mentioned and the facts left open to conjecture. But if anyone stirs up this hornets' nest they'll take swift revenge in their public sermons, pointing out their enemy by insinuations and allusions so artfully veiled that no one who knows anything can fail to know who is meant. And you'll have to throw your sop to Cerberus before they'll make an end of barking.[118]

Is there a comedian or cheapjack you'd rather watch than them when they hold forth in their sermons? It's quite absurd but highly enjoyable to see them observe the traditional rules of rhetoric. Heavens, how they gesticulate and make proper changes of voice, how they drone on and fling themselves about,

117. The Abraxasians were a gnostic sect believing in 365 spheres or heavens, a number they arrived at by totting up the numerical equivalents for the Greek letters in the word abraxas.

118. The reference to the 'sop for Cerberus' alludes to the *Aeneid*, 6, 419.

Certain canonical privileges, particularly associated with confessional jurisdiction, attached to mendicant status. The sacrament of penance, demanding auricular confession, was attacked by all the reformers. Some of the late medieval handbooks, with their insistence on specifying the last theological sub-species of guilt for validity of absolution, explain why Calvin, for instance, found it so distasteful. Erasmus wrote a good deal about the sacrament and seems himself to have confessed regularly, if rarely. In general he emphasizes not the sacramental validity but the occasion offered by the sacrament for obtaining advice and direction. It was of course forbidden under the most rigorous canonical penalties for a confessor to reveal anything which could connect a penitent with a sin.

rapidly putting on different expressions and confounding everything with their outcry! This is a style of oratory which is handed
down in person from brother to brother like a secret ritual. I'm
not one of the initiated, but I'll make a guess at what it's like.

They start with an invocation, something they've borrowed
from the poets. Then if they're going to preach about charity
their exordium is all about the Nile, a river in Egypt, ⟨or if they
intend to recount the mystery of the cross they'll happily
begin with Bel, the Babylonian dragon. If fasting is to be their
subject they make a start with the twelve signs of the Zodiac,
and if they would expound the faith they open with a discussion on squaring the circle.[119] I myself have heard one notable
fool – I'm sorry, I meant to say scholar – who set out to reveal
the mystery of the Trinity to a large congregation. In order to
display the exceptional quality of his learning and to satisfy the
ears of the theologians he made a novel beginning, starting
with the alphabet, syllable, and sentence, and going on to the
agreement of noun with verb, adjective with noun and substan-
tive. There was general astonishment amongst his listeners,
some of whom whispered to each other the quotation from
Horace, "What's the point of all this stink?" Finally he reached
the conclusion that a symbol of the Trinity was clearly expressed in the rudiments of grammar, and no mathematician
could trace a figure so plain in the sand. And that great
theologian had sweated eight whole months over this discourse, so today he is blinder than a mole, all his keenness of
sight doubtless gone to reinforce the sharp edge of his intellect.
But the man has no regrets for his lost sight; he even thinks it
was a small price to pay for his hour of glory.

I've heard another one, an octogenarian and still an active
theologian, whom you'd take for a reincarnation of Scotus
himself, set out to explain the mystery of the name of Jesus.

119. Bel is the dragon of Daniel xiv.
The signs of the Zodiac are not totally without relevance to fasting. The
Lenten fast, roughly coinciding with the sun's entry into the segment Aries,
was occasionally justified by reference to the change in the humours
coincident on the astronomical event.
In the next paragraph Folly refers to Horace, Satires 2, 7, 21.

He proved with remarkable subtlety how anything that could be said about this lay hidden in the actual letters of his name. For the fact that it is declinable in three different cases is clearly symbolic of the threefold nature of the divine. Thus, the first case (*Jesus*) ends in *s*, the second (*Jesum*) in *m*, the third (*Jesu*) in *u*, and herein lies an 'inexpressible' mystery; for the three letters indicate that he is the sum, the middle, and the ultimate. They also concealed a still more recondite mystery, this time according to mathematical analysis. He divided *Jesus* into two equal halves, leaving the middle letter *s* broken by a caesura. Then he showed that this was the letter 𝖂 in Hebrew, pronounced *syn*; and *syn* sounds like the word I believe the Scots use for the Latin *peccatum*, that is, sin. Here there is clear proof that it is Jesus who takes away the sins of the world. This novel introduction left his audience open-mouthed in admiration, especially the theologians present, who very nearly suffered the same fate as Niobe. As for me, I nearly split my sides like the fig-wood Priapus who had the misfortune to witness the nocturnal rites of Canidia and Sagana, and with good reason; for when did Demosthenes in Greek or Cicero in Latin think up an 'exordium' like that? These orators held the view that an introduction which was irrelevant to the main theme was a bad one – even a swineherd with no one but Nature for a teacher wouldn't open a speech in such a way.⟩ But our masters of learning think that their preamble, as they call it, will show special rhetorical excellence if it's wholly unconnected with the rest of the subject, so that the listener will marvel and say to himself "Now where's that taking him?"[120]

120. The proverb 'blind as a mole' is discussed in the *Adages*. Ovid (*Metamorphoses*, 6, 152 ff.) recounts how Niobe's seven sons were all killed by Apollo's darts and her seven daughters by Diana before she herself was turned to stone as a punishment for scorning Leto, mother of Apollo and Diana.

The figwood Priapus which cracked in fright at the rites of Canidia and Sagana comes from Horace (*Satires*, 1, 8). The phrase 'where's that taking him?' comes from Virgil (*Bucolics*, 3, 19).

The introduction to the sermon based on the letters of the name Jesus is reminiscent of the number mysticism and caballistic interpretations still popular in the early sixteenth century. Even though many of the humanists wrote occasionally in this style, Erasmus was firmly opposed to it.

In the third place, by way of an exposition, they offer no more than a hasty interpretation of a passage from the gospel as an aside, so to speak, though this should really be their main object. And fourthly, with a quick change of character they propound some theological question the like of which 'has never been known on earth or in heaven', and they imagine this is a further indication of their expertise. At this point there really is a display of theological arrogance, as they bombard the ears of their listeners with such high-sounding titles as Worthy Doctors, Subtle or Most Subtle Doctors, Seraphic Doctors, Cherubic Doctors, Holy Doctors, and Incontrovertible Doctors. Then they let fly at the ignorant crowd their syllogisms, major and minor, conclusions, corollaries, idiotic hypotheses, and further scholastic rubbish. There remains a fifth act, in which an artist can really surpass himself. This is where they trot out some foolish popular anecdote, from the *Mirror of History*, I expect, or the *Deeds of the Romans* and proceed to interpret it ⟨allegorically, tropologically, and anagogically⟩. In this way they complete their chimaera, a monstrosity which even Horace never dreamt of when he wrote "Add to the human head" and so on.[121]

121. The phrase for what 'has never been known on earth or in heaven' comes from Lucian's *Alexander* which Erasmus had translated.

The great scholastics acquired honorific titles by which they were known to later generations. Thomas Aquinas was the 'doctor angelicus', Scotus the 'doctor subtilis', Bonaventure the 'Pater seraphicus', Ockham the 'doctor invincibilis'. 'Irrefragabilis' was used only of Alexander of Hales.

The famous *Mirror* of Vincent of Beauvais, like the *Gesta Romanorum*, is a popular thirteenth-century handbook printed in the late fifteenth century and often used as a source of *exempla*.

The middle ages classified commentaries on scripture into four categories of interpretation, so that each text could have a literal meaning, an allegorical meaning (drawing the religious lesson), a tropological (moral) meaning and an anagogical (mystical) meaning. The four-fold possibility of each text was summarized in the famous rhyme.

> *Littera gesta docet; quid credas allegoria;*
> *Moralis, quid agas; quid speres, anagogia.*

The *Enchiridion* contains several examples of the allegorical exegesis of the Old Testament.

But they've heard from someone that the opening words of a speech should be restrained and quietly spoken. As a result they start their introduction so softly they can scarcely hear their own voices – as if it really did any good to say what is intelligible to none. They've also heard that emotions should be stirred by frequent use of exclamations, so they speak in a low drone for a while and then suddenly lift their voices in a wild shout, though it's quite unnecessary. You'd swear the man needed a dose of hellebore, as if it didn't matter where you raise your voice. Moreover, as they've heard that a sermon should warm up as it goes along, they deliver the various sections of the beginning anyhow, and then suddenly let out their voices full blast, though the point may be of no importance, and finally end so abruptly that you might think them out of breath.

Last of all, they've learned that the writers on rhetoric mention laughter, and so they're at pains to scatter around a few jokes. O 'sweet Aphrodite', what polish and pertinence, a real case of 'the ass playing the lyre'! They sometimes try satire too, but it's so feeble that it's laughable, not wounding, and they never sound so servile as when they're anxious to give an 'impression of plain speaking'. In fact their entire performance might have been learned from the cheapjacks in the market squares, who are a long way their superiors, though the two types are so alike that they must have learned their rhetoric from each other.

Even so, thanks to me, they find people who'll listen to them and believe they hear a genuine Demosthenes or Cicero, especially among merchants and silly women, whose ears they are particularly anxious to please. For the merchants have a habit of doling out small shares of their ill-gotten gains if they're suitably flattered, and the friars find favour with women for many reasons, the main one being that a priest can provide a bosom

---

The reference to Horace alludes to the opening of the *Ars poetica*: 'Supposing a painter chose to put a human head on a horse's neck . . . could you help laughing?'

The words 'allegorically, tropologically, and anagogically' were added to the text in 1522.

where a woman can pour out her troubles whenever she quarrels with her husband.

Now I think you must see how deeply this section of mankind is in my debt, when their petty ceremonies and silly absurdities and the noise they make in the world enable them to tyrannize over their fellow men, each one a Paul or an Antony[122] in his own eyes. For my part, I'm only too glad to leave these hypocrites, who are as ungrateful in their attempts to conceal what they owe to me ⟨as they're unscrupulous⟩ in their disgraceful affectations of piety.

I've long been wanting to say something about kings and their courtiers, who cultivate me quite openly, with the candour one expects from those of gentle birth. Indeed, nothing would be so dismal and as much to be shunned as the life they lead if they had even a grain of good sense. No one would think power worth gaining, at the cost even of perjury or parricide, if he seriously considered the burden that has to be shouldered by the man who wants to exercise true sovereignty. Once he is at the helm of government he has to devote himself to public instead of his personal affairs, and must think only of the well-being of his people. He can't deviate by so much as a hair's breadth from the laws he has promulgated and set up himself, and he has to guarantee personally the integrity of every magistrate and official. Every eye is trained on him alone, and he can either be a beneficial star, should his character be blameless, and the greatest salvation to mankind, or a fatal comet leaving a trail of disaster in his wake. Other men's vices are neither so well-known nor so far-reaching in their effects, but a sovereign's position is such that if he falls short of honesty in the slightest degree, corruption spreads throughout his people like a plague. Then too, a sovereign's lot brings with it many seductions to lead him from the path of virtue, such as pleasures, independence, flattery, and luxury, so that he must strive the harder and be more keenly on the watch lest he prove to have failed in his duty even if he is only deceived. Finally, to say nothing of the plotting and enmity

---

122. On the 'ass with the lyre' see note 49, p. 40. The saints Antony and Paul referred to were both fourth-century hermits.

and all the other perils or fears which beset him, there stand over him that true King who before long will demand a reckoning of every one of his slightest transgressions, with severity proportionate to the degree of power he held. These are the considerations, I say, and many more like them, which would rob the prince of all his pleasure in sleep or food did he but reflect on them, as he would if he were wise.

But as it is, with my help, princes leave all these concerns in the lap of the gods. Their own concern is for a soft life, and so in order to keep their minds untouched by care they give audience only to men who know how to say what is pleasant to hear. They believe they properly fulfil all the duties of a prince if they devote themselves to hunting and keep a stable of fine horses, if they sell magistracies and commands at a profit to themselves, if they devise new methods every day for reducing the wealth of their subjects and sweeping it up into their own purse – but all under appropriate forms and suitably contrived pretexts, so that their practices preserve a façade of justice however iniquitous they are. They take care too to add a word of flattery with a view to putting popular sentiment under obligation to themselves. Picture the prince, such as some of them are today: a man ignorant of the law, well nigh an enemy to his people's advantage while intent on his personal convenience, a dedicated voluptuary, a hater of learning, freedom, and truth, without a thought for the interests of his country, and measuring everything in terms of his own profit and desires. Then give him a gold chain, symbol of the concord between all the virtues, a crown studded with precious stones to remind him that he must exceed all others in every heroic quality. Add a sceptre to symbolize justice and a wholly uncorrupted heart, and finally, the purple as an emblem of his overwhelming devotion to his people. If the prince were to compare these insignia with his way of life, I'm sure he would blush to be thus adorned, and fear that some satirist would turn all these trappings into a subject for mockery and derision.[123]

123. The political thought of Erasmus scarcely changed throughout his career and is conveniently summarized in the 1516 treatise *On the Education*

Now what shall I say about the courtiers? ⟨For the most part⟩ they're the most obsequious, servile, stupid, and worthless of creatures, and yet they're bent on appearing foremost in everything. There's only one matter in which they have no pretensions: they're quite happy to go around displaying the gold, jewels, purple, and all the other emblems of virtue and wisdom on their persons while leaving any interest in what these symbolize to others. They count themselves extremely fortunate to be permitted to call the king "Sire", to know how to address him in three words, to pile up courtesy titles like "Serene Highness", "your Lordship", "your Majesty", to shed all sense of shame and make themselves agreeable with flattery, for these are the skills becoming to nobleman and courtier. But if you look more closely into their whole pattern of life you'll find they're no better than Phaeacians or "Penelope's suitors" – you know the rest of the poem ⟨which Echo can quote for you better than I can⟩. They sleep till midday, when a wretched little hired priest waiting at their bedside runs quickly through the mass before they're hardly out of bed. Then they go to breakfast, which is scarcely over before there's a summons to lunch. After that follow dice, draughts, fortune-telling, clowns, fools, whores, idle games, and dirty jokes, interspersed with one or two snacks. Then comes dinner, followed by a round of drinks, or more than one, you

---

of a Christian Prince, written for the future Charles V. Its main characteristics are the insistent pursuit of peace in all circumstances, a consequent dislike of treaties and pacts, a preference for the arbitrated settlement of disputes, for a limited monarchy under a prince himself subject to the laws, and a state where social harmony is erected on economic prosperity and controlled by sumptuary laws. There is also a clear view of the dangers of hereditary succession.

Underneath Folly's depiction of the dangers faced by princes emerges a portrait of the ideal prince, subject to his own laws, devoted to the welfare of his people, intent on the suppression of corruption and mindful of his own salvation.

Deviating 'by a hair's breadth' from the norm is a proverb discussed in the *Adages*. The Latin for 'leave all these concerns in the lap of the gods' is taken from Horace (*Odes*, 1, 9, 9).

At the beginning of the next paragraph the qualification 'for the most part' was introduced in 1522.

may be sure. In this way, hours, days, months, years, and centuries are frittered away without a moment's boredom. For my part, whenever I see them 'giving themselves airs' I've generally had enough of it and make off; meanwhile each ⟨of the ladies⟩ thinks herself pretty well a goddess according to the length of the train she's trailing, and ⟨the noblemen⟩ elbow past each other to be seen standing close to Jove. Their self-satisfaction rests on the weight of the chain their necks have to carry, as if they have to show off their physical strength as well as their riches.[124]

Such practices of princes have long been zealously adopted by supreme pontiffs, cardinals, and bishops, and indeed, have almost been surpassed. Yet if any of these were to reflect on the meaning of his linen vestment, snow-white in colour to indicate a pure and spotless life; or of his two-horned mitre, both peaks held together by a single knot, signifying perfect knowledge of both Old and New Testaments; of his hands, protected by gloves, symbolic of purity, untainted by any contact with human affairs, for administering the sacrament; of his crozier, a reminder of his watchful care of the flock entrusted to his keeping, or the cross carried before him as a symbol of his victory over all human passions – if, I say, any of them were to reflect on these and many kindred matters, wouldn't his life be full of care and trouble? But as things are, they think they do well when they're looking after themselves, and responsibility for their sheep they either trust to Christ himself or delegate to their vicars and those they call brothers. They don't even remember that the name 'Bishop', which means 'overseer', indicates work, care, and concern. Yet when it comes to netting their revenues into the bag they can play the overseer well enough – no 'careless look-out' there.[125]

124. Flattery is of course a recurrent theme in Folly's declamation, as in Erasmus's works. The second chapter of the treatise *On the Education of a Christian Prince* is entitled 'The Avoidance of Flatterers'.

The Phaeacians (*Odyssey*, 6, 8), were noted for luxurious living. Penelope's suitors are dismissed as idle and luxurious layabouts by Horace in the poem Folly refers to (*Epistles*, 1, 2).

125. The phrase for 'careless look-out', in Greek in the text, combines an allusion to an Homeric usage (e.g. *Iliad*, 10, 515) with a pun on the literal sense of 'episkopos' or overseer.

Similarly, the cardinals might consider how they are the successors of the apostles and are expected to follow the example of their predecessors, and that they are not the lords but the stewards of the spiritual riches for every penny of which they will soon have to render an exact account. They could also reflect for a moment on their vestments and ask themselves these questions: what meaning has this whiteness of surplice for them if not total and supreme purity in life? And the purple beneath, if not a burning love for God? And again, this cloak on top, spreading out in capacious folds to envelop the entire mule of the most reverend father (and quite big enough to cover a camel) – doesn't it signify the boundless charity which should be at the service of every man, with instruction, exhortation, comfort, chastisement, or admonishment, settling wars and opposing evil princes, and freely spending not wealth alone but their very life-blood on behalf of Christ's flock? And what need have they of wealth at all if they take the place of the apostles who were poor men? If, as I say, they would ask themselves these questions, they would either renounce their ambitions for the office they hold and resign without further regrets, or else they would surely lead a life as arduous and anxious as that of the original apostles.

Then the supreme pontiffs, who are the vicars of Christ: if they made an attempt to imitate his life of poverty and toil, his teaching, cross, and contempt for life, and thought about their name of "pope", which means "father", or their title of "Supreme Holiness", what creatures on earth would be so cast down? Or who would want to spend all his resources on the purchase of their position, which once bought has to be protected by the sword, by poison, by violence of every kind? Think of all the advantages they would lose if they ever showed a sign of

Folly is of course right in pointing out that liturgical ceremonial and ecclesiastical protocol were developed under the influence of court proced-ures. Cardinals, in particular, grew from parish priests of the Roman titular churches, a status which still gives them the right to elect the bishop of Rome, into ecclesiastical princes, with privileges of jurisdiction and dress to match their new status.

In the *Enchiridion* and elsewhere, Erasmus frequently makes the point that ecclesiastical titles denote not power or status but function.

wisdom! Wisdom, did I say? Rather a grain of the salt Christ spoke of would suffice to rid them of all their wealth and honours, their sovereignty and triumphs, their many offices, dispensations, taxes, and indulgences, all their horses and mules, their retinue, and their countless pleasures. (You'll note how much trafficking and harvesting and what a vast sea of profiteering I've covered in a few words.) In place of all this it would bring vigils, fasts, tears, prayers, sermons, study, sighs, and a thousand unpleasant hardships of that kind. Nor must we overlook what this will lead to. Countless scribes, copyists, clerks, lawyers, advocates, secretaries, muleteers, grooms, bankers, and pimps (and I nearly added something rather more suggestive, but was afraid of being too blunt for your ears) – in short, an enormous crowd of people now a burden on the Roman see (I'm sorry, I meant 'now an honour to') would be left to starve. A monstrous abominable crime! And even more execrable, the supreme princes of the church, the true lights of the world, would be reduced to taking up scrip and staff.

But as things are today, any work that has to be done they can leave to Peter and Paul, who have plenty of time on their hands, while claiming all the pomp and pleasure for themselves. Consequently, and again, thanks to me, practically no class of man lives so comfortably with fewer cares; for they believe they do quite enough for Christ if they play their part as overseer by means of every kind of ritual, near-theatrical ceremonial and display, benedictions and anathemas, and all their titles of "your Beatitude", "Reverence", and "Holiness". For them it's out of date and outmoded to perform miracles; teaching the people is too like hard work, interpreting the Holy Scriptures is for schoolmen, and praying is waste of time; to shed tears is weak and womanish, to be needy is degrading; to suffer defeat is a disgrace and hardly fitting for one who scarcely permits the greatest of kings to kiss his sacred feet; and finally, death is an unattractive prospect, and dying on a cross would be an ignominious end.

All they have left are the weapons and fine-sounding benedictions to which Paul refers (and these they certainly scatter around with a lavish hand) along with interdicts, suspensions, repeated excommunications and anathemas, painted scenes of judgement, and that dreaded thunderbolt whereby at a mere nod they can dispatch the souls of mortal men to deepest Tartarus. This the holy fathers in Christ, who are in fact the vicars of Christ, launch against none so savagely as those who at the devil's prompting seek to nibble away and reduce the patrimony of Peter. Lands, cities, taxes, imposts, and sovereignties are all called Peter's patrimony, despite the words of the Gospel, "We have forsaken all and followed thee." Fired with zeal for Christ they will fight to preserve them with fire and sword, and Christian blood flows freely while they believe they are the defenders, in the manner of the apostles, of the church, the bride of Christ, through having boldly routed those whom they call her foes.[126] As if indeed the deadliest enemies of the church were not these impious pontiffs who allow Christ to be forgotten through their silence, fetter him with their mercenary laws, misrepresent him with their forced interpretations of his teaching, and slay him with their noxious way of life!

Moreover, since the Christian church was founded on blood, strengthened by blood, and increased in blood, they continue to manage its affairs by the sword as if Christ has perished and can no longer protect his own people in his own way. War is something so monstrous that it befits wild beasts rather than men, so crazy that the poets even imagine that it is let loose by Furies, so deadly that it sweeps like a plague through the world, so unjust that it is generally best carried on by the worst type of bandit, so impious that it is quite alien to Christ; and yet they leave everything to devote themselves to war alone. Here even

126. The 'grain of salt' Christ spoke of refers to Matthew v, 13.

The 'fine-sounding' benedictions to which St Paul refers are those of the spreaders of dissension and deceivers of guileless hearts who offer 'flattering talk' and 'pious greetings' (Romans xvi, 18).

The 'painted scenes of judgement' depicted the fate of the damned. Interdicts, suspensions and anathemas were, like excommunication, canonical penalties. Their efficacy however was in the order not of grace but of ecclesiastical organization, a point which neither Folly nor the middle ages as a whole properly appreciated.

The 'dreaded thunderbolt' is presumably either excommunication or perhaps the solemn curse.

The quotation 'we have forsaken all' comes from Matthew xix, 27.

decrepit old men can be seen showing the vigour of youths in their prime, undaunted by the cost, unwearied by hardship, not a whit deterred though they turn law, religion, peace, and all humanity completely upside down. And there's no lack of learned sycophants to put the name of zeal, piety, and valour to this manifest insanity, and to think up a means whereby it is possible for a man to draw a murderous sword and plunge it into his brother's vitals without loss of the supreme charity which in accordance with Christ's teaching every Christian owes his neighbour.[127] I still find it difficult to make up my mind whether certain German bishops have set an example or are following one, in the way in which they have abandoned pomp and benedictions and other such ceremonial matters and carry on as secular lords, even to the extent of believing that it is almost a mark of cowardice and unbecoming to a bishop to render up his warrior soul to God elsewhere than on the battlefield.

Then the rank and file of priests think it wrong to fall short of the standard of holiness set by their masters. They battle for ⟨their rights to⟩ a tithe with swords, spears, stones, and every force of arms in fine soldier style, while the sharp-eyed amongst them look to see if they can extract anything from the writings of the ancients with which to intimidate the wretched people into agreeing that more than a tithe is their due. It never occurs to them how much can be read everywhere about the duty they owe the people in return. Nor does the tonsure serve as any reminder to them that a priest should be free from all the desires of this world and have his thoughts fixed on heaven. On the contrary, these fine fellows insist that they've properly performed

127. The connexion between war and the Furies refers to the *Aeneid*, 7, 323. The reference to 'decrepit old men' alludes clearly to Julius II who was over 60 when he acceded to the papacy. For the next ten years he made war, even allying himself with the Turks, and revalued the depreciated silver coinage of the papacy, thereby considerably improving the papal income. Erasmus, who had had to get out of the way of the papal army, was witheringly contemptuous, as Folly's satirical portrait makes clear. The attribution to Erasmus of the Lucianic dialogue about Julius's attempt to enter heaven, the *Julius exclusus*, written in 1513, is no longer disputed. Lijster, who is perpetually apologizing for Erasmus's audacities, thinks him restrained on the subject of Julius II.

their duty if they reel off perfunctorily their feeble prayers, which I'd be greatly surprised if any god could hear or understand, seeing that they can scarcely do either themselves even when bawling them at the top of their voice.

But there's one thing priests have in common with laymen. When it comes to harvesting their gains they're all on the alert, every one of them an expert in the law. Yet if there's a burden to be borne they deliberately shift it on to another's shoulders, passing it on like a ball from hand to hand. Just as lay princes delegate some of their administrative duties to deputies who keep passing these on from one to another, they leave ⟨any⟩ concern for piety, doubtless in their modesty, to ordinary folk. These pass it on to those they call 'ecclesiastics', as if they themselves had no connection at all with the church and the vows taken at baptism meant nothing. Then the priests who call themselves 'secular' (as if they'd been consecrated to the world, not to Christ) push the burden on to the 'regulars', and they pass it on to the monks; the less strict monks shift it on to the stricter orders, and the whole lot of them leave it to the mendicants; and from there it goes to the Carthusians, amongst whom alone piety lies hidden and buried, hidden in fact so well that you can scarcely ever get a glimpse of it. In the same way, the pontiffs who are so occupied with their monetary harvests delegate all their more apostolic work to the bishops, the bishops to the heads of the churches, and these to their vicars; they in their turn push it on to the mendicant friars, who put it in the hands of those who will shear the sheep's wool.

But it's not my purpose here to go into details of the lives of pontiff or priest. I don't want to look as though I'm writing satire when I should be delivering a eulogy, nor anyone to think that in praising bad ⟨princes⟩' I mean to censure good ones. I touched briefly on these matters only to make it clear that no mortal can live happily unless he is initiated in my rites and is sure of my favours.[128]

For how could it be otherwise, seeing that the goddess of

128. Erasmus, always conscious of the abuse of hierarchical function as the source of power or wealth, held that ecclesiastical preferment demanded an increasing likeness to Christ. He used this argument in a lost essay on the

Rhamnus, Nemesis herself, who directs the fortunes of mankind, gets on so well with me that she has always shown herself the bitterest enemy of the wise, while bestowing every advantage on fools even in their sleep? You know about Timotheus, the meaning of the name given him, and the saying about 'The creel catches fish while the owner sleeps.' Then there's 'The owl is on the wing,' and references to 'being born on the fourth' and to having Sejanus' nag or the lost gold of Toulouse, which are clearly aimed at the wise. But enough of 'quoting proverbs'; I don't want you to imagine I've been plundering the notebooks of my friend Erasmus.[129]

To return to the point. Fortune favours the injudicious and the venturesome, people who like to say 'the die's cast'. But wisdom makes men weak and apprehensive, and consequently you'll generally find the wise associated with poverty, hunger, and the

---

war waged by Julius II. Towards the end of this paragraph 'princes' replaced 'pontiffs' in 1514.

'Seculars' differ from 'religious' (who need not be priests) in that, although obliged to celibacy, they do not take the three formal vows of poverty, chastity and obedience. The ancient orders, exempt from hierarchical jurisdiction, are responsible only through their own superiors to the pope. Not all religious or 'regulars' are monks. In the early sixteenth century all regulars were exempt from diocesan jurisdiction.

Folly implies that the mendicants, who include the Franciscans, pass for less worldly than the monks, who were at any rate probably richer. The Carthusians were the most severe, and the most contemplative of all the monastic orders. Thomas More seriously considered joining them. They are normally considered not to have been in need of reform, even at this date.

129. In the paragraph preceding this one, Folly, realizing she is not supposed to be writing satire makes play of the fact that she has been speaking with Erasmus's voice. Nemesis, who personifies avenging justice, presided over the punishment of pride and the avenging of injustice in the world. The various phrases in Greek in the original text come from a series of adages, with another allusion by Folly to the identity of her inventor.

Timotheus was an Athenian general of the fourth century BC whose denial that he owed his victories to Fortune brought swift retribution. His name means 'favoured by God'. The first two adages refer to man's inability to help himself and his need to rely on Fortune. 'Being born on the fourth (month)' like Hercules presaged labours and trials. 'Sejanus' nag' brought misfortune to its owners, while whoever touched the gold of Toulouse died in agony (Aulus Gellius, 3, 9, 6–7).

reek of smoke, living neglected, inglorious, and disliked. Fools, on the other hand, are rolling in money and are put in charge of affairs of state; they flourish, in short, in every way. For if a man finds his happiness in pleasing princes and spending his time amongst those gilded and bejewelled godlike creatures, he'll learn that wisdom is no use at all to him, and is indeed decried above all by people like this. If he wants to get rich, how much money can he make in business if he lets wisdom be his guide, if he recoils from perjury, blushes if he's caught telling a lie, and takes the slightest notice of those niggling scruples wise men have about thieving and usury? And then if anyone aspires to ecclesiastical wealth or preferment, a donkey or a buffalo would get there faster than a wise man. If you're after pleasure, then women (who play the biggest part in the comedy) are wholeheartedly for the fools, and flee in horror from a wise man as from a scorpion. Finally, all who look for a bit of gaiety and fun in life keep their doors firmly shut against the wise, more than anything – they'll open it to any other living creature first. In short, wherever you turn, to pontiff or prince, judge or official, friend or foe, high or low, you'll find nothing can be achieved without money; and as the wise man despises money, it takes good care to keep out of his way.[130]

For my own praises, on the other hand, there's neither measure nor limit. Even so, there has to be a limit sometime to a speech, and I shall come to an end, though first I must show you briefly that there are plenty of great authors who testify to me in their writings and behaviour alike. I don't want to be thought so foolish as to please only myself, or be wrongly accused by the lawyers of having no evidence to produce. So I'll take them as a model for what I cite – which will be 'nothing to the point'.

To start with, everyone accepts the truth of the well-known saying "Where fact is lacking, fiction is best", and so children are properly taught from the start the line "To play the fool in season is the height of wisdom". You can see now for yourselves what a great blessing Folly is when even her deceptive shadow and

130. The 'die is cast' is another proverb discussed in the *Adages*. The reference a few lines later to 'pleasing princes' alludes to Horace (*Epistles*, 1, 17, 35), who thinks there are greater titles to fame.

semblance win such high praise from learned men. Still more frankly does the plump, sleek porker from Epicurus' herd tell us to "Mix folly with counsel", though he's not so clever when he adds it should be "only for a while". Then he says "It is sweet to be silly in season", and again, elsewhere, he prefers "to seem artless and foolish than be wise and short-tempered". In Homer, too, Telemachus wins the poet's praise in every way, but is now and then called childish, and the dramatists apply the same epithet freely, like a good omen, to children and young people. And what is the subject of that divine poem the *Iliad* if not the passions of foolish kings and peoples? Moreover, Cicero's famous tribute is surely quite unqualified: "The world is full of fools!" For everyone knows that the more widespread a blessing, the more effective it is.[131]

However, it may be that these authorities carry little weight with Christians, so if you like we'll find further support for my praises in the evidence of the Holy Scriptures, or give them a proper foundation as the learned do. Let me begin first by asking permission from the theologians to make sure they give their approval. Then, since we're tackling such a difficult subject and possibly presuming too far in asking the Muses to come down again from Helicon, a long journey for them, especially for something which isn't really their concern, maybe while I'm playing the theologian and treading such a thorny path, I ought

131. Here ends the central section on Folly's followers. Folly now announces the final section of the declamation, devoted to the wise who have praised her and, in particular, to Pauline folly.

Since this Christian folly is praised without a trace of irony, the *Praise of Folly* ends with a remarkable feat of double irony as it transforms itself from a mock encomium into a real one.

The introductory paragraph to the final section is still bantering in tone, as in logic. The line about playing the fool in season comes from one of Cato's distichs, learned by heart by every grammar-school child in the middle ages. The 'sleek porker from Epicurus' herd' is an expression Horace uses of himself (*Epistles*, 1, 4, 16). His advice to mix folly with counsel is in *Odes*, 4, 12, 27–8. The other Horatian reference is to *Epistles*, 2, 2, 126.

Homer called Telemachus a silly child (*Odyssey*, 11, 449).

The quotation from Cicero comes from the letters (*To his friends*, 9, 22, 4).

to call on the spirit of Scotus (which is far thornier than any porcupine or hedgehog) to leave his precious Sorbonne and occupy my breast, but only for a while — it can soon return wherever it likes, 'to the devil' for all I care. I only wish I could change my face and don a theologian's garb![132] Still, if I had too many of the trappings of theology I'm afraid someone might take me for a thief and accuse me of secretly pillaging the desks of our masters. But it oughtn't to be so remarkable if I've acquired something from my long-standing association with the theologians, considering how close it has been. Even that figwood god Priapus listened to his master reading and remembered a few Greek words. And the cock in Lucian had no difficulty in understanding human speech simply from having lived with men so long.[133]

But now if the auspices are good, let's get back to our subject. Ecclesiastes wrote in his first chapter that "the number of fools is infinite", ⟨and in making the number infinite doesn't he appear to embrace all mankind, apart from a handful of individuals whom I doubt if anyone has ever met? Jeremiah is even more explicit in his chapter 10, when he says that "every man is made a fool by his own wisdom." To God alone he allowed wisdom, leaving folly to all mankind. A little earlier he says: 'Man should not glory in his own wisdom." Now why don't you want man to glory in his own wisdom, my dear Jeremiah? The answer's simple: because man has no wisdom.⟩ But to return to Ecclesiastes. When he cries Vanity of vanities, all is vanity,- what else do you suppose he means except what I've said, that the life of man is nothing but a sport of folly? And thereby he casts his vote for Cicero's tribute: ⟨in which the

132. Folly is about to embark on the serious panegyric of Pauline folly. The reference to her apparel is a last mock disclaimer that what she says is intended seriously.

133. Folly has already once invoked the Muses from Helicon, remembering the *Aeneid* (7, 641). The Sorbonne was the seat of the Paris faculty of theology, not especially Scotist in its views but reactionary and sharing with Scotist theology the presuppositions about the extrinsic nature of human perfection which Erasmus most disliked.

The reference to Priapus recalls Horace (*Satires*, 1, 8, 1).

words I quoted above are rightly celebrated:⟩ "The world is full of fools." Again, when the great sage ⟨Ecclesiasticus⟩ said "The fool changes as the moon, but the wise man is steadfast like the sun," what he was suggesting was surely that the entire mortal race is foolish and the epithet of wise applies to God alone. By moon they understand human nature, by the sun the source of all light, that is, God. This is confirmed by what Christ himself says in the Gospel, that no one is to be called good save one, that is, God. Then if whoever is good is wise, as the stoics say, and anyone who is not wise is a fool, it must follow that all men are fools. Again, Solomon says in Proverbs chapter 15 "Folly is joy to the fool" which is clearly an admission that nothing in life is enjoyable without folly. There is a similar reference in the text "He who increases knowledge increases sorrow, and in much understanding is much grievance." ⟨Surely too the famous preacher has openly expressed the same idea in his chapter 7: "The heart of the wise is the home of sadness, and the heart of the foolish is the home of joy." That is why he thought that full knowledge of wisdom was still incomplete without understanding of me as well. If you doubt me, here are his own words, which he wrote in chapter 1: "And I gave my heart to know wisdom and learning, and also madness and folly." Note that when Ecclesiastes wrote this he named folly last, and intended it as a tribute, for this, as you know, is the order followed by the church, where the person who comes first in status takes the last place, in this point at least in accordance with the evangelist's teaching.

Indeed, Ecclesiasticus, whoever he was, makes it quite clear in his chapter 44 that folly is better than wisdom, though I'm not going to quote his words until you'll help with the 'development of the argument' with suitable replies, like those who join in discussions with Socrates do in the dialogues of Plato. Now, which is it better to hide away, things which are rare and valuable or those which are common and cheap? Have you nothing to say? Even if you pretend ignorance, there's a Greek proverb to answer for you – 'the water-pot is left lying on the doorstep' – and in case anyone doesn't accept that with proper respect, let me tell you it's quoted by

Aristotle, the god of our teachers. Are any of you so foolish as to leave gold and jewels lying in the road? I'm sure you're not. You hide them away in the innermost room of your house, you do more, you secrete them in the furthest corners of your best-locked chest. It's the mud that you leave lying in the street. So if what is precious is hidden, and what is worthless is left exposed to view, isn't it obvious that the wisdom which Ecclesiasticus forbids to be hidden is worth less than the folly he orders to be kept concealed? Hear the evidence of his own words: "Better is a man who hides his folly than a man who hides his wisdom."

Consider too how the Holy Scriptures attribute honesty of mind also to the fool, while the wise man believes that no one is his equal. For this is how I interpret what Ecclesiastes wrote in chapter 10. "But a fool walking along the road, since he is foolish, thinks all men are fools." Now don't you think it indicative of exceptional honesty to think every man your equal, and in a world given to self-aggrandizement to share your merits with all?⟩ And so the great king was not ashamed of being named like this when he said in chapter 30, "I am the most foolish of men." Nor was Paul, the great teacher of the heathen, reluctant ⟨in his Epistle to the Corinthians⟩ to accept the name of fool. "I speak as a fool, I am more," he said, just as if it were a disgrace to be outdone in folly.[134]

⟨But at this point I hear an outcry from certain Greek pedants who are bent on pecking crows' eyes, or rather, catching out the many theologians of today by blinding them with the smoke-screen of their own commentaries. The second place in this flock, if not the actual leadership, certainly belongs to my

134. Erasmus quotes scripture from memory and is frequently inaccurate. The long catena of scriptural quotations begins in these three paragraphs with the following: Ecclesiastes i, 17; Jeremiah x, 14; x, 7; Jeremiah ix, 23; Ecclesiastes i, 2; Ecclesiasticus xxvii, 12; Matthew xix, 17; Proverbs xv, 21; Ecclesiastes i, 18; Ecclesiastes vii, 4; Ecclesiastes i, 17. The reference to Ecclesiasticus xliv is wrong. It should be xli, 18. Ecclesiasticus xx, 33; Ecclesiastes x, 3; Proverbs xxx, 2; 2 Corinthians xi, 23. There follows at this point another reference to Erasmus by Folly.

The reference to Aristotle is to the *Rhetoric* I, 6, 23. The proverb is discussed in the *Adages*.

friend Erasmus, whom I mention by name from time to time by way of a compliment. What a foolish thing to quote, they cry, just what you'd expect from Folly! The Apostle's meaning is quite different from what you imagine. He didn't intend by these words that he should be thought more foolish than anyone else, but when he said "They are ministers of Christ; so am I," as if he had made a boast of putting himself on a level with the others in this, he went on to correct himself by adding "I am more," aware that he was not only the equal of the other apostles in his ministry for the Gospel but to a large extent their superior. He wanted this to carry conviction without his words sounding arrogant and offensive, so he made folly his pretext to forestall objections, writing "I speak as a fool" because it is the privilege of fools to speak the truth without giving offence.

But what Paul had in mind when he wrote this, I leave to the pedants to dispute. For my part I follow the large, fat, stupid, and popularly most highly thought of theologians with whom the majority of scholars would rather be in the wrong, 'by Zeus,' than hold a correct view along with your experts in three tongues. Not one of these thinks of your Greek pedants as more than jackdaws, especially since a certain renowned theologian (renowned perhaps in his own eyes?) whose name I have the sense to suppress, lest some of our jackdaws are quick off the mark with the Greek taunt of the 'ass playing the lyre', has expounded this passage in masterly theological style. Starting from the words "I speak as a fool, I am more" he opens a new chapter such as could only be possible by calling on the full forces of dialectic, and makes a new subdivision, with the following interpretation (I'll quote his argument exactly, his actual words as well as their substance): "I speak as a fool, that is, if I seem to you a fool in making myself the equal of false apostles, I shall seem even more of a fool in your eyes by setting myself above them." However, a little later he appears to forget himself and slips into a different interpretation.[135]

135. The experts in the three tongues (Latin, Greek and Hebrew) were the humanists who insisted that a knowledge of the ancient tongues was the

But I don't know why I bother to defend myself with a single example, seeing that it's the generally accepted privilege of theologians to stretch the heavens, that is, the Scriptures, like tanners with a hide. According to St Paul, there are words which can do battle for Holy Scripture, though in their context they don't do so, if we are to trust Jerome, that 'master of five tongues'. Paul once happened to see an inscription on an altar in Athens and twisted its meaning into an argument for the Christian faith. He left out all the words which would have damaged his case and selected only the last two, *ignoto deo* "to the unknown god". Even in this he made some alteration, since the complete inscription read "to the gods of Asia, Europe, and Africa, the unknown and foreign gods". His, I believe, is the precedent our present-day 'sons of theology' follow when they pick out four or five words from different contexts, and if necessary even distort their meaning to suit their purpose, though those which come before and after may be either totally irrelevant or actually contradictory. This they do with such carefree impudence that theologians are often the envy of the legal experts.[136]

---

indispensable tool for theological studies in furtherance of an evangelically based religion. Trilingual foundations were made notably at Cologne, Louvain and Alcala, while the ideal that inspired them also inspired foundations elsewhere, as at Oxford. François I put out feelers to Erasmus with a view to his making such a foundation in France, but nothing came of the project until the institution of the royal lectureships from 1530 onwards.

The theologian referred to and barely disguised in the reference to the ass and the lyre was Nicholas of Lyra who died in 1349. It was said in the sixteenth century, that if Lyra had not played his lyre, Luther would not have danced (*Si Lyra non lyrasset, Luther non saltasset*). He wrote a series of *Postillae Litterales* on the Old and New Testaments, carefully distinguishing between literal and mystical senses of the text. They were immensely influential and were the first commentary on the Bible to be printed (1471–2). Folly is of course making clear in her reference to Erasmus and trilingual pedantry that she is conferring only an ironic compliment on Nicholas of Lyra by embracing his view.

136. The incident of St Paul and the inscription at Athens is recounted in Acts xvii, 23. What Folly says is narrated by Jerome in his commentary. Jerome's 'five tongues' were Greek, Latin, Hebrew, Chaldean and Dalmatian.

They can go to any lengths now that the great – I nearly blurted out his name but that Greek saying stopped me again – has extracted a meaning from some words of Luke which is as compatible with the spirit of Christ as fire with water. For as the hour of the supreme peril approached, a time when loyal servants would rally round their master and 'fight his fight' with all the resources they could muster, Christ's intention was to remove from the hearts of his disciples any reliance on defences of this kind, and so he asked them whether they had lacked anything when he had sent them out so unprovided, with neither shoes to protect their feet against injury from thorns and stones nor purse as a guard against hunger. When they replied that they had lacked nothing, he went on: "But now, he who has a bag, let him take it, and likewise a purse; and he who has no sword must sell his coat and buy one." Since the whole of Christ's teaching is directed towards instilling gentleness, patience, and contempt of life, the meaning of this passage should be clear to all. Christ wanted to disarm his emissaries still further, so that they would not only spurn shoes and purse but also cast off their coats in order to set out on their mission of the Gospel naked and unencumbered, providing themselves with nothing but a sword – not the sword which serves robbers and murderers, but the sword of the spirit which penetrates into the innermost depths of the bosom and cuts out every passion with a single stroke, so that nothing remains in the heart but piety.

Now, pray, see how our renowned theologian distorts this. He interprets the sword as a defence against persecution, the bag as an adequate supply of provisions, just as if Christ had reversed his beliefs and recanted his former teaching when his emissaries appeared to be setting out insufficiently equipped 'in royal style.' Or he seems to have forgotten that he said they would be blessed when afflicted with insults, revilement, and persecution, and forbade them to resist evil since only the meek are blessed, not the pugnacious; forgotten that he had called on them to consider the example of the sparrows and the lilies, so that he is now so reluctant to see them go out without a sword that he even bids them sell their coat to buy one, preferring them to go naked rather than unarmed. Moreover, just as anything which serves to repel violence comes under the head of "sword", "pouch" covers any of the necessities of life. And so this interpreter of the divine mind fits out the apostles with spears, crossbows, slings, and catapults, and leads them forth to preach the crucified. He also loads them up with coffers and trunks and packs – as if they'll always have to move on from an inn on an empty stomach. He isn't even disturbed by the fact that though Christ once ordered a sword to be bought, he soon afterwards sharply ordered one to be sheathed; nor has anyone heard it said that the apostles used swords and shields against attack from the heathen, which they would have done had Christ intended what our interpreter says he did.[137]

There's another of them, whom with due respect I won't name, though his reputation stands high, who has taken Habakkuk's words about tents ("The hides of the land of Midian shall be taken") to refer to the flayed skin of Bartholomew. And I was recently present myself (as I often am) at a theological debate where someone asked what authority there was in the Scriptures for ordering heretics to be burnt instead of refuted in argument. A grim old man, whose arrogance made it clear he was a theologian, answered in some irritation that the apostle Paul had laid down this rule saying, 'A man who is a heretic, after the first and second admonition, reject [devita],' and he went on thundering out this quotation again and again while most of those present wondered what had happened to the man. At last he explained that the heretic was to be removed from life [de vita]. Some laughed, though there were plenty of others who found this fabrication sound theology; but when several expressed their disagreement, our 'lawyer from Tenedos', as they say, our irrefutable authority continued thus: 'Pay attention. It is written that thou shalt not

137. The text of Luke whose interpretation Folly accuses Nicholas of Lyra of distorting is xxii, 35–6.

The texts about swords to which Folly refers are presumably Matthew xxvi, 52 and John xviii, 11, but nowhere does Christ order a sword to be bought.

*Turn?
PO?*

let the evildoer [*maleficus*] live. Every heretic is an evildoer;
therefore,' etc. The entire audience marvelled at the man's
reasoning power and came over to his way of thinking,
hotfoot. It occurred to no one that this law applied only to
sorcerers, wizards, and magicians, whom the Hebrews call
mekaschephim in their own tongue, a word we translate as
malefici. Otherwise the death penalty would have to be applied
to fornicators and drunkards.[138]

But it's foolish of me to continue with these examples so
numberless that the volumes of Chrysippus and Didymus
could never hold them all. I only wanted to remind you of the
licence granted those saintly scholars, so that you would show
me the same indulgence as a 'blockhead theologian' if my
quotations aren't always quite accurate. Now let me get back
to Paul.⟩ "You suffer fools gladly", he says, speaking of himself.
⟨And again, "Receive me as a fool," and "I do not speak according
to God but as if I were foolish," and elsewhere too he says,
"We are fools for Christ's sake." This is high tribute to folly
from a great authority.⟩ Moreover, he is an open advocate of
folly ⟨as a prime necessity and a great benefit⟩. "Whoever
among you thinks himself wise must become a fool to be truly
wise." ⟨And according to Luke, Jesus addressed the two disciples
whom he joined on the road to Emmaus as fools.⟩ Should we
be surprised at this, seeing that that ⟨godlike⟩ Paul attributes

---

138. The second theologian appears to be the hermit of St Augustine,
Jordan of Quedlinburg (sometimes called Jordan of Saxony, but not to be
confused with the Dominican general of that name), a mystical writer and
preacher who died in 1380 or 1370. The reference to Habakkuk is iii, 7.
There are different traditions about the death of St Bartholomew, who may
have been beheaded. St Paul's use of *devita* is from the letter to Titus (iii, 10)
and the reference to the *maleficus* is in Deuteronomy xiii, 5, (where the Latin
term is '*fictor somniorum*'). The Greek word for *devita* means in fact 'avoid'.
In his translation of the New Testament, Erasmus says 'flee'.

There was in fact technically no death penalty for heresy as such, since
heresy is an ecclesiastical crime. Heretics were delivered to the secular power
and put to death normally for 'blasphemy'. The effect was the same, and the
Church was quite capable of forcing the secular power to do its will by the
application of spiritual sanctions. The 'man from Tenedos' is discussed in the
Adages.

some folly even to God? "God's foolishness", he says, "is wiser than men." Origen subsequently objected in his commentary that we cannot really explain this folly by reference to the views held by men, as we can in the passage "The doctrine of the cross is folly to those that are perishing."[139]

⟨But there is no need to worry about producing all this evidence to prove my point when Christ openly says to his Father in the sacred Psalms 'Thou knowest my foolishness.'⟩ It is also significant that fools have always given great pleasure to God, and this, I fancy, is the reason. Great princes eye men who are too clever with hostility and suspicion, as Julius Caesar did Brutus and Cassius, though he had no fear of drunken Antony, and as Nero did Seneca and Dionysius did Plato, though they delighted in men of duller and simpler wits. In the same way, Christ always loathes and condemns those 'wiseacres' who put their trust in their own intelligence; as Paul bears witness in no uncertain words when he says "God has chosen the foolish things of the world," and again "God chose to save the world through folly," since it could not be redeemed by wisdom. God himself makes this clear enough when he proclaims through the mouth of the prophet "I will destroy the wisdom of the wise and reject the intelligence of the intelligent." So does Christ, when he gives thanks because the mystery of salvation had been hidden from the wise but revealed to little children, that is, to fools. ⟨⟨The

139. Chrysippus is said to have written more than seven hundred works. Didymus, the Greek contemporary of Augustus, is said to have written 3,500 or 4,000, of which none has survived.

The texts of St Paul referred to in this paragraph are 2 Corinthians xi, 19; xi, 17 and 1 Corinthians iv, 10; iii, 18; i, 25; i, 18.

The reference to Luke is to xxiv, 25.

Origen, the third-century Greek Father whose understanding of Christian dogma within a neoplatonist framework later caused his work to be condemned, was a very important figure for the evangelical humanists. Pico della Mirandola had defended him (in a thesis which in turn was condemned), and the early sixteenth century saw a real attempt to replace the authority of the anti-Pelagian Augustine with that of a rehabilitated Origen, whose doctrine clearly harmonized more easily with the humanist determination to understand Christian perfection in terms of moral fulfilment. Erasmus was notably favourable to Origen.

Greek word for a child, νήπιος means "foolish", and is the opposite of σοφός "wise"). ⟩ There are also some relevant passages in the Gospel where Christ attacks Pharisees and scribes and teachers of the Law while giving his unfailing protection to the ignorant multitude. ⟨What else can "Woe unto you, Scribes and Pharisees" mean but "Woe unto you who are wise"?⟩[140] But Christ seems to have taken special delight in little children, women, and fishermen, while the dumb animals who gave him the greatest pleasure were those furthest removed from cleverness and cunning. So he preferred to ride a donkey, though had he chosen he could safely have been mounted on a lion; and the Holy Spirit descended in the form of a dove, ⟨not of an eagle or a hawk,⟩ while throughout the Scriptures there is frequent mention of harts, young mules, and lambs. Moreover, he calls those who are destined for eternal life his sheep, though there is no animal so stupid: witness the proverbial expression in Aristotle, 'sheeplike character', which he tells us is derived from the slow-wittedness of the animal and is commonly used as a taunt against dull and stupid men. Yet Christ declares himself the shepherd of this flock, and even takes pleasure himself in the name of Lamb, as when John reveals him in the words 'Behold the Lamb of God.' The same expression often appears in the Apocalypse.[141]

All this surely points to the same thing: that all mortals are fools, even the pious. Christ too, though he is the wisdom of the

140. See psalm lxviii, 6 (R.S.V. lxix, 5)
Caesar's fear of Brutus and Cassius who were pale and thin is reported by Plutarch (*Life of Caesar*, 62), as is his failure to fear the sleek Antony. Shakespeare draws on the same passage of Plutarch in *Julius Caesar*, I, ii, 194–5,

> Yond Cassius has a lean and hungry look,
> He thinks too much: such men are dangerous.

Tacitus says that Nero distrusted his former tutor Seneca (*Annals*, 15, 62 ff.). The tyrant Dionysius of Syracuse sent Plato away in disgrace.

The scripture quotations in this section are 1 Corinthians i, 27 and 21, Isaiah xxix, 14 (but Folly confuses this text with 1 Corinthians i, 19) and Matthew xxiii, 13–15 and 23–7.

141. The ass is mentioned in Matthew xxi, 2 and the dove in Matthew iii, 16. The parable of the good shepherd is in John x. Aristotle's proverb is discussed in the *Adages*. The expression 'the Lamb of God' appears in John i, 29 and 36 and throughout the Apocalypse (Revelation).

Father, was made something of a fool himself in order to help ⟨the folly of mankind⟩ when he assumed the nature of man and was seen in man's form, just as he was made sin so that he could redeem sinners. Nor did he wish them to be redeemed in any other way save by the folly of the cross and through his simple, ignorant apostles, to whom he unfailingly preached folly. He taught them to shun wisdom, and made his appeal through the example of children, lilies, mustard-seed, and humble sparrows, all foolish, senseless things, which live their lives by natural instinct alone, free from care or purpose. And then when he forbade his disciples to worry about how they should answer the charges of the governors and told them not to seek to know times and seasons, it was surely because he wanted them not to rely on their own intelligence but be wholly dependent on him. This also explains why God the creator of the world forbade man to eat of the tree of knowledge, as if knowledge was poisonous to happiness. So Paul openly condemns knowledge for building up conceit and doing harm, and I believe St Bernard had him in mind when he interpreted the mountain on which Lucifer set up his seat as the mount of knowledge.

⟨Then perhaps we shouldn't overlook the argument that Folly finds favour in heaven because she alone is granted forgiveness of sins, whereas the wise man receives no pardon. So when men pray for forgiveness, though they may have sinned in full awareness, they make folly their excuse and defence. If I remember rightly, that is how Aaron in the Book of Numbers intercedes against the punishment of his sister: "I beseech you, master, do not charge us with this sin, which we committed foolishly." Saul uses the same words in praying David to forgive his fault: "For it is clear that I acted foolishly." And again, David himself tries to placate the Lord by saying." "I beseech thee, O Lord, take away the iniquity of thy servant, for I have acted foolishly," as if he could only win forgiveness by pleading folly and ignorance. Still more forceful is the argument that when Christ prayed on the cross for his enemies, "Father, forgive them", he made no other excuses for them but their ignorance: "For they know not what they do." Paul writes to Timothy in the same vein, "But I was granted God's mercy because I acted ignorantly, in unbelief." What else is acting ignorantly but acting foolishly, with no evil intent? And when Paul speaks of being granted mercy, he clearly implies that he would not have been granted it had he not had folly to plead in his defence. The sacred psalmist, whom I forgot to quote in his proper place, also speaks for us all when he says, "Remember not the sins of my youth and my ignorances," and you will have marked that his two excuses are youth, which finds in me a constant companion, and ignorances which are numbered as plural so that we may appreciate the full power of folly.⟩[142]

142. The remarkable animation of this passage in its plea for learned or spiritual ignorance derives from the tradition of unlettered piety which Erasmus absorbed from the *devotio moderna* and the Brethren of the Common Life, and which it was his personal achievement to integrate with Christian humanism.

In this final section of the *Praise of Folly* Erasmus takes advantage of the ironic form to put his ideal with total seriousness into the sort of paradoxes in which the evangelists recount the moral teaching of Christ. However, what Folly says here does not exclude the need for learning, required to justify this reading of the Christian message, which Erasmus thought should itself be instantly accessible to everyone.

The references here are to: 1 Corinthians i, 18 and 24 (Christ's folly the wisdom of God); Philippians ii, 7 (assuming the form of man); 2 Corinthians v, 21 (made sin); 1 Corinthians i, 21 (the folly of the Cross).

Children are mentioned for instance in Matthew xviii, 3; lilies for instance in Matthew vi, 28; mustard seed in Matthew xiii, 31; sparrows in Matthew x, 29; governors in Matthew x, 18; times and seasons in Acts i, 7; the tree of knowledge in Genesis ii, 17. St Paul's association of knowledge with conceit is in 1 Corinthians viii, 1. St Bernard's identification of Lucifer's sin with a desire for knowledge is in his commentary on Isaiah xiv, 12. The reference to Numbers is to xii, 11, to Saul 1 Samuel xxvi, 21 and to David 2 Samuel xxiv, 10. Christ's prayer for those who crucified him is in Luke xxiii, 34, and the reference to Timothy comes from 1 Timothy i, 13. The Psalm quoted is xxiv, 7 (Vulgate; R.S.V. xxv, 7).

Not all these quotations bear the weight which Folly puts on them. In particular it is difficult to read Genesis as condemning knowledge. But Erasmus deliberately attaches Folly to a tradition of exegesis with which the Brethren of the Common Life had made him familiar. The wisdom Folly goes on to attack is conventional and worldly rather than spiritual, but she does renew Christ's insistence that his wisdom is folly to the world.

To sum up (or I shall be pursuing the infinite), it is quite clear that the Christian religion has a kind of kinship with folly ⟨in some form⟩, though it has none at all with wisdom. If you want proofs of this, first consider the fact that the very young and the very old, women and simpletons are the people who take the greatest delight in sacred and holy things, and are therefore always found nearest the altars, led there doubtless solely by their natural instinct. Secondly, you can see how the first founders of the faith were great lovers of simplicity and bitter enemies of learning. Finally, the biggest fools of all appear to be those who have once been wholly possessed by zeal for Christian piety. They squander their possessions, ignore insults, submit to being cheated, make no distinction between friends and enemies, shun pleasure, sustain themselves on fasting, vigils, tears, toil, and humiliations, scorn life, and desire only death – in short, they seem to be dead to any normal feelings, as if their spirit dwelt elsewhere than in their body. What else can that be but madness? And so we should not be surprised if the apostles were thought to be drunk on new wine, and Festus judged Paul to be mad.[143]

But now that I have donned the 'lion skin', let me tell you another thing. The happiness which Christians seek with so many labours is nothing other than a certain kind of madness and folly. Don't be put off by the words, but consider the reality. In the first place, Christians come very near to agreeing with the Platonists that the soul is stifled and bound down by the fetters of the body, which by its gross matter prevents the soul from being able to contemplate and enjoy things as they truly are. Next, Plato defines philosophy as a preparation for death because it leads the mind from visible and bodily things, just as death does. And so as long as the mind makes proper use of the organs of the body it is called sane and healthy, but once it begins to break its bonds and tries to win freedom, as if it were planning an escape from prison, men call it insane. If this happens

143. The qualification 'in some form' was added in 1523. The apostles were thought to be drunk in Acts ii, 13 and Festus' reaction to St Paul is in Acts, xxvi, 24. 'Donning the lionskin' means undertaking a great task and is a proverb discussed in the *Adages*.

through disease or some organic defect, by general consent it is called insanity. Even so, we see this type of person foretelling the future, showing a knowledge of languages and literature they had never previously learned, and giving clear indication of something divine. Undoubtedly this happens because the mind is beginning to free itself from contamination by the body and exercise its true natural power. I think this also explains why those who are struggling at the hour of death often have a somewhat similar experience, so that they speak wonders as if inspired.

Again, if this happens through pious fervour, it may not be quite the same kind of insanity, but is so like it that most people make no distinction, especially as the number of folk who differ in their whole way of life from the general run of mankind is very small. And so we have a situation which I think is not unlike the one in the myth in Plato, where those who were chained in a cave marvelled at shadows, whereas the man who had escaped and then returned to the cavern told them that he had seen real things, and they were much mistaken in their belief that nothing existed but their wretched shadows. This man who has gained understanding pities his companions and deplores their insanity, which confines them to such an illusion, but they in their turn laugh at him as if he were crazy and turn him out. In the same way, the common herd of men feels admiration only for the things of the body and believes that these alone exist, whereas the pious scorn whatever concerns the body and are wholly uplifted towards the contemplation of invisible things. The ordinary man gives first place to wealth, the second to bodily comforts, and leaves the last to the soul – which anyway most people believe doesn't exist because it is invisible to the eye. By contrast, the pious direct their entire endeavour towards God, who is absolute purity, and after him towards what is closest to him, the soul. They have no thought for the body, despise wealth and avoid it like trash, and if they are obliged to deal with such matters they do so with reluctance and distaste, having as if they did not have, possessing as if they did not possess.[144]

144. Folly makes it clear that neoplatonist, and especially Plotinian, systems can serve as a substructure to explain and understand the Christian

There are moreover in each of these things widely differing degrees. To begin with, though all the senses have some kinship with the body, some of them are grosser, such as touch, hearing, sight, smell, and taste, while other faculties are less physical, for instance, memory, intellect, and will. The power of the soul depends on its inclinations. Since, then, all the power of the pious soul is directed towards what is furthest removed from the grosser senses, these become blunted and benumbed. The vulgar crowd of course does the opposite, develops them very much and more spiritual faculties very little. That explains what we have heard happened to several saints, who drank oil by mistake for wine.

Again, take the affections of the soul. Some have more traffic with the grossness of the body, such as lust, desire for food and sleep, anger, pride, and envy, and on these the pious wage unceasing war, while the crowd thinks life impossible without them. Then there are what we could call intermediate affections, which are quasi-natural to all, like love for one's ⟨country⟩, and affection for children, parents, and friends. The crowd sets great store by these, yet the pious strive to root them too from their soul, or at least to sublimate them to the highest region of the soul. They wish to love their father not as a father, for he begot nothing but the body, and this too is owed to God the Father, but as a good man and one in whom is reflected the image of the supreme mind, which alone they call the *summum bonum* and beyond which they declare nothing is to be loved or sought.[145]

---

revelation. Folly's Platonism remains notable however for the reference to prophetic insanity, one of the four sorts of divine *furor* discussed by Ficino in his commentary on Plato's *Symposium* which stimulate the process by which the soul is reunified and, progressively weaned from dependence on matter, reunited to God. The idea that philosophy is a preparation for death is also discussed by Cicero, the source from whom Montaigne took the title of his famous essay *Que philosopher, c'est apprendre à mourir*. Erasmus in the *Enchiridion* takes it from Socrates in the *Phaedo*.

The phrase 'possessing as if they did not possess' is a reminiscence of St Paul, 1 Corinthians vii, 29-30.

145. It is recounted of St Bernard that, meditating on scripture, he drank oil without noticing that it was not water.

Folly is presenting a modified neoplatonist psychological system, drawing on Origen's commentary on St Paul and the seventh chapter of the

This is the rule whereby they regulate all the remainder of life's duties, so that anything visible, if it is not wholly to be despised, is still valued far less than what cannot be seen. They also say that even in the sacraments and the actual observances of their religion, both body and spirit are involved. For example, they think little of fasting if it means no more than abstaining from meat and a meal – which for the common man is the essential of a fast. It must at the same time reduce the passions, permitting less anger or pride than usual, so that the spirit can feel less burdened by the matter of the body and can aim at tasting and enjoying the blessings of heaven. It is the same with the Eucharist: the ritual with which it is celebrated should not be rejected, they say, but in itself it serves no useful purpose or can be positively harmful if it lacks the spiritual element represented by those visible symbols. It represents the death of Christ, which men must express through the mastery and extinction of their bodily passions, laying them in the tomb, as it were, in order to rise again to a new life wherein they can be united with him and with each other. This then is how the pious man acts, and this is his purpose. The crowd, on the other hand, thinks the sacrifice of

---

Enchiridion in which Erasmus expounds Origen's view. The ascription of passions to the body rather than the soul is Plotinian, although it became common in the neo-stoic moralists of the Renaissance. In Christian authors it normally leads to a trichotomist psychological system, based on 1 Thessalonians v, 23, and distinguishes body, soul and spirit. For Folly, as for Pico della Mirandola, the soul can determine itself either to achieve spiritual and angelic status or to remain immersed in the material world.

Folly carefully distinguishes the passions, belonging to the senses in which the 'vulgar crowd' is enmeshed, from the higher affections, however hesitant she may remain about these. They are 'intermediate', 'quasi'-natural, capable of being transferred to the highest point of the soul. The uncertainty is transferred from the *Enchiridion*, where some of the affections come near to being virtuous. Erasmus, far too empirically minded to systematize his teaching, does in fact move towards a greater sympathy with these 'intermediary' affections. The identification of the *summum bonum* with the divine mind is expressed in terms reminiscent of Ficino's commentary on the *Symposium*.

Erasmus changed 'love for one's father' to 'love for one's country' in 1532.

the mass means no more than crowding as close as possible to the altars, hearing the sound of the words, and watching other small details of such ritual.

I quote this only as one example; in fact the ⟨pious man⟩ throughout his whole life withdraws from the things of the body and is drawn towards what is eternal, invisible, and spiritual. Consequently, there is total disagreement between the two parties on every point, and each thinks the other mad; though in my view, the epithet is more properly applied to the pious, not the common man. This will be clearer if I do as I promised, and show briefly how the supreme reward for man is no other than a kind of madness.[146]

First consider how Plato imagined something of this sort when he wrote that the madness of lovers is the highest form of happiness. For anyone who loves intensely lives not in himself but in the object of his love, and the further he can move out of himself into his love, the happier he is. Now, when the soul is planning to leave the body and ceases to make proper use of its organs, it is thought to be mad, and doubtless with good reason. This, surely, is what is meant by the popular expressions "he is beside himself", "he has come to", and "he is himself again". Moreover, the more perfect the love, the greater the madness — and the happier. What, then, will life in

146. Folly, having drawn almost unguardedly on the Plotinian tradition, is now at pains to modify the neoplatonist paradigm by insisting on the positive, if still relatively slight, value of the material world, especially with regard to the sacraments.

Elsewhere, Erasmus is caustic about such 'works' as fasting. Here, however, Folly points out the purposes of the ascetic practices elaborated in earlier centuries, which was to discipline the passions. It is possible that the human nervous system has become more complex since the early middle ages, and the pain threshold lower. Folly, at any rate, does not use absolutes but prefers to talk in terms of more and less. She insists only on not allowing the ritual, material element in religious practice to submerge the spiritual content.

The Christian death with Christ crucified and rebirth with Christ in glory are here interpreted, as by the neoplatonist Fathers, in terms of the conquest of passion, promoting a greater hegemony of spirit over senses and hence, on neoplatonist presuppositions, a greater likeness to God. See note 22, p. 20.

heaven be like, to which all pious minds so eagerly aspire? The spirit will be the stronger, and will conquer and absorb the body, and this it will do the more easily partly because it is, as it were, in its own kingdom, partly for having previously in life purged and weakened the body in preparation for this transformation. Then the spirit will itself be absorbed by the supreme Mind, which is more powerful than its infinite parts. And so when the whole man will be outside himself, and happy for no reason except that he is so outside himself, he will enjoy some ineffable share in the supreme good which draws everything into itself.

Although this perfect happiness can only be experienced when the soul has recovered its former body and been granted immortality, since the life of the pious is no more than a contemplation and foreshadowing of that other life, at times they are able to feel some foretaste and savour of the reward to come. It is only the tiniest drop in comparison with the fount of eternal bliss, yet it far exceeds all pleasures of the body, even if all mortal delights were rolled into one, so much does the spiritual surpass the physical, the invisible the visible. This is surely what the prophet promises: "Eye has not seen nor ear heard, nor have there entered into the heart of man the things which God has prepared for those that love him." And this is the part of Folly which is not taken away by the transformation of life but is made perfect. So those who are granted a foretaste of this – and very few have the good fortune – experience something which is very like madness. They speak incoherently and unnaturally, utter sound without sense, and their faces suddenly change expression. One moment they are excited, the next depressed, they weep and laugh and sigh by turns; in fact they truly are quite beside themselves. Then when they come to, they say they don't know where they have been, in the body or outside it, awake or asleep. They cannot remember what they have heard or seen or said or done, except in a mist, like a dream. All they know is that they were happiest when they were out of their senses in this way, and they lament their return to reason, for all they want is to be mad for ever with this kind of madness. And this is only the merest taste of the happiness to come.[147]

But I've long been forgetting who I am, and I've 'overshot the mark'. If anything I've said seems rather impudent or garrulous, you must remember it's Folly and a woman who's been speaking. At the same time, don't forget the Greek proverb 'Often a foolish man speaks a word in season', though of course you may think this doesn't apply to women.

I can see you're all waiting for a peroration, but it's silly of you to suppose I can remember what I've said when I've been spouting such a hotchpotch of words. There's an old saying, 'I hate a fellow-drinker with a memory', and here's a new one to put alongside it: 'I hate an audience which won't forget.'

And so I'll say goodbye. Clap your hands, live well, and drink, distinguished initiates of FOLLY.[148]

The End

147. Plato speaks of the madness of lovers in the *Phaedrus* (245b). Love was another of the four Platonist *furores* which stimulated the soul's ascent to beatitude. The idea of living in the object of one's love is Platonist too although also a commonplace of Christian tradition. The promise starting 'eye has not seen' comes from 1 Corinthians ii, 9. The reference to the 'good part' of Folly (*Moriae*) is a deliberate allusion to the 'best part' of Mary (*Mariae*) which Christ said should not be taken from her in spite of Martha's plea (Luke x, 42). The folly being praised by Folly has become religious fulfilment and, as such, totally serious. The last paragraph derives from St Paul's account of his own ecstasy at the beginning of 2 Corinthians xii.

148. The last paragraph begins with a quotation from Lucian's *The Dream or the Cock*. The ironic mask is resumed and Folly remembers she is a garrulous woman, even if she can speak 'a word in season' (a proverb discussed in the *Adages*). A last adage is mentioned about a fellow-drinker with a memory. The final reference to drink recalls the earlier serious Bacchus before, in Holbein's wood-cuts, Folly finally leaves her pulpit. 'Clap your hands' is the conventional Ending to a Roman comedy. 'The End' is in Greek.

LETTER TO

MAARTEN VAN DORP

1515

ERASMUS OF ROTTERDAM
TO THE DISTINGUISHED THEOLOGIAN
MAARTEN VAN DORP[1]

I haven't had your letter, but a friend in Antwerp showed me a copy. I don't know how he came by this. I see you think that the publication of *Folly* was unfortunate, warmly approve of my painstaking restoration of the text of Jerome, and are against my bringing out an edition of the New Testament. You are far from offending me by this letter of yours, my dear Dorp, indeed you are now much dearer to me, dear though you always were before, such is the candour of your advice, the friendliness of your admonitions and the affectionate tone of your criticism. Christian charity has the gift of retaining its natural sweetness even when it is most severe. I receive many letters daily from learned men which hail me as the glory of Germany, as the sun or the moon, and pile on such splendid titles by way of a compliment, and I really find this rather overwhelming. I swear on my life that not one of them has given me so much pleasure as that censorious letter from my friend Dorp. As Paul rightly says, charity is never at fault. If she praises, she wishes to do good, if she takes offence her intention is the same, and I only

---

1. On Maarten van Dorp and the circumstances of Erasmus's letter, see the third section of the Introduction, pp. xxxvii–liii, Erasmus, having just returned from England, was on his way to Strasbourg and Basle. This letter was first printed by Froben at Basle in August 1515 with three other important letters. All four were considerably expanded versions of what had actually been sent. However, even if we do not know the length of the original letter, Erasmus's references to sickness and fatigue have a touch of the conventional disclaimer about them.

The letter to Dorp, written at Antwerp in 1514, has regularly been printed as an appendix to the *Folly*, from 1516. Like *Folly*, it underwent a series of additions and corrections during Erasmus's lifetime.

The letter from Dorp was printed with this reply in October 1515 at Antwerp. Both were printed together from June 1524 in most important editions of the *Folly*, as Erasmus calls it.

wish I could answer your letter at my leisure and acquit myself properly to such a friend. I am very anxious for your approval in all I do, for I think so highly of your almost god-like ability, your exceptional learning and your outstandingly perceptive judgement, that I would rather have a single vote from Dorp in my favour than a thousand from elsewhere. At the moment I'm still feeling rather sick from the channel crossing and tired from being on horseback, and I also have a lot to do sorting out my bits of baggage, but I thought it better to send a reply of sorts than to leave a friend thinking as you do – whether you formed your opinion unaided or it was put into your head by others who prevailed on you to write your letter so that they could masquerade under another name.[2]

First of all, then, to be frank, I almost regret myself that I published *Folly*. That little book has brought me fame, or reputation, if you prefer. But I've no use for fame combined with odium, and heaven knows, what is popularly called fame is nothing but an empty name and a legacy from paganism. Several expressions of this kind linger on amongst Christians, who give the name of immortality to the reputation one leaves to posterity, and virtue to a taste for the arts of any kind. My sole aim in publishing all my books has always been to do something useful by my industry, and if I can't achieve that, at least to do no harm. There are plenty of examples of men (even great ones) who abuse their learning to serve their passions, one singing his foolish loves, another using flattery to win favour, a third hitting back with his pen when provoked by insult, a fourth blowing his own trumpet and outdoing Thraso or Pyrgopolynices in singing his own praises. Now my own talent is slender and my education scanty, but at least I've always aimed at doing good, if I could, or anyway at hurting no one. Homer worked off his hatred for Thersites by drawing a cruel picture of him in the *Iliad*. Plato censured a lot of people by name in his dialogues, and whom did Aristotle spare, when he had no mercy for Plato and Socrates? Demosthenes could vent his fury on

2. The reference to St Paul in this paragraph alludes to 1 Corinthians xiii, 4–8 but is inexact.

Aeschines, Cicero on Piso, Vatinius, Sallust and Antony, and many names mentioned by Seneca are the victims of his ridicule and scorn. To turn to more recent examples, Petrarch similarly took up his pen against a doctor, Lorenzo against Poggio, and Politian against Scala. Can you name me a single person whose self-restraint is sufficient to stop him writing a harsh word against anyone? Even Jerome, serious and pious as he was, sometimes couldn't prevent himself from flaring up against Vigilantius, or from excessive abuse of Jovinian and bitter attacks on Rufinus. The learned have always been in the habit of committing their joys and sorrows to paper, as a faithful companion into whose bosom they can pour out all the turbulence of the heart. Indeed, there are people to be found whose sole purpose in starting to write a book is to find an outlet for their emotions and thus transmit these to posterity.[3]

3. Thraso is the boasting soldier of Terence's *Eunuch* who hopes to attract his girl by vaunting his prowess. Pyrgopolynices was the name of Plautus' boastful soldier. Homer's attack on Thersites is in the *Iliad* (2, 215 ff.). Aristotle's disrespect for Plato and Socrates rests only on calumny and conjecture. Aeschines was an orator of the fourth century BC accused by Demosthenes of accepting bribes. Lucius Calpurnius Piso, consul and governor of Macedonia, was accused by Cicero of peculation and maladministration in 55 BC. The other victims of Cicero mentioned are Vatinius, with whom Cicero was reconciled after a political dispute, Sallust, who opposed him at Milo's trial for murder in 52 BC and Antony, against whom Cicero wrote the *Philippics* in 44 BC. About 1355 Petrarch wrote his invective *Against a Doctor* to defend himself against attack. Lorenzo Valla carried on a sustained battle with his fellow-humanist Poggio in the fifteenth century. Politian's dispute on Latin usage with the Florentine Chancellor Bartolomeo Scala took place in the late fifteenth century.

Vigilantius' late-fourth-century attack on the cult of martyrs' relics and miracles is today known only through Jerome's attacks on him. St Jerome also attacked Jovinian for denying the value of celibacy and Rufinus for defending Origen after Jerome had come to regard him as heretical.

In his letter, now signed with his own name, Erasmus preserves echoes of Folly's voice. The abjuration of the pursuit of fame as pagan and the denunciation of Christians who confuse immortality with posthumous reputation and a taste for the arts suggest that Erasmus, while no doubt sincere, is concerned that the image he is projecting should in some degree accord with the paradoxes of the final pages of the satire. Deprecatory remarks about his education and talent fit into the same mould but the burden of his apologia

But in my case, in all the many volumes I have published to date, in which I have praised so many in all sincerity, can you tell me anyone whose reputation I have damaged or besmirched in the slightest? What nation, class of person or individual have I ever censured by name? Yet you little know, my dear Dorp, how often I have been on the point of doing so under provocation from insults which no one should be expected to endure. However, I have always controlled my resentment and thought more of how posterity would judge me than of what the wickedness of my detractors deserved. If the true facts had been known to others as they were to me, no one would have judged me a too sharply censorious, but rather a just, restrained and reasonable man. Then I wonder why others concern themselves with my personal sentiments, or how any criticism of mine can have any influence on other countries or future times. I shall have done what was right for me, not them. Moreover, I've no enemy whom I wouldn't prefer to make my friend, if I could. Why should I bar the way to this, or write against an enemy what I might afterwards regret too late having written against a friend? Why should my pen blacken a character whose purity I could never restore even if it were deserved? I would rather err on the side of praising the undeserving than castigating where blame is due. Unmerited praise passes for ingenuousness on the part of the giver, but if you paint in his true colours someone whose conduct calls for nothing but censure, this is attributed to your own sick judgement and not to his deserts. I'll say nothing here of how a serious war can sometimes break out as a result of injuries leading to reprisals and how a dangerous fire is often sparked off by insults bandied to and fro, but if it is unchristian to repay injury with injury, so equally is it undignified to work off resentment by exchange of abuse in the way women do.

It was arguments like these which convinced me that I should

---

is clear: he uses his learning in the interests of good, and he does not attack individuals by name, as Dorp had attacked him. Even Julius II is not named in the *Folly*. The list of classical and modern precedents for personal attacks fills a prefatory function here analogous to the list of mock encomia in the letter-preface to More.

keep my writings free from malice and cruelty, unspoilt by naming wrongdoers. My aim in *Folly* was exactly the same as in my other works. Only the presentation was different. In the *Enchiridion* I simply outlined the pattern of Christian life. In my little book *The Education of the Prince* I offered plain advice on how to instruct a prince. In my Panegyric I did the same under the veil of eulogy as I had done elsewhere explicitly. And in *Folly* I expressed the same ideas as those in the *Enchiridion*, but in the form of a joke. I wanted to advise, not to rebuke, to do good, not injury, to work for, not against, the interests of men. The philosopher Plato, serious-minded though he is, approves of fairly lavish drinking-matches at banquets because he believes that there are certain faults which austerity cannot correct but the gaiety of wine-drinking can dispel. And Horace thinks that joking advice does as much good as serious. 'What stops a man who can laugh,' he says, 'from speaking the truth?' This was surely well understood by the famous sages of antiquity who chose to present the most salutary counsel for life in the form of amusing and apparently childish fables, because truth can seem harsh if unadorned, but with something pleasurable to recommend it can penetrate more easily the minds of mortals. No doubt this is the honey which doctors in Lucretius smear on the rim of a cup of wormwood which they prescribe for children. And the sort of fools which princes of former times introduced into their courts were there for the express purpose of exposing and thereby correcting certain minor faults through their frank speech which offended no one. It would perhaps seem inappropriate to add Christ to this list, but if divine matters are at all comparable with human, his parables have surely some affinity with the fables of the ancients. The truth of the gospel slips more pleasantly into the mind and takes firmer grip there if it is attractively clothed than it would if it were presented undisguised, something which St Augustine amply confirms in his work *On Christian Doctrine*. I saw how ordinary men were corrupted by opinions of the most foolish kind in every walk of life. I longed to find a remedy more than I hoped for success. And then I believed I had found a means whereby I could somehow insinuate myself into these over-indulged souls and cure them by giving them pleasure. I had often observed how a gay and amusing form of advice like this had happy results in many cases.[4]

If you answer that the character I assumed is too frivolous to provide a mouthpiece for a discussion on serious matters, I am ready to admit that I may be at fault. It's the charge of excessive severity I protest against, not that of being foolish, though I could defend myself well against this too, if only by quoting the example of the many serious men whom I listed in the short preface to the book itself. What else could I do? I was on my way back from Italy, staying as a guest in the house of my friend More, where an attack of kidney trouble kept me several days indoors. My books hadn't yet arrived, and even if they had, my illness prevented concentrated application to serious studies. With nothing to do, I began to amuse myself with a eulogy of folly,

4. On the *Enchiridion* and *The Education of the Prince*, see the Introduction (pp. xi–liii) and note 123 p.105. The reference to Plato and drinking-matches alludes to the *Symposium*. The line from Horace is quoted from the *Satires* (1, 1, 24–5) and the reference to Lucretius alludes to the *de rerum natura*, 1, 935 ff.

Erasmus's defence of his *Folly* contains some special pleading. He is trying to win Dorp's support in the controversy which the publication of the Greek New Testament is bound to raise. In claiming that he is reasonable and sweet-tempered, that he has been misjudged and that the *Folly* does not go beyond the *Enchiridion*, Erasmus is admitting to less than the whole truth. In quoting Plato, Horace and Lucretius, he is protecting himself behind a little Folly-like banter.

Dorp's letter explained Augustine's advice (in the *de doctrina christiana*) to have recourse to the Greek sources by the absence at that date of any officially received Latin text of scripture. Since Augustine's day the Greek text, too, had probably become corrupt. Dorp was worried about what Erasmus's Greek text, with its revelations of the Vulgate's inadequacies, would do to the authority of scripture and, by later calling Augustine a 'dialectician', he showed that he wished to use his authority in an anti-humanist sense.

Erasmus, however, knew that Augustine also taught in the *de doctrina christiana* both the necessity of consulting Hebrew and Greek texts and the necessity of grammatical correction. He therefore here unnecessarily mentions the *de doctrina christiana*, as if announcing his intention of making Dorp's weapon boomerang on him. In his reply, Dorp juggles with quotations to try to turn Jerome's authority against Erasmus.

The idea that truth requires to be wrapped in fable if it is to be understood by the simple is neoplatonist. It is exploited later in the century by Dorat and Ronsard.

with no idea of publication but simply as a distraction from the pain of my complaint. Once started, I let some close friends have a look at what I'd done, so as to add to my amusement by sharing the joke. They were delighted, and urged me to continue. I did as they asked, and spent a week, more or less, on the job: too long, I'm sure, for such a lightweight subject. Then the friends who had persuaded me to write undertook to take the book to France, and there it was printed, though from a faulty and mutilated copy. Proof of its popularity, or lack of it, is the fact that within a few months it was reprinted seven times, in several places. I was amazed myself at the way people liked it. If you call this being foolish, my dear Dorp, I can only plead guilty or at least offer no defence. I played the fool when I had nothing to do and my friends persuaded me, and it's the first time in my life I've done so. Who is wise all the time? You admit yourself that all my other works have been the kind to win warm approval from pious and learned men everywhere. Who are your stern censors or rather, Areopagites who won't forgive a man a single lapse into foolishness? They must be remarkably captious if they are so offended by a single humorous book that they immediately despoil a writer of the credit won from so many previous long hours of serious work. I could produce many fooleries from other sources which are far more foolish than this one, even from the great theologians who think up tedious subjects to provoke argument and then do battle among themselves for these futile futilities as if for hearth and home. Moreover, they play out these ridiculous farces which are far sillier than the Atellan without masks, whereas I show much more modesty. When I wanted to play the fool, I assumed the character of Folly, and just as in Plato Socrates masks his face in order to sing the praises of love, I too have played my comedy in character.[5]

You say that even the people who dislike the subject admire my intelligence, learning and eloquence, but are offended by my

5. On the mixture of truth and falsehood in Erasmus's account of the circumstances of the *Folly*'s composition, see the Introduction (pp. xliv-xlv). Erasmus always attributed his trouble with kidney stone to the wine he had had to drink while staying at Venice with Aldus in 1507-8. The Areopagites were members of the Areopagus, the Athenian political council which was

outspoken severity. Your critics pay me higher compliments than I want. I've no use for praise like this, especially coming from those in whom I find neither intelligence, learning nor eloquence — if they were better endowed in these respects, believe me, my dear Dorp, they wouldn't be so put out by jokes which aim at doing good rather than giving a display of learning and wit. In the Muses' name, I beg you to tell me what sort of eyes and ears and taste these people have if they are offended by severity in that book. In the first place, what severity can there be when no name is singled out for attack except my own? They might have remembered what Jerome is always saying, that a discussion of faults which is general injures no individual. But if anyone does take offence, he has nothing to complain about to the author — he can claim redress for his wrongs from himself, if he likes, for he's his own betrayer in seeing a personal attack in words which were addressed to everyone and so to no one in particular, unless someone wants to claim them for himself. You must have noticed that all the way through I was so careful not to mention any names of persons that I was even unwilling to criticize any nation too sharply, for in the passage where I review the forms of self-love which are special to each country, I assign military glory to the Spaniards, culture and eloquence to the Italians, good looks and fine food to the English, and so on, all things which anyone can recognize in himself without displeasure or indeed can hear about with a smile. And then when I am going through all the types of men, in accordance with the plan I set myself for my theme, and noting the faults peculiar to each, do I ever let fall a word which is venomous or unpleasant to hear? Where do I uncover a cesspool of vice or stir up the secret Camarina of human life? We all know how much could be said against evil pontiffs, wicked bishops and priests and vicious princes, against any class of society, in fact, if, like Juvenal, I had not been ashamed to commit to paper what many are not ashamed to do. All I have done is to recount what is comic and

---

also a bench of judges, later proverbial for its severity. Atella was the town from which the improvised, masked and often licentious 'Atellan' farces took their name. The reference to Plato alludes to the beginning of the *Phaedrus*.

absurd in man, not the unpleasant, but in such a way that in passing I often touch on serious things and give advice which it is important for people to hear.[6]

I know you haven't time to descend to trifles like this, but if you ever have a spare moment, do try to look more carefully at those absurd jokes of Folly's. I'm sure you'll find them much more in accordance with the views of the evangelists and apostles than the dissertations of certain persons are, however splendid they think them and however worthy of the great masters. You admit yourself in your letter that most of what I wrote is true. But you believe it does no good to 'wound the delicate ear with sharp-edged truth'. If you think that one should never speak freely and that truth should only be told when it gives no offence, why do doctors prescribe bitter drugs and count hier-apicra amongst their most valuable remedies? If those who cure the ills of the body use these methods, surely we should do the same when we would heal the diseases of the soul. Make your appeal, says Paul, argue and reprove, in season and out of season. If the apostle wants faults to be attacked in every possible way, do you really want no sore spot to be touched, even when this is done so gently that no one could possibly be hurt unless he deliberately sets out to hurt himself? Now, if there is any way of mending men's faults without offence to anyone, by far the easiest way is to publish no names. Next best is to restrain oneself from mentioning things which are repugnant to the ears of decent men, for just as some incidents in a tragedy are too horrible to be presented to the eyes of the audience and are better only reported, men have certain traits of character which are too obscene to be related with decency. Finally, put everything into the mouth of a comic character so that it will amuse and divert, and the humour of the spoken word will remove any offensive-ness. We have all seen how an appropriate and well-timed joke can sometimes influence even grim tyrants. What pleas or serious speech do you think could have calmed the rage of the great king Pyrrhus as easily as the joke the soldier made? 'Why, if only our bottle hadn't given out,' he said, 'we'd have said far worse things

6. Folly deals with national characteristics on pp. 68–9. On the mud of Camarina, see note 106, p. 86.

about you.' The king laughed and pardoned him. And the two greatest orators, Cicero and Quintilian, had every reason for laying down rules for raising a laugh. Speech which has wit and charm has such power to please that we can enjoy a well-turned phrase even if it is aimed at ourselves, as history relates of Julius Caesar.[7]

Now, if you admit that what I've written is true, is enjoyable, and is not obscene, what better means can be devised for mending the common ills of men? In the first place, pleasure is what catches a reader's attention and holds it when caught. In other respects no two readers look for the same thing, but pleasure wins over all alike, unless someone is too stupid to be sensitive to the pleasures of the written word. And then those who can be offended by a book where no names are mentioned seem to me to react in much the same way as those silly women who get worked up whenever anything is said against a loose-living woman as if it were a personal insult to them all, and conversely, if a word of praise is spoken about virtuous women they are as pleased with themselves as if a tribute paid to one or another applies to the whole sex. Men should be far removed from silliness of this kind, learned men further still, and theologians furthest of all! If I come upon a charge of which I am innocent, I don't take offence, I congratulate myself on having escaped the evils to which I see many fall victim. But if something is touched on and I see myself mirrored there, that's no reason either for taking offence. If I'm wise I'll hide my feelings and not give myself away. If I'm honest I'll take warning and make sure that I'm not subsequently confronted by name with a reproach which I saw levelled there in general terms. Can't we at least allow my little book what even the ignorant crowd permits popular comedies? How many taunts are freely thrown out there against monarchs, priests, monks, wives, husbands – against anyone in

7. The quotation about wounding the delicate ear with sharp-edged truth comes from Persius (*Satires*, 1, 107). 'Hierapicra' is a wonder-working but bitter drug. The reference to St Paul alludes to 2 Timothy iv, 2. The anecdote concerning Pyrrhus is narrated by Plutarch in his *Life* of Pyrrhus. Cicero discusses humour towards the end of the second book of the *de Oratore* and Quintilian in the *Institutio oratoria* (6, 3). Julius Caesar's willingness to forgive is remarked on by Suetonius in his *Lives of the Caesars*.

fact? Yet because no one is attacked by name everyone laughs, and either frankly admits or wisely conceals any weakness of his own. The most violent tyrants put up with their clowns and fools, though these often made them the butt of open insults. The emperor Vespasian didn't retaliate when someone said his face looked as if he were excreting. Then who are these ultra-sensitive people who can't bear to hear Folly herself joking about the common life of men with no personal reproach? The Old Comedy would never have been hissed off the stage if it had refrained from publishing abroad the names of well-known men.

But you, my dear Dorp, write as if my little book of Folly had set the entire body of theologians against me. 'Why ever did you have to attack theologians so bitterly?' you ask, and you deplore the fate which awaits me. 'Hitherto everyone was all eagerness to read your works and longed to meet you in person. Now Folly, like Davos, has upset everything.'[8] I know you write this with the best intentions, and I'll give you a straight answer. Do you really think that the whole theological order is disturbed if anything is said against foolish or bad theologians who don't deserve the name? If that were the prevailing law, no one could say a word against criminal men without making the entire human race his enemy. Has any king had the presumption to deny that there have been several bad kings who were unworthy of their position? Or any bishop been too arrogant to admit the same about his own order? Are the theologians the only order to have amongst their large numbers no one who is stupid, ignorant or quarrelsome? Do we find they are all Pauls, Basils or Jeromes? On the contrary, the more eminent a profession, the fewer people in it can answer to the name. You'll find more good skippers than good princes, more good doctors than good bishops. That is no reproach to an order, but rather a tribute to the few who have conducted themselves nobly in the noblest of orders. So please tell me why should the theologians take more offence, if they really are offended, than kings, nobles, or magistrates, than bishops, cardinals and supreme pontiffs? Or

8. The description of Vespasian's face derives from Suetonius' *Lives of the Caesars*. Davos is the slave of Horace who told him during the Saturnalia what he felt to be the truth about him (*Satires*, 2, 7).

than tradesmen, husbands, wives, lovers and poets, for Folly doesn't omit any type of mortal, unless they are so stupid as to apply to themselves any general criticism of bad men?

St Jerome addressed his book *On Virginity* to Julia Eustochium, and in it depicted the character of bad virgins so clearly that a second Apelles couldn't set it so vividly before our eyes. Did Julia take offence? Was she angry with Jerome for disparaging the order of virgins? Not a bit. And why not? Because a sensible virgin would never assume that criticism of her bad sisters was directed at herself. She would in fact welcome such an admonition, whereby the good could take warning against letting themselves deteriorate, and the bad could learn how to change their ways. Jerome wrote *On the Life of Clerics* for Nepotian, and *On the Life of Monks* for Rusticus. He painted a colourful picture of both orders, with some extremely shrewd criticism of their faults. Neither of the two he addressed took offence, for they knew none of it applied to them. Why doesn't William Mountjoy, by no means the lowest of the nobility at court, break off our friendship because of Folly's numerous jokes about courtiers? Because he is as eminently sensible as he is virtuous, and quite rightly thinks that criticism of nobles who are bad and stupid has nothing to do with him. How many jokes does Folly make at the expense of bad and worldly bishops? And why is the Archbishop of Canterbury not offended? Because he is a man who is an absolute model of all the virtues and concludes that none of them is aimed at himself.[9]

But I needn't go on naming sovereign princes and all the other bishops, abbots, cardinals, and distinguished scholars, not one of whom so far has shown the slightest sign of estrangement because of *Folly*. And I simply can't believe that any theologians

9. Julia Eustochium took a vow of virginity at the age of eighteen in AD 383, the date of St Jerome's treatise for her. She later directed a convent at Bethlehem. Apelles was the celebrated Greek painter mentioned by Folly (p. 72). Nepotian was a young officer of the imperial guard who became a monk. Jerome wrote to him in 394 at his request and, on his early death of fever, he wrote a consolatory letter to his uncle. Rusticus was a monk who corresponded with Jerome from Gaul.

Erasmus is quite aware that Folly included among her followers more

are annoyed by this book, unless there are a few of them who fail to understand it or are envious or so grudging by nature that nothing meets with their approval. There are some individuals amongst them, as is well known, who start off with such wretched ability and judgement that they're unsuited for any form of study, and least of all theology. Then when they've learned up a few rules of grammar from Alexander of Villedieu and dabbled in some sort of sophistic nonsense, they go on to memorize without understanding them ten propositions of Aristotle and the same number of topics from Scotus and Ockham. Anything else they hope to get out of the *Catholicon*, the *Mammetrectus*, and other dictionaries of the same sort which will serve them as a Horn of Plenty.[10] But now just look how high they carry their heads! Nothing is so arrogant as ignorance. These are the persons who despise St Jerome as no more than a grammarian, for they fail to understand him. They pour scorn on Greek and Hebrew, even on Latin, and though they're as stupid as pigs and totally lacking in common sense, they imagine they occupy the citadel of all wisdom. They all censure, condemn and pass sentence; they've no doubts nor hesitations, and there's nothing

---

than that proportion of theologians corresponding to the proportion of criminals in the human race and more than 'several' kings. He now justifies himself by arguing that the higher the rank, the fewer to be found to fill it worthily, so ironically twisting the theologians' tails again.

He now goes on tellingly to name the people who have not taken offence. In his letters of the winter 1517–18, when he can add Leo X to the list, he will make more of this argument. For William, Lord Mountjoy, see the Introduction (pp. xl, xli, xliv). The Archbishop of Canterbury was Erasmus's patron, William Warham.

10. Alexander of Villedieu's thirteenth-century grammar or *Doctrinale* in rhymed hexameters was a much-used medieval textbook printed a hundred times before 1500. At the end of his treatise on education *de pueris . . . instituendis* (1529), Erasmus is not far from paying it a compliment, perhaps because he must have known it at Deventer. The *Catholicon* of the thirteenth-century Dominican John Balbi of Genoa was a Biblical encyclopaedia printed as early as 1460 and called *Summa grammaticalis valde notabilis, quae Catholicon nominatur*. The *Mammetrectus* was a glossary on the Bible, the lives of the saints and other devotional writings, compiled by one Marchesinus of Reggio of very uncertain date. It was printed in 1470.

they don't know. Yet these two or three individuals often create considerable disturbances, for there's nothing so shameless or so obstinate as their ignorance. It is they who are bent on conspiring against good learning. They aspire to be something in the senate of theologians, and they are afraid that if good learning is reborn and the world given new life, they will be shown up as knowing nothing though hitherto they were generally believed to know all. Theirs is the outcry and opposition, theirs the combined attack on men who devote themselves to good learning. They are the ones who dislike *Folly*, because they understand neither Greek nor Latin. If a harsh word is spoken against these bogus theologians who are only putting on an act, what has that to do with the true theologians, an order of genuine distinction? For if it is their pious fervour which makes them upset, why is their anger specially directed against *Folly*? How much impiety, indecency and invective is there in Poggio's writings? Yet he is cherished everywhere as a Christian author and translated into nearly every language. Doesn't Pontano attack the clergy with insult and abuse? But he is read for his elegance and wit. How much obscenity is there in Juvenal? But people think he provides a useful lesson even in the pulpit. Tacitus wrote insultingly and Suetonius with hostility against Christians: Pliny and Lucian both scorned the idea of the immortality of the soul; yet they are read by everyone for their learning, and rightly so. It is only Folly who is unacceptable, simply because she amused herself with witticisms not at the expense of true theologians who are worthy of their name, but against the trivial disputes of the ignorant and the absurd title of Our Master.[11]

11. Gian Francesco Poggio Bracciolini (1380–1459), whose invective against Lorenzo Valla Erasmus has already been referred to (see note 3, p. 139), spent his life as a layman in the service of the Roman Curia and unearthed unknown manuscripts of many important ancient authors. He was devoted to classical studies but, like many of the humanists, also wrote works of history. His collection of largely indecent satirical material known as the *Facetiae* and aimed particularly at monks and priests was widely translated by 1500.

Giovanni Pontano (1429–1503) was the Latinist president of the Naples academy which later bore his name. His voluminous writings included a

Two or three of these charlatans, tricked out in theological fashion, are trying to stir up resentment against me on the grounds that I have injured and alienated the order of theologians. For my part, I value theological learning so highly that I give the name of learning to nothing else. I admire and revere the whole order so much that I am enrolled as a member of it alone, and wish for nothing more, though modesty forbids me to assume such a distinguished title. I know the standards of learning and life which the name of theologian requires. There is something in the profession of theology which is beyond human capacity. It is an honour which belongs to bishops, not to people like me. For me it's enough to have learned the Socratic maxim that we know nothing at all, and to apply my efforts to helping others with their studies as far as I can. And I really don't know where to look for those two or three godlike theologians who you say have so little sympathy with me. I've stayed in several places since the publication of *Folly*, lived in many universities and many large towns. I have never found any theologian angry with me, apart from one or two of the sort who are hostile to any liberal studies, and even these have never uttered a word of protest in my hearing. What they say behind my back doesn't worry me much, especially as I have the opinion of so many good men to support me. If I weren't afraid this would look more like personal pride than sincerity, my dear Dorp, I could quote you numbers of theologians, all renowned for the sanctity of their lives, outstanding in their learning and pre-eminent in rank, several of them bishops, who have never shown me greater friendliness than since the publication of *Folly*, and take more pleasure in that little book than I do myself. I could cite them all

---

series of lively Lucianic dialogues. Dorp's reply to Erasmus particularly objected to his invocation of Poggio and Pontano as models.

Erasmus goes on to allude to Juvenal's well-known obscenities, to the anti-Christian passages of Tacitus (*Annales*, 15, 44) and Suetonius (*Life of Nero*), to Pliny's materialism and to Lucian's flippant treatment of religious beliefs.

The absurd title of 'Magister Noster' refers to p. 95 of *Folly*. The first of Ulrich von Hutten's *Letters of Obscure Men* (1515) makes considerable play of it.

with their names and titles at this point if I didn't fear that your three theologians would extend their hostility on Folly's account even to men as great as these. One of those responsible for this unhappy situation is with you now, I think, though I'm only guessing, and if I cared to paint him in his true colours no one would be surprised that Folly displeases him.[12] Indeed, if she didn't, she wouldn't please me. Of course she doesn't really please me, but she's certainly less displeasing for not pleasing minds like his. I set more store by the opinion of theologians who are wise and learned and so far from accusing me of over-severity that they even praise my sincerity and the restraint with which I handled a somewhat licentious subject without undue licence and amused myself with a humorous theme without malice. And if I'm to address myself only to the theologians, as you say they're the only people to take offence, everyone knows how much more is common talk about the habits of bad theologians. Folly doesn't touch on any of that. She does no more than make fun of their time-wasting trivial discussions, though she doesn't simply disapprove of these but condemns men who base what's called the 'poop and prow' of theology on them, and who are so taken up with these battles of words, as St Paul named them, that they haven't a moment to spare for reading the words of the evangelists, the prophets or the apostles.

I only wish, my dear Dorp, that there were fewer of them guilty of this charge. I could show you some who've passed their eightieth year and wasted so much of their life in nonsense like this that they've never even opened the gospels. I discovered this for myself and in the end they admitted it. And even in the character of Folly I didn't dare to say what I often hear the theologians themselves deplore, and here I mean true theologians, that is, honest, serious and learned scholars who have drunk deeply of the teaching of Christ at its very source. Whenever they are among people with whom they can give free voice to

12. There is no mention of three theologians in Dorp's letter. P. S. Allen conjectures that the single adversary referred to may be John Briard, who was a leader of conservative theological opinion at Louvain but who approved the *Novum Instrumentum* on its publication. Erasmus was on cordial terms with him except for a short period early in 1519.

their thoughts they deplore the new kind of theology which has come into the world and regret the passing of the old one, which was so much more holy and sacred and so well able to reflect and recall the heavenly teachings of Christ. But quite apart from the baseness and monstrosity, the barbarity and artificiality of its vocabulary, its total unawareness of liberal studies and ignorance of languages, this new-fangled theology is so adulterated by Aristotle, by petty human inventions and profane regulations, that I doubt if it knows anything of the genuine, pure Christ.[13] For in fixing its eyes too firmly on man-made instruction it loses sight of the archetype. Consequently the more prudent theologians are often obliged to speak differently in public from what they think in their hearts or say to their close friends, and there are times when they are uncertain what answer to give those who consult them, realizing that Christ taught one thing and man's inherited teaching prescribes another. What, I ask you, has Christ to do with Aristotle, or the mysteries of eternal wisdom with subtle sophistry? What purpose is served by that maze of debatable issues, so many of which are a waste of time or a noxious evil, if only because of the strife and dissension they

13. Running through Erasmus's letter is the assumption, which he elsewhere makes explicit, that the contentiousness of the scholastics is connected with the barbarity of their Latin and their Aristotelian logic. What Erasmus earlier described as the 'rebirth' of liberal studies (or perhaps 'good learning': the Latin phrase *bonae litterae* which occurs frequently in the letter has no exact modern equivalent) was felt by him not only to open the way back to a more spiritual Christianity based on the values of the scriptures and the early Fathers, but also of itself to promote with elegance of style humanity of behaviour.

This view of the moral benefits to be derived from the cultivation of *bonae litterae*, quite apart from the examples and values contained in classical literature, was widely shared by Erasmus's humanist contemporaries. Some of them, like Budé, who regarded *humanitas* as a quality of behaviour rather than a type of erudition, based their view on a passage of Aulus Gellius (*Noctes Atticae*, 13, 17) which identifies *humanitas* with both the Greek educational ideal and learning and instruction in the liberal arts (*artes liberales*). The rebirth of *bonae litterae* which, at its narrowest, means classical studies, was felt by the humanists to be an event of immense cultural significance, a view to which our own use of the term 'Renaissance' to describe Erasmus's period partly subscribes.

create? Some points need elucidating and some decisions have to be taken, I don't deny, but on the other hand there are a great many questions which are better ignored than investigated, seeing that part of our knowledge lies in accepting that there are some things we cannot know, and a great many more where uncertainty is more beneficial than a firm standpoint. Finally, where there has to be a decision, I should like to see it taken with reverence, not with a feeling of superiority, and in accordance with the holy scriptures, not the fabrications of men's petty minds. Today there's no end to futile investigations which are the root of all the discord between sect and party, and every day one pronouncement leads to another. In short, we have come to the point when the basis of the issue involved rests not so much on Christ's teaching as on the schoolmen's definitions and the power of the bishops, such as they are. Consequently everything is now so complicated that there is not even a hope of recalling the world to true Christianity.

All this and many other such things are clearly seen and deplored by those theologians who are outstanding for their sanctity and scholarship, and they refer the prime cause of everything to the effrontery and irreverence of the modern type of theologian. If only you could penetrate my mind, my dear Dorp, and read my thoughts in silence, you would appreciate only too well how much I am careful to leave unsaid at this point. And *Folly* doesn't touch these questions either, or only very lightly, for I didn't want to offend anyone. I was equally cautious on every point, not wishing to write anything distasteful or personally libellous or factious, or what could be taken as an insult to any class of people. If anything is said there about veneration of saints, you'll find that it always has some qualification to make it clear that what is criticized is the superstition of those who venerate saints in the wrong way. Similarly, where I said anything against princes, bishops or monks, it was never without some indication that this was not intended as an insult to the whole order but as a reproach to its corrupt and unworthy members, so that I could censure their faults without hurting any good man. And in doing so without mentioning any names I did my best to avoid a personal affront even to a bad man. Finally, in working out my theme by means of jokes and witticisms through the mouth of a fictitious and comic character, I thought that even the critics who are normally sour and ill-disposed would take in good part.

But then, you say, I am condemned not so much for over-severity in my satire as for impiety. How are pious ears to accept my calling the happiness of the life to come a sort of madness? Dear Dorp, you are naturally open-minded, and I should like to know who has taught you this artful method of misrepresentation, or rather, which I think more likely, what master of cunning has suborned your true honesty to put up this malicious charge against me? The method adopted by those pernicious perverters of the truth is to pick out a couple of words and take them out of context, even changing the meaning at times and ignoring anything which would tone down and explain a phrase which would otherwise seem harsh. This is a device which Quintilian notes and teaches in his *Institutions*, telling us to present our case to full advantage by means of supporting assertions and anything which can soften or extenuate or otherwise assist our cause; but on the other hand, to quote our adversaries' arguments stripped of all this and in the most odious terms possible. Your friends have learned this device not from Quintilian's teaching but from their own evil disposition, and it is often the reason why words which would have been a pleasure to hear if they had been quoted as they were written are offensive when misrepresented. I do beg you to reread the passage and to look closely at the stages and development of the argument which leads to my conclusion that this happiness is a form of madness. Take note too of the words I use to explain this. What you will find there is far from being offensive to pious ears and will give them genuine pleasure. Anything at all offensive is not in my book but in your version of it.[14]

For when Folly was arguing that her name could be extended to cover the whole world and showing that the sum of all human happiness depends on her, she went through every type

14. The reference to Quintilian alludes to the fifth book of the *Institutio oratoria*. The phrase 'offensive to pious ears' was a quasi-official if relatively mild formula of ecclesiastical disapprobation (see note 112, p. 94).

of man up to kings and supreme pontiffs, then went on to the apostles themselves and even to Christ, to whom we find a kind of folly attributed in the holy scriptures. There is surely no danger of anyone's imagining that the apostles and Christ were fools in the literal sense. Yet in them too there is some sort of weakness due to human affections which in comparison with the pure eternal wisdom can be seen to be not wholly wise.[15] This is the folly which triumphs over all the wisdom of the world. That is why the prophet compares all the justice of mortal men with the soiled linen of a menstruating woman; not because the justice of good men is polluted, but because whatever is purest among men is somehow impure when compared with the ineffable purity of God. Thus, in showing a folly which is wise, I also showed an insanity which is sane and a madness which retains its senses. To soften what followed about the happiness of the blessed, I first cited the three forms of madness prescribed by Plato, where the happiest is that of lovers, for it takes them out of themselves. In the case of the pious, this ecstasy is only a foretaste of the happiness to come, in which we shall be wholly absorbed into God and be more in him than in ourselves. Now Plato calls it madness when anyone is carried out of himself and exists in the object of his love where he finds his happiness. Can't you see then how careful I was in the passage which follows to distinguish between types of folly and insanity so that no literal-minded reader could misunderstand my words?[16]

15. The question of whether or not there were 'passions' in Christ is an ancient one. It was acute during the Christological disputes of the fifth century. In 1499 Erasmus had firmly maintained against Colet that Christ in his human nature was subject to fear. The prophet is Isaiah (lxiv, 6).

16. Erasmus (see note 72, p.58) is careful here to use the term *furor* for the sort of madness described by Plato which is ecstatic in that it takes people out of themselves. In Ficino's largely Plotinian commentary on Plato's *Symposium*, there is a four-fold divine *furor* which sets the soul on its quest for progressive reunification as it moves through the four degrees of creation towards the vision of God. The poetic (and musical) *furor* is the gift of the Muses, the religious *furor* of Dionysus, the prophetic *furor* of Apollo and the erotic *furor* of Venus. This theory, which was well known in the Renaissance, gives Erasmus an impeccable precedent for accepting the morally elevating properties of some sorts of folly, even before he goes on to argue from the authority of St Paul.

But this is not the real issue, you say. It's my actual wording which offends the ears of the pious. Then why aren't they equally offended when they hear Paul speak of 'God's foolishness' and 'the folly of the Cross'? Why don't they call St Thomas to account? He writes of Peter's ecstasy that 'in his pious foolishness he began a sermon on tabernacles'. By foolishness he means Peter's holy and ecstatic happiness; and his words are chanted in churches. Why, I wonder, did they not quote one of my own prayers in which I referred to Christ as a worker of spells and charms? St Jerome calls Christ a Samaritan, although he was a Jew. Paul also calls him 'sin', which would be stronger than 'sinner', and also 'a cursed thing'.[17] What an impious sacrilege, if anyone wished to interpret this with evil intent! But if it is taken in the spirit in which Paul wrote, it is a pious tribute. Similarly, if anyone were to call Christ a robber, an adulterer, a drunkard or a heretic, wouldn't all good men stop their ears? But if he expresses this in proper terms, and as his argument develops gently leads his listener by the hand, so to speak, to an understanding of how Christ triumphed through the Cross to restore to his Father the body he snatched from the jaws of hell; how he took to himself the synagogue of Moses, like the wife of Uriah, so that from it could be born a peaceful people; how drunk with the sweet wine of charity he gave himself freely for us; how he introduced a new form of teaching, far removed from the tenets of wise and unwise alike – how, I ask, could anyone be offended, especially when we often find in the holy scriptures each one of these words used in a good sense? And this reminds me, in the *Chiliades* I called the apostles Sileni, indeed, I said that Christ himself was a sort of Silenus. Now this would be intolerable if some prejudiced critic dismissed it briefly with an unpleasant interpretation, but anyone who is

17. The reference to St Thomas may be to the *Commentary* on Matthew (xvii, 5). The prayer in which Erasmus refers to Christ in the terms mentioned is the *Precatio ad Virginis Filium Jesum*, certainly before 1499. Saint Jerome refers to Christ as a Samaritan in the homilies on Luke (xxxiv) and Paul says of Christ that he was made sin in 2 Corinthians v, 21. At Galatians iii, 13 the Vulgate has *maledictum* while Erasmus prefers *exsecratio*.

fair-minded and pious, if he reads what I wrote, will appreciate the allegory.[18]

I'm really surprised your friends haven't noticed how cautiously I express myself, and how careful I am to tone down my words with a qualification. This is what I wrote: 'But now that I have donned "the lionskin", let me tell you another thing. The happiness which Christians seek with so many labours is nothing other than a certain kind of madness and folly. Don't be put off by the words, but consider the reality.' You see how at the start, as Folly is to speak about something so sacred, I lighten the tone with the proverb about wearing a lionskin. And I don't refer simply to folly or madness but to 'a kind of folly and madness', so that it will be understood that I mean pious folly and happy madness, in accordance with the distinction I go on to make. Not satisfied with this, I add 'certain', so that it is quite clear that I'm speaking figuratively, not literally. Still not satisfied, I guard against any offence that may be given by the sound of the words by asking for more attention to be paid to what I say than to how I say it. All this is stated at once in the opening words of my argument. Then when I develop the subject, do I ever use a word which is not pious and circumspect, and indeed, more reverent than in keeping with the character of Folly? But here I preferred to forget consistency for a while, rather than to fall below the dignity of the subject. I chose to offend rhetoric, not to injure piety. And finally, when my exposition was complete, so as not to upset anyone because I made a comic character like Folly speak on such a sacred subject, I excused myself like this: 'But I've long been forgetting who I am, and I've "overshot the mark". If anything I've said seems rather impudent or garrulous, you must remember it's Folly and a woman who's been speaking.'

You can see that everywhere I've always been careful to avoid

18. David's sin with Bathsheba, the wife of Uriah the Hittite, is recounted in 2 Samuel xi. *Adagiorum Chiliades* was the title given to the book of adages from the Aldine edition of 1508 to the Froben edition of 1523. Before 1508 the work was called *Adagiorum Collectanea* and from 1526 *Adagiorum Opus*. The 1536 edition reverts to *Chiliades*. On the Silenus figure, see note 10, p. 13, and note 53, p. 44.

anything which could be at all offensive. But those whose ears are open only to propositions, conclusions and corollaries pay no heed to that. What was the point of arming my little book with a preface which I hoped would forestall misrepresentations? I don't doubt that it will satisfy any open-minded reader, but what's to be done with those who don't want to be satisfied either through their natural obstinacy or because they're too stupid to understand what is there to satisfy them? Simonides said that the Thessalians were too dull-witted to deceive, and here we have people too stupid to placate. And it's not surprising if a subject for misrepresentation can be found if all one looks for is something to misrepresent. If anyone reads the works of Jerome in a similar spirit he'll come up with a hundred places open to misrepresentation, and there are passages which can be called heretical in the most Christian of all scholars of the Church, to say nothing for the moment of Cyprian and Lactantius and their like.[19] Finally, who ever heard of a humorous essay being subjected to a theologian's scrutiny? If this is approved practice, why don't they equally apply this rule to all the writings and witticisms of the poets of today? They'll find plenty of obscenities there, and much that smells of the old paganism. But as these aren't classed as serious works none of the theologians thinks they're his concern.

However, I wouldn't want to seek shelter behind an example like this. I shouldn't wish to have written anything, even in fun, which could offend Christian piety in any way. I only ask for someone to understand what I wrote, someone fair-minded and honest who brings a true concern to comprehend, not a fixed intention to misrepresent. But if one were to count up first those who have no natural ability and less judgement, then those who have never come in contact with liberal studies but are infected rather than educated in a limited and confused doctrine, and lastly those who are hostile to anyone who knows what they

19. Simonides of Ceos was a lyric and elegiac poet of the sixth century BC and Erasmus is referring to a passage about him in Plutarch. The Thessalians of northern Greece were considered dull-witted by their political and military rivals in the south. Cyprian and Lactantius were both orthodox early Christian apologists.

don't know themselves and set out to misrepresent anything and everything which comes to their notice, a man could only be sure of escaping calumny by writing nothing at all. There are also a lot of people who make these false accusations simply out of a desire to win reputation, for nothing is so vain-glorious as ignorance combined with confidence in one's own learning. Then when their thirst for fame can't be satisfied by honest means, instead of a life of obscurity they prefer to imitate the young man of Ephesus who distinguished himself by setting fire to the most celebrated lighthouse in the whole world. As they can't publish anything worth reading of their own, they concentrate on picking holes in the works of distinguished men.

By these I don't mean myself, for I'm a mere nothing, and I think so little of *Folly* that no one need suppose I'm upset by this. It's not surprising that the sort of people I've been describing pick on several points in a long work and make them appear scandalous or irreverent or impious or smelling of heresy – all faults which they introduce themselves and aren't to be found there.[20] It would be far more conciliatory and more in keeping with Christian sincerity to support and encourage the industry of learned men, and where they inadvertently slip into error either to let it pass or to interpret it sympathetically, rather than to keep a hostile lookout for points to criticize and to behave like a professional informer instead of a theologian. It would also be a far happier state of affairs if we could teach or learn by combining our forces, and in Jerome's words, if we could skirmish on the field of letters without doing each other harm. What is surprising about such people is that for them there's no middle course. In some of the authors they read they can find a trivial pretext for defending even the grossest of errors which come to their notice, while against others they are so prejudiced that nothing can be said with sufficient circumspection to escape their trumped-up accusations. Instead of behaving like this, tearing others to pieces and then being torn themselves, wasting their time and everyone else's, how much better it would be if they would learn Greek or

---

20. 'Smelling of heresy' (*haeresim sapiens*) is another technical formula of ecclesiastical condemnation.

Hebrew, or Latin at least! Knowledge of these languages is so important for understanding the holy scriptures that it seems to me gross impertinence for anyone to assume the name of theologian if he is ignorant of them.

And so, dear Maarten, in my concern for your own interests I shall continue to beg you, as I've done often enough before, to extend your studies at least to learning Greek. You are blessed with rare intellectual gifts, and your style of writing is firm and vigorous, fluent and richly worded. This indicates a mind which is both sound and fertile in ideas. You are not only in the prime of life but at the peak of your developing powers, and you have just completed your general course of studies with success. If you added a knowledge of Greek as the finishing touch to the distinguished start you have made, you may be sure that I should be emboldened to promise myself and everyone else to expect from you what no present-day theologian has hitherto achieved. You may take the view that all human learning is contemptible in comparison with love for true piety and believe that you will arrive at such wisdom more quickly by being transformed through Christ. You may also believe that anything worth understanding is more fully comprehended through the light of faith than from the books of men, and I can readily share your opinion. But if in the present state of the world you persuade yourself that you can have a true understanding of theology without a knowledge of languages, especially of the one in which most of the holy scriptures have come down to us, you are entirely wrong.

I only wish I could convince you of this as much as I want, for I want it as warmly as I love you and interest myself in your studies, and you know that I love you with all my heart and my interest knows no bounds. But if I can't persuade you, please listen to these pleas from a friend at least enough to give what I'm asking a trial. I'll bear any blame, as long as you'll admit that my advice was friendly and disinterested. If you value my love for you at all, if you feel you owe anything to our common homeland or to what I wouldn't call my learning but at least to my laborious training in good learning, or to my age (for if it were only a matter of years I could be your father) – grant me my wish, and let my position or the good will between us convince you if my arguments can't. You have often praised my eloquence, but I shan't believe in it unless I can persuade you now. If I succeed then we'll both be happy, I for having given my advice and you for having taken it, and though you're already the dearest of my friends you'll be dearer still to me because I've made you dearer to yourself. If I fail, I fear that as you advance in age and experience you'll come to appreciate the advice I gave and condemn your present attitude, and then, as generally happens, you'll see your mistake only when it is too late to correct it. I could give you the names of a great many men who had to make a start like children on this language when their hair was white, because at long last they realized that all scholarship was blind and crippled without it.

But I've said too much on this subject. To return to your letter: you think that the only way I can pacify the theologians' hostility and recover their former good will is by producing a sort of 'recantation' in praise of Wisdom to counter my praise of Folly. You strongly advise and beg me to do this. My dear Dorp, I'm a man who despises no one but himself and wants nothing so much as to be at peace with the world, nor would I shrink from embarking on such a task if I didn't foresee what the result would be. Any hostility which may have arisen amongst a handful of prejudiced, uneducated people certainly wouldn't be removed but would be still more inflamed. I think it's better to 'let sleeping dogs lie and not touch this Camarina'. It would be wiser, unless I'm mistaken, to let this evil die away in time.[21]

Now for the second part of your letter. You much admire my care in restoring the text of Jerome, and you urge me to continue with similar work. Well, you're spurring on a willing

21. On the mud of Camarina, see note 106, p. 86.

This whole passage is noteworthy for several reasons. Erasmus willingly admits the inconsistency of his satire. He quite sincerely states his continuing belief in the primacy of piety over learning and faith over knowledge, but by 1515 he no longer feels the need to explore the possibility that these views invalidate his learned and humanistic theological work. He is much more confident and sure of touch. And he here reverses the letter's earlier disclaimers to accept the role of a senior scholar old enough to be Dorp's father. Dorp was exactly thirty and Erasmus not yet fifty.

horse, though it's not so much encouragement I need as assistance, for the work is proving very difficult. But never believe me in future if I'm not speaking the truth now: your theologians who are so offended by *Folly* won't like my edition of Jerome. And they aren't much more kindly disposed towards Basil, Chrysostom or Gregory of Nazianzus than they are to me, though in my case their fury is unrestrained. However, in their more exasperated moments they don't hesitate to speak insultingly even of those lights of learning. They're afraid of liberal scholarship and fearful for their own tyranny. Let me tell you that this is no rash pronouncement of mine. When my work had started and news of it had spread, certain individuals who passed for serious scholars and believed themselves outstanding theologians hastened to implore the printer, in the name of everything sacred, not to allow the insertion of a single word of Greek or Hebrew; these languages were fraught with immense danger and offered no advantage, and served only to satisfy men's curiosity. And previously, when I was in England, I happened to be dining with a Franciscan, a follower of Scotus (the first of that name) who has a popular reputation for learning and in his own opinion knows all there is to know. When I told him what I was trying to do in Jerome he expressed astonishment that there was anything in Jerome's books which the theologians didn't understand, though his own ignorance is such that I should be surprised if he properly understands three lines in the whole of Jerome's works. This agreeable person went on to say that if I was in any difficulty over my introduction to Jerome, Briton had made everything clear in his commentary.[22]

Now what can one make of theologians like that, my dear Dorp, or what can one wish for them except perhaps a good doctor to prescribe for their brains? And yet it is often men of this type who make most outcry in a theologians' assembly, and they are the ones who make pronouncements on Christianity. They fear and dread what they see as an evil and a mortal

22. The 'first' Scotus was John Scotus Eriugena, the ninth-century neoplatonist philosopher with monist tendencies. Briton was a learned thirteenth-century Dominican theologian. Erasmus recounts his meeting with the Franciscan at greater length in his notes on Jerome.

danger, though this is the very thing which St Jerome and Origen himself in his old age toiled so hard to acquire in order to be a true theologian. And Augustine, when he was already a bishop and advanced in years, regrets in his *Confessions* that as a young man he had been unwilling to learn what would have been so useful to him for interpreting the holy scriptures. If there is danger, I am not afraid to take a risk which was sought by men of such wisdom. If it's a question of curiosity, I've no wish to be holier than Jerome, and those who call what he did no more than curiosity may judge for themselves what service they do him.

There still exists an ancient decree of the Pontifical Senate on the appointment of doctors to give public instruction in languages, though there is no mention anywhere of provision for learning sophistic or Aristotelian philosophy, apart from the doubts expressed in the decrees whether these should lawfully be learned or not. And many great authors disapprove of them as a subject for study. Then why do we neglect what pontifical authority has ordered and apply ourselves to what is doubtfully recommended or positively discouraged? None the less Aristotle suffers the same fate as the holy scriptures. Nemesis is everywhere at hand, ready to exact vengeance for our contempt for language, and here too the theologians indulge in their dreams and fantasies, producing fresh enormities as they fasten on some points and fail to see others. We owe it to these splendid theologians that of all the writers whom Jerome lists in his *Catalogue* so few survive, simply because they wrote what Our Masters can't understand. To them we owe the corrupt and defective condition in which we now have St Jerome, so that others have to work harder restoring his words than he did when he wrote them.[23]

I come now to the third part of your letter concerning the New Testament. I really do wonder what has happened to you

23. Origen is known to have taken up very late the study of Hebrew to help his study of scripture. Erasmus's attitude to him had been notably favourable since Vitrier had introduced him to Origen's work, condemned for the doctrine of the non-eternity of Hell and for his view on the comparatively mild effects of original sin. On the significance of Erasmus's use of Augustine as an authority, see note 4, p. 142. The *Catalogue* of Jerome

and where you are applying your wits which used to be so keen. You don't want me to make any changes, except where the meaning may be clearer in the Greek text, and you won't admit there are any faults in the version we generally use. You think it sacrilege to pick holes in something which has been confirmed by the approval of so many centuries and by so many councils of the Church. If you, with all your learning, my dear Dorp, are right on this point, can you explain why the quotations in Jerome, Augustine and Ambrose often differ from the text we have? Why does Jerome criticize and correct word by word many passages which still appear in our version? What will you do in the face of such a consensus of evidence, I mean when the Greek texts have a different reading which Jerome quotes as proof, the earliest Latin texts read the same, and the sense fits in much better with the general context? You surely can't intend to ignore all this and follow your own text which may be corrupt through a copyist's errors. No one is claiming that anything in the holy scriptures is a lie, if that is the inference you draw, and none of this has anything to do with the personal conflict between Augustine and Jerome. But the truth demands, what is plain even for the blind to see, that there are often passages where the Greek has been badly translated because of the inexperience or carelessness of the translator, and often a true and faithful reading has been corrupted by uneducated copyists, something we see happening every day, or sometimes even altered by half-educated scribes not thinking what they do. Then who is giving his support to a lie – the man who corrects and restores these texts or the man who would rather accept an error than remove it? Especially

---

was the treatise *On Famous Men*. Erasmus was about to edit the letters of Jerome, patron of the Brethren of the Common Life.

Erasmus had earlier referred to the decrees of the 'Pontifical Senate' in a letter to Christopher Fisher of 1505. It is a Constitution of Clement V after the Council of Vienne (1311–12) ordaining the appointment of two teachers in each of the three languages, Hebrew, Arabic and Chaldaean in each of the four universities, at Paris, Oxford, Bologna and Salamanca. Greek was presumably omitted because the Constitution was aimed at promoting the conversion of the infidels, a category which did not include the schismatic Greeks.

when it is a characteristic of corrupt texts that one mistake leads to another. Moreover, the emendations I have made generally concern the implications of a passage rather than its actual meaning, though there are often places where the implication is a major part of the meaning, and not infrequently the whole passage has gone astray. In cases like this, what did Augustine, Ambrose, Hilary and Jerome have recourse to if not the Greek sources? And although this practice has also been approved by ecclesiastical decrees, you can still prevaricate, and try to refute or rather to wriggle out of the argument by hair-splitting.

You say that in their time the Greek texts were more accurate than the Latin, but that today the situation is reversed, and we should not trust the writings of those who disagreed with the teaching of the Roman Church. I find it hard to believe that this is your considered opinion. Really! Aren't we then to read the works of those who didn't hold the Christian faith? Then why allow so much authority to Aristotle, a pagan who never had anything to do with faith? The entire Jewish race disagrees with the teaching of Christ; so are the Prophets and the Psalms, written in their own tongue, to have no meaning for us? Now count up all the points in which the Greeks differ from the orthodox Latin beliefs. You'll find nothing there which originates in the words of the New Testament or refers to them. The dispute between the two rests only upon the word *hypostasis*, on the procession of the Holy Spirit, the ceremonies of consecration, the poverty of priests and the power of the Roman pontiff.[24]

24. The first three heads of the dispute between Latins and Greeks listed by Erasmus involve complex issues. The fifth century had seen bitter disputes about the correct usages of the terms 'nature' and 'hypostasis' (which Latin theology came to translate as 'person') when applied to Christ and the Trinity. The Council of Chalcedon made it necessary after 451 to speak of one nature and three persons in God, but one person and two natures in Christ. Unhappily, the meaning of both terms was still shifting at the time of the definition and there are examples of orthodox thought expressed subsequently in heterodox terminology and heterodox thought expressed in orthodox terminology.

The Latins argued on the second point the procession of the Holy Spirit from Father *and* Son (adding the word *Filioque* to the Creed), which the Greeks rejected. It is a mark of Latin theology to reject the term 'generation'

None of these is supported by arguments from corrupt texts. What will you say when you find the same interpretation in Origen, Chrysostom, Basil and Jerome? Surely not that someone has altered the Greek texts even in their times! Has anyone ever found a single passage where the Greek texts have been falsified? Why ever should they want to do this when they make no use of them to defend their beliefs? And then we have evidence from Cicero, who is otherwise prejudiced against the Greeks but always admits that in every branch of learning Greek texts were more accurate than the ones we have, for the different lettering, the accents and the sheer difficulty of writing Greek make it less easy for faults to arise and easier to correct them if they do.

In saying that I shouldn't diverge from the current version which has won the approval of so many councils, you behave like one of those popular theologians who always give ecclesiastical authority to anything which has crept into common usage. But can you produce a single assembly in which this version has been approved? Who would have approved it, when no one knows its author? It wasn't Jerome, as Jerome's own prefaces bear witness. But even if some assembly did approve it, did it also refuse to allow any emendation in accordance with the Greek sources? Did it approve all the errors which could creep in in various ways? I suppose the Fathers worded their decision like this: 'We approve of this version, though we do not know its author. We will allow no changes even if the most accurate Greek texts have a different reading, or Chrysostom, Basil, Athanasius or Jerome read something different, which may accord better with the meaning of the gospels; although in all other respects we have a high regard for these authorities. Furthermore, we set the seal of our approval on any error or corruption, any addition or omission which may subsequently arise by any means whatsoever through ignorance or presumption of scribes or through their incompetence, drunkenness or

---

applied to the Holy Spirit and to insist on 'procession'. On the third point, the Latins attached much less importance than the Greeks to the function in the rite of consecration of the invocation to the Holy Spirit or 'epiclesis'. For centuries indeed the Roman rite contained no explicit epiclesis.

negligence. We grant permission to no one to change the text once it is accepted.' An absurd pronouncement, you say. But it must have been something like this if you invoke the authority of an assembly to deter me from the task I have set myself.

Finally, what are we to say when we see that there are variations even in the copies of this version? Could an assembly really have approved these contradictions, foreseeing no doubt the alterations which different hands would make? How I wish, my dear Dorp, that the Roman pontiffs could find time to issue salutary pronouncements on these points, whereby provision could be made for restoring the noble works of the great authors and for preparing and issuing emended editions. Yet I shouldn't wish to see as members of any such council those so-called theologians who are unworthy of the name and whose only purpose is to give status to their own learning. But is there anything in their learning which is not completely irrelevant and confused? If these petty despots had their way the world would be compelled to reject the best authorities and to treat their stupid utterances as divinely inspired, though these men are so lacking in true learning that so long as they acquire no better scholarship I would rather be a humble artisan than the best among them. These are the people who want no changes in a text, for fear of exposing their own ignorance. It is they who oppose me with the fictitious authority of assemblies and exaggerate the serious crisis in the Christian faith. They spread rumours about the peril of the Church (which I suppose they support on their own shoulders, though they'd do better propping up a common cart) and other such hazards in the hearing of the ignorant and superstitious crowd who take them for real theologians and hang on their lips. They fear that when they misquote the holy scriptures as they frequently do, someone will confront them with the authority of the truth in Greek or Hebrew, and then it will be apparent that their so-called oracles are no more than idle nonsense. St Augustine, who was a great man and a bishop, was not unwilling to learn from a year-old infant. But people like this prefer to throw everything into confusion rather than allow themselves to appear ignorant of any detail concerning absolute knowledge, though I see nothing in this which concerns the sincerity of Christian faith. If it did, it would be a further reason for my labours.

Surely there can be no danger that the world will immediately abandon Christ if someone happens to hear that a passage has been found in the holy scriptures which has been corrupted by an ignorant or a drowsy copyist or wrongly rendered by some translator. There are other reasons for this danger, but I'm being careful to say nothing of them here. It would show a far more Christian spirit if every man would set argument aside and make what voluntary contribution he can to the common interest, acting in all sincerity; putting off his pride to learn what he does not know and ridding himself of jealousy to teach what he knows. If there are any too illiterate to teach anything properly or too proud to be willing to learn, they are few in number and can be ignored, while we concern ourselves with those whose abilities are good or at any rate promising. I once showed my annotations while they were still unrevised, still hot from the forge, as they say, to certain unprejudiced men, to eminent theologians and learned bishops. They all declared that even these rudimentary outlines were highly illuminating for their understanding of the holy scriptures.

Then you tell me that Lorenzo Valla has undertaken this work before me. I knew this, for I was the first to publish his *Notes on the New Testament*. I have also seen the *Commentaries* of Jacques Lefèvre on the letters of Paul. I only wish that their labours had made my own efforts unnecessary. I certainly believe that Valla merits the highest praise, if more for his rhetoric than for his theology, for in his work on the holy scriptures he devoted himself to comparing the Greek with the Latin texts, although there are quite a number of theologians who have never read straight through the complete Testament. However, I disagree with his conclusions in several places, especially where they touch on points of theology. Jacques Lefèvre was engaged in writing his commentaries while my own work was in preparation, and it's a pity that even in our most intimate conversations neither of us thought of mentioning what we were doing. I didn't know what he had been busy with until his work appeared in print. I very much admire his undertaking, though here again

I disagree with him in several places – reluctantly, for I'd gladly be 'of one mind' with such a friend in all respects. But truth must count for more than friendship, especially with regard to the holy scriptures.[25]

However, I'm not quite clear why you confront me with these two authors. Is it to dissuade me from a task you believe has already been performed? But it will be apparent that I had good reason for undertaking this work even if I came after two such great men. Or do you mean that the theologians disapprove even of their activities? I personally can't see how Lorenzo could have met with such continuing resentment, and I'm told that Lefèvre is universally admired. Have you considered that I'm attempting something quite different? Lorenzo, it seems clear, limited himself to annotating certain passages as he came to them and with what is commonly called a light touch. Lefèvre has only published commentaries on the letters of Paul, which he translated in his own way and then added notes in passing where there were matters of dispute. What I have done is to translate the entire New Testament from the Greek texts, putting the Greek opposite for easy reference. I have added notes which are separate from the text, in which I show partly through examples and partly through the authority of the early theologians that I have changed nothing in my revision without due consideration, in the hopes that my work of correction will inspire confidence and my emendations can't easily be changed. If only my painstaking efforts could be certain of success! For as far as relations with the Church are concerned, I shall have no hesitation about dedicating this humble product of my working hours to any bishop or cardinal or even to any Roman pontiff, provided he is like the one we have now. Finally, although you discourage me from publication at present, I'm quite sure that you too will

25. On Jacques Lefèvre d'Étaples and Lorenzo Valla, see the Introduction (pp. xi-liii). Until shortly after the date of this letter, Erasmus's relations with Lefèvre were cordial, though scarcely intimate. There was however a dispute after the publication of the *Novum Instrumentum* and, once Luther had been condemned, the group of reformers in the diocese of Meaux, led by Lefèvre as vicar general *in spiritualibus* to the bishop Guillaume Briçonnet, was never to trust Erasmus.

congratulate me when the book is out, once you've had a mere taste of the learning without which a true judgement on these questions is impossible.[26]

So you see, my dear Dorp, you've won gratitude twice over for a single service — from the theologians in whose name you have conscientiously carried out your mission, and from me for having given clear proof of your affection in the friendly tone of your admonition. You in your turn will surely take my equally frank explanation in good part, and if you are wise, will listen more readily to advice from me, who have only your interests at heart, than from those who are anxious to win over to their party a talent born for the highest things such as yours, but only in order to strengthen their forces by the addition of such a distinguished leader. Let them choose a better part, if they can; but if they can't, you yourself can choose the best. If you can't make them better men, as I hope you'll try to do, at least you can ensure they don't make you worse. Make sure you put my case to them with the same conviction you brought to putting theirs to me. You will placate them, as far as it's possible to do so, and make them see that I act as I do not with any intention of insulting those who do not share my learning but in the general interest of all mankind. This is something which will be open to anyone to make use of, if he wishes, without putting anyone under compulsion who prefers to dispense with it. Tell them too that if anyone comes forward with the ability or the desire to offer better guidance than I can, I intend to be the first to tear up and destroy my work and to adopt his way of thinking.

Give my best regards to Jean Desmarais, and be sure to let him see this defence of *Folly*, on account of the commentary on it which my friend Lijster dedicated to him. Remember me warmly to the learned scholar Nevius and my kind friend Nicholas of Beveren, priest-in-charge of St Peter's. You pay splendid tribute to the abbot Menard, and knowing your honesty, I'm sure this is wholly genuine. It inspires me to feel affection and regard for him on your account, and I won't fail to make

26. On Erasmus and Leo X, see the Introduction (pp. xi–liii).

honourable mention of him in my works at the first favourable opportunity.[27]

A fond farewell to you, my friend, dearest of mortal men.

Antwerp, 1515

27. Jean Desmarais was rector of Louvain and had taught Gerard Lijster, who dedicated to him the commentary on *Folly*. Nevius was the principal of the Collège du Lis at Louvain and Nicholas of Beveren (also Nicholas of Burgundy) was the illegitimate son of Anthony of Burgundy (1421–1504) and a member of the powerful Veere family which had sporadically provided Erasmus with patrons. The abbot Menard of Egmond, praised by Cornelius Gerard for his antiquarian interests, had provided Dorp with a benefice. Erasmus mentions him warmly in 1516 when dedicating a minor work to one of his relations.

INDEX

Theseus 63n.
Thessalians 159 & n.
Thetis 17n.
Thomism xxii–xxiii, xxxi, lii,
    85n., 88, 89n., 90n., 94 & n.,
    102n., 157 & n.
Thoth 50 & n.
Thraso 138, 139n.
Thrasymachus 83 & n.
Timon of Athens 40 & n.
Timotheus 113 & n.
Tithonus 24n., 25, 26n.
Toulouse, lost gold of 113 & n.
Trent, Council of xxxiv
Trophonius 9 & n.
Tryphe (Sensuality) 18, 19n.
Tudor kings (of England):
    ancestors of 67n.; see also
    Henry VIII
Turin xliv
Turks 69; war against 6 & n.,
    64n., 93
Tyard, Pontus de 18n.
Tyndale, William xxxv

Ulysses see Odysseus
Utica 39n.
Utrecht xxxvii

Valerius Maximus 41n.
Valla, Lorenzo xli, xlviii, li, 139
    & n., 150n., 169, 170
Varro, Marcus Terentius 15n.
Vatinius 139 & n.
Veere family 172n.
Venice xx, xxvii, xliv, xlv, xlvi,
    69, 81n., 143n.
Venus 21 & n., 25, 26n., 27 &
    n., 58 & n., 73, 75 & n., 86n.,
    156n.
Vespasian, Emperor 147 & n.

Vienne, Council of 165n.
Vigilantius 139 & n.
Villedieu, Alexander of 149 &
    n.
Vincent of Beauvais: Mirror of
    History 102 & n.
'vinculum Mundi' 34n.
Virgil xxxii, 5 & n., 20n., 22n.,
    26n., 37n., 46nn., 53n., 66n.,
    73n., 75n., 79, 83n., 99n.,
    101n., 111n.
virgins 148
Vitrier, John xli, 164n.
votive offerings 65–6
Vulcan 16n., 27 & n., 28, 29n.,
    86 & n., 95 & n.
Vulgate, Latin ix, xli, xlvii–xlix,
    li, lii, 142n.

war 37 & n., 110–11 & n.
Warham, William xlii, xliv,
    xlvi, xlix, 148
Whittington, Richard 4n.
William of Ockham xxiv, 89n.,
    102n., 149
Wilson, John xii
Wittenberg theses xxxiv, 64n.
women xvi, 30–31 & n., 32, 48–
    9, 57, 103–4, 114, 146, 148
works, religion of xxv, 15n.,
    132n.
worship 90–91 & nn.
writers 81–3 & n., 138–9, 150,
    159

Xenocrates 47, 48n.
Ximenes de Cisneros,
    Cardinal xlix

youth 22–6
Youthfulness xvi, 16n.

READ MORE IN PENGUIN

In every corner of the world, on every subject under the sun, Penguin represents quality and variety – the very best in publishing today.

For complete information about books available from Penguin – including Puffins, Penguin Classics and Arkana – and how to order them, write to us at the appropriate address below. Please note that for copyright reasons the selection of books varies from country to country.

In the United Kingdom: Please write to *Dept. EP, Penguin Books Ltd, Bath Road, Harmondsworth, West Drayton, Middlesex UB7 ODA*

In the United States: Please write to *Consumer Sales, Penguin USA, P.O. Box 999, Dept. 17109, Bergenfield, New Jersey 07621-0120.* VISA and MasterCard holders call 1-800-253-6476 to order Penguin titles

In Canada: Please write to *Penguin Books Canada Ltd, 10 Alcorn Avenue, Suite 300, Toronto, Ontario M4V 3B2*

In Australia: Please write to *Penguin Books Australia Ltd, P.O. Box 257, Ringwood, Victoria 3134*

In New Zealand: Please write to *Penguin Books (NZ) Ltd, Private Bag 102902, North Shore Mail Centre, Auckland 10*

In India: Please write to *Penguin Books India Pvt Ltd, 706 Eros Apartments, 56 Nehru Place, New Delhi 110 019*

In the Netherlands: Please write to *Penguin Books Netherlands bv, Postbus 3507, NL-1001 AH Amsterdam*

In Germany: Please write to *Penguin Books Deutschland GmbH, Metzlerstrasse 26, 60594 Frankfurt am Main*

In Spain: Please write to *Penguin Books S. A., Bravo Murillo 19, 1° B, 28015 Madrid*

In Italy: Please write to *Penguin Italia s.r.l., Via Felice Casati 20, I–20124 Milano*

In France: Please write to *Penguin France S. A., 17 rue Lejeune, F–31000 Toulouse*

In Japan: Please write to *Penguin Books Japan, Ishikiribashi Building, 2–5–4, Suido, Bunkyo-ku, Tokyo 112*

In Greece: Please write to *Penguin Hellas Ltd, Dimocritou 3, GR–106 71 Athens*

In South Africa: Please write to *Longman Penguin Southern Africa (Pty) Ltd, Private Bag X08, Bertsham 2013*

READ MORE IN PENGUIN

A CHOICE OF CLASSICS

Netochka Nezvanova Fyodor Dostoyevsky

Dostoyevsky's first book tells the story of 'Nameless Nobody' and introduces many of the themes and issues which dominate his great masterpieces.

Selections from the Carmina Burana
A verse translation by David Parlett

The famous songs from the *Carmina Burana* (made into an oratorio by Carl Orff) tell of lecherous monks and corrupt clerics, drinkers and gamblers, and the fleeting pleasures of youth.

Fear and Trembling Søren Kierkegaard

A profound meditation on the nature of faith and submission to God's will, which examines with startling originality the story of Abraham and Isaac.

Selected Prose Charles Lamb

Lamb's famous essays (under the strange pseudonym of Elia) on anything and everything have long been celebrated for their apparently innocent charm. This major new edition allows readers to discover the darker and more interesting aspects of Lamb.

The Picture of Dorian Gray Oscar Wilde

Wilde's superb and macabre novel, one of his supreme works, is reprinted here with a masterly Introduction and valuable Notes by Peter Ackroyd.

Frankenstein Mary Shelley

In recounting this chilling tragedy Mary Shelley demonstrates both the corruption of an innocent creature by an immoral society and the dangers of playing God with science.

READ MORE IN PENGUIN

A CHOICE OF CLASSICS

The House of Ulloa   Emilia Pardo Bazán

The finest achievement of one of European literature's most dynamic and controversial figures – ardent feminist, traveller, intellectual – and one of the great nineteenth century Spanish novels, *The House of Ulloa* traces the decline of the old aristocracy at the time of the Glorious Revolution of 1868, while exposing the moral vacuum of the new democracy.

The Republic   Plato

The best-known of Plato's dialogues, *The Republic* is also one of the supreme masterpieces of Western philosophy, whose influence cannot be overestimated.

The Duel and Other Stories   Anton Chekhov

In these stories Chekhov deals with a variety of themes – religious fanaticism and sectarianism, megalomania, and scientific controversies of the time, as well as provincial life in all its tedium and philistinism.

Metamorphoses   Ovid

A golden treasury of myths and legends, which has proved a major influence on Western literature.

A Nietzsche Reader   Friedrich Nietzsche

A superb selection from all the major works of one of the greatest thinkers and writers in world literature, translated into clear, modern English.

Madame Bovary   Gustave Flaubert

With *Madame Bovary* Flaubert established the realistic novel in France while his central character of Emma Bovary, the bored wife of a provincial doctor, remains one of the great creations of modern literature.

READ MORE IN PENGUIN

A CHOICE OF CLASSICS

John Aubrey	**Brief Lives**
Francis Bacon	**The Essays**
George Berkeley	**Principles of Human Knowledge and Three Dialogues between Hylas and Philonous**
James Boswell	**The Life of Johnson**
Sir Thomas Browne	**The Major Works**
John Bunyan	**The Pilgrim's Progress**
Edmund Burke	**Reflections on the Revolution in France**
Thomas de Quincey	**Confessions of an English Opium Eater**
	Recollections of the Lakes and the Lake Poets
Daniel Defoe	**A Journal of the Plague Year**
	Moll Flanders
	Robinson Crusoe
	Roxana
	A Tour through the Whole Island of Great Britain
Henry Fielding	**Amelia**
	Jonathan Wild
	Joseph Andrews
	Tom Jones
Oliver Goldsmith	**The Vicar of Wakefield**

READ MORE IN PENGUIN

A CHOICE OF CLASSICS

George Herbert	**The Complete English Poems**
Thomas Hobbes	**Leviathan**
Samuel Johnson/	
James Boswell	**A Journey to the Western Islands of Scotland and The Journal of a Tour to the Hebrides**
Charles Lamb	**Selected Prose**
Samuel Richardson	**Clarissa**
	Pamela
Richard Brinsley	
Sheridan	**The School for Scandal and Other Plays**
Christopher Smart	**Selected Poems**
Adam Smith	**The Wealth of Nations**
Tobias Smollett	**The Expedition of Humphrey Clinker**
Laurence Sterne	**The Life and Adventures of Sir Launcelot Greaves**
	A Sentimental Journey Through France and Italy
Jonathan Swift	**Gulliver's Travels**
Thomas Traherne	**Selected Poems and Prose**
Sir John Vanbrugh	**Four Comedies**

READ MORE IN PENGUIN

A CHOICE OF CLASSICS

Honoré de Balzac	**The Black Sheep**
	The Chouans
	Cousin Bette
	Eugénie Grandet
	A Harlot High and Low
	Lost Illusions
	A Murky Business
	Old Goriot
	Selected Short Stories
	Ursule Mirouet
	The Wild Ass's Skin
Marquis de Custine	**Letters from Russia**
Corneille	**The Cid/Cinna/The Theatrical Illusion**
Alphonse Daudet	**Letters from My Windmill**
René Descartes	**Discourse on Method and Other Writings**
Denis Diderot	**Jacques the Fatalist**
	Nun
	Rameau's Nephew and D'Alembert's Dream
Gustave Flaubert	**Bouvard and Pecuchet**
	Madame Bovary
	The Sentimental Education
	The Temptation of St Anthony
	Three Tales
Victor Hugo	**Les Misérables**
	Notre-Dame of Paris
Laclos	**Les Liaisons Dangereuses**
La Fontaine	**Selected Fables**
Madame de Lafayette	**The Princesse de Clèves**
Lautrémont	**Maldoror and Poems**

A CHOICE OF CLASSICS

Molière	The Misanthrope/The Sicilian/Tartuffe/A Doctor in Spite of Himself/The Imaginary Invalid
	The Miser/The Would-be Gentleman/That Scoundrel Scapin/Love's the Best Doctor/Don Juan
Michel de Montaigne	Essays
Marguerite de Navarre	The Heptameron
Blaise Pascal	Pensées
	The Provincial Letters
Abbé Prevost	Manon Lescaut
Marcel Proust	Against Sainte-Beuve
Rabelais	The Histories of Gargantua and Pantagruel
Racine	Andromache/Britannicus/Berenice
	Iphigenia/Phaedra/Athaliah
Arthur Rimbaud	Collected Poems
Jean-Jacques Rousseau	The Confessions
	A Discourse on Equality
	The Social Contract
Jacques Saint-Pierre	Paul and Virginia
Madame de Sevigné	Selected Letters
Stendhal	Lucien Leuwen
Voltaire	Candide
	Letters
	Philosophical Dictionary
Emile Zola	L'Assomoir
	La Bête Humaine
	The Debacle
	The Earth
	Germinal
	Nana
	Thérèse Raquin

READ MORE IN PENGUIN

A CHOICE OF CLASSICS

Leopoldo Alas	**La Regenta**
Leon B. Alberti	**On Painting**
Ludovico Ariosto	**Orlando Furioso** (in 2 volumes)
Giovanni Boccaccio	**The Decameron**
Baldassar Castiglione	**The Book of the Courtier**
Benvenuto Cellini	**Autobiography**
Miguel de Cervantes	**Don Quixote**
	Exemplary Stories
Dante	**The Divine Comedy** (in 3 volumes)
	La Vita Nuova
Bernal Diaz	**The Conquest of New Spain**
Carlo Goldoni	**Four Comedies (The Venetian Twins/The Artful Widow/Mirandolina/The Superior Residence)**
Niccolò Machiavelli	**The Discourses**
	The Prince
Alessandro Manzoni	**The Betrothed**
Emilia Pardo Bazán	**The House of Ulloa**
Benito Pérez Galdós	**Fortunata and Jacinta**
Giorgio Vasari	**Lives of the Artists** (in 2 volumes)

and

Five Italian Renaissance Comedies
   (Machiavelli/**The Mandragola**; Ariosto/**Lena**; Aretino/**The Stablemaster**; GI'Intronati/**The Deceived**; Guarini/**The Faithful Shepherd**)
The Poem of the Cid
Two Spanish Picaresque Novels
   (Anon/**Lazarillo de Tormes**; de Quevedo/**The Swindler**)

READ MORE IN PENGUIN

A CHOICE OF CLASSICS

Jacob Burckhardt	**The Civilization of the Renaissance in Italy**
Carl von Clausewitz	**On War**
Friedrich Engels	**The Origins of the Family, Private Property and the State**
Wolfram von Eschenbach	**Parzival**
	Willehalm
Goethe	**Elective Affinities**
	Faust Parts One and Two (in 2 volumes)
	Italian Journey
	The Sorrows of Young Werther
Jacob and Wilhelm Grimm	**Selected Tales**
E. T. A. Hoffmann	**Tales of Hoffmann**
Henrik Ibsen	**The Doll's House/The League of Youth/The Lady from the Sea**
	Ghosts/A Public Enemy/When We Dead Wake
	Hedda Gabler/The Pillars of the Community/The Wild Duck
	The Master Builder/Rosmersholm/Little Eyolf/John Gabriel Borkman
	Peer Gynt
Søren Kierkegaard	**Fear and Trembling**
	The Sickness Unto Death
Georg Christoph Lichtenberg	**Aphorisms**
Friedrich Nietzsche	**Beyond Good and Evil**
	Ecce Homo
	A Nietzsche Reader
	Thus Spoke Zarathustra
	Twilight of the Idols and **The Anti-Christ**
Friedrich Schiller	**The Robbers** and **Wallenstein**
Arthur Schopenhauer	**Essays and Aphorisms**
Gottfried von Strassburg	**Tristan**
August Strindberg	**The Father/Miss Julie/Easter**